HISTORIC
CORSTORPHINE
AND ROUND ABOUT

Kramond ynch

Lyth Roade

E

Mainshou
Kottmoor
Craggy hal
Fair Kraigy
Bridgs
Nether Kramont
Grantoun
Weirdy
Laurencetoun
Nether Bartoun
Pilmuse
Moore hous
Newhaven
Over Kramons
W. Dryley
Warchry
Nether Lany
Kannock
Over Barnetoun
E. Dryley
Türlig
Lyth
Over Lany
Southfield
Gracruik
Inner Lyth
Broughtoun
Restalrig
Revelstoun
Silver mill
E. Craigs
Craig Den mills
Needons feild
Coldham
Haus
Newbridge
Darry
West creigs
Hill
Korstorphin
Wriht hous
Holirudhous
Magdalen
Nether Gogar
Warfter C.
Sauchtoun
Edenburgh
Arthur's ſeat
Gogar mil
Brome house
Sauchtoun
Goray
Marchiston
The Parck
Easter dudly
Hermiſtoun
Luchna Burn
Schich
Brunstoun
Rydthewes
Gorgymill
Tippertin
Blaſsford
Wester
E. Hales
Craghous
Grange
Duddigtoun
YRE
Balbertoun
Kray
Rydd hall
Priestfield
Kainron
Wester Hales
Cohntoun
Over Brail
Bridard
Ricartoun
Burr. house
Woodhall
Oxtoun
Nether Libertou
Nyddri Marshal
Keyrhill
Coldeun
Mortoun hall
Over Libertou
Craigmiller
Wauyſtoun
Boncly
Mortoun
North hous
Foullbrigs
Daimahoy
Curry
Over Curry
Store hous
Edmondstoun
Killyth
Hilend
Stratoun
Southhous
Pilmoore
Curry hill
Lunçhoy
Stratoun
Wowmet
Newtoun
Desdridge
Byrney
Pentland hill
Lyips
Penthland
Stratoun hall
Long Gilmoortoun
Palace
Harelaw
Roſlyn more
Cotſtek
Guters
Grange
Colchurn
Logennes
Catharins
Paradiſc
Louhead
Dilketh C.
Brucly
Glen croce
Castel law
G. Collidge
Pryden
Lystoe
Achindinny
N. house
over
Butlonds
Gartſyid
Kirk
Mileoun
Greenlan
Roslyin
Leswod
Leswood D
Huſe in the moor
Woodhousty
Woodhousley
Hilhead
Hachrondale
Pennycook
Karkettill
Pendrieech
Coits
Achindyuny
Pendourith
Lukenes
Whyt hill
Brounſtoun
Over yr ſyit
Skewu den
New Battel
Revenscheuk
Fatlipps
Dalhousy
Cotts
Halles
Coldhal
Karingtoun
Cockpen
oulwood
Karingtoun barns
Terſunte
Newbyres
Welſtoun
Headſtone
Schanch
Hywmyl burn
Achincork

EDEN
B

HISTORIC
CORSTORPHINE
AND ROUND ABOUT

VOLUME 1
THE CHURCH AND PARISH LIFE

A. S. Cowper
B.A. HONS., F.L.A., F.S.A. SCOT

Published by
THE CORSTORPHINE TRUST
2003

OPPOSITE TITLE PAGE
Timothy Pont: Shires of Lothian and Linlithgow, 1636.
(Courtesy NLS, *ref. Newman 988)*

FIRST EDITION

Copyright © A.S. Cowper, published 1991

SECOND (ILLUSTRATED) EDITION

published in Great Britain in 2003
by The Corstorphine Trust
The Corstorphine Heritage Centre,
St. Margaret's Park
Corstorphine, Edinburgh,
EH12 7SX

Copyright © The Corstorphine Trust 2003

ALL RIGHTS RESERVED.
No part of this publication may be reproduced, stored
in a retrieval system or transmitted in any form or by any means,
electronic, mechanical, photocopying, recording or otherwise,
without prior permission in writing from the publisher.

All Illustrations copyright The Corstorphine Trust
unless otherwise acknowledged.

ISBN: 0-9544757-0-4

British Library Cataloguing-in-Publication Data
A Catalogue record for this book is available on request

Design and layout by Mark Blackadder

Printed and bound in Scotland by the Bath Press Ltd, Glasgow

*DEDICATED TO THOSE
WHO HAVE GONE BEFORE*

About 1760 William Erskine was a ploughman at Golfhall Gogar. His granddaughter Isabella, born at Carlourie, 1817, married John Couper at Cramond Kirk 1834. In time the spelling of the surname changed and a grandson of Isabella and John was James McLean Cowper born at Linlithgow 1877, a craftsman of no mean ability.
He was my father.

A. S. COWPER
B.A. HONS., F.L.A., F.S.A. SCOT.

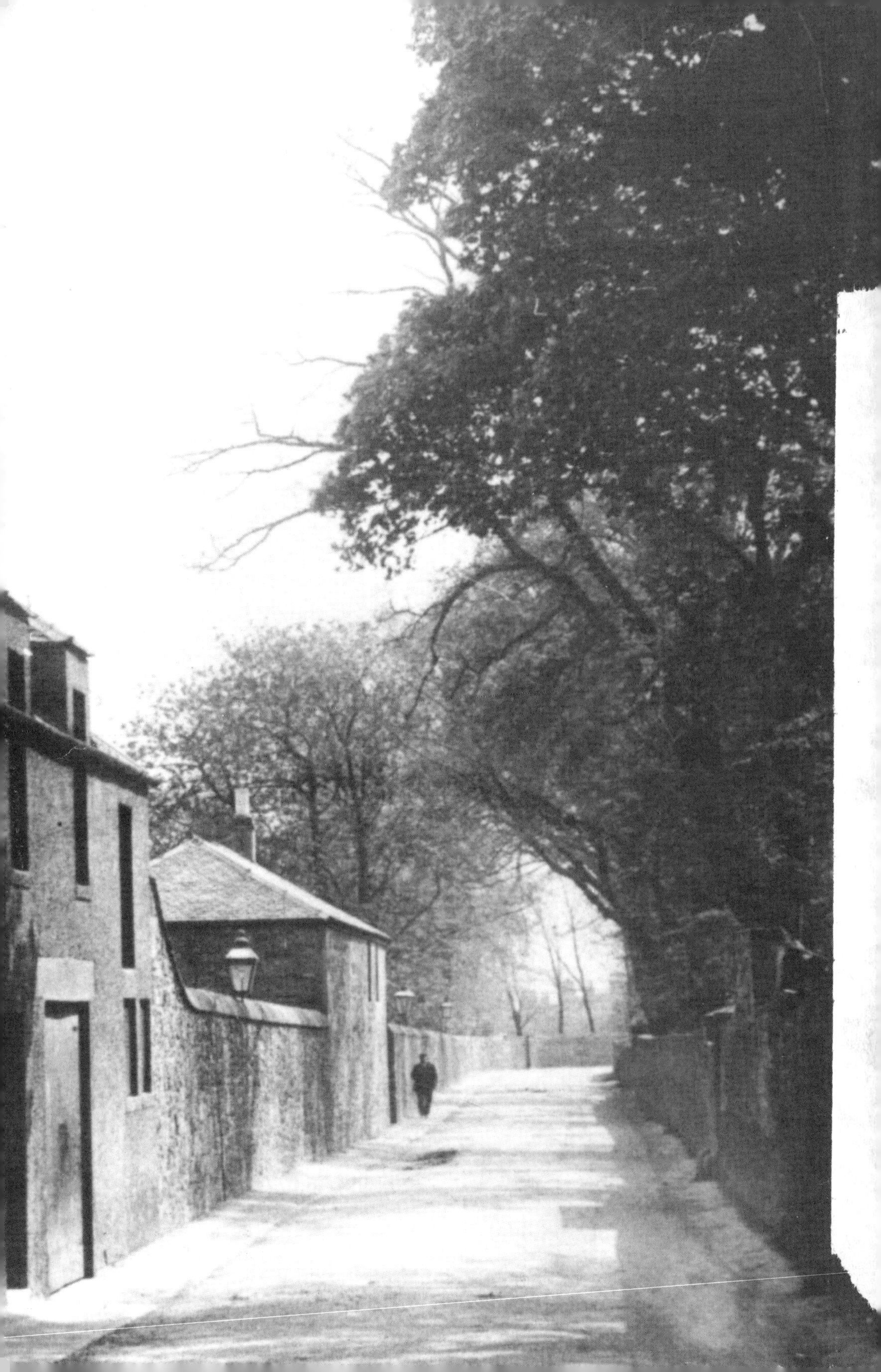

CONTENTS

DEDICATION	V
ACKNOWLEDGEMENTS, 1ST EDITION	IX
ACKNOWLEDGEMENTS, 2ND EDITION	X
EXTRACT FROM LETTER RECEIVED BY MISS COWPER FROM THE LATE PROFESSOR EMERITUS GORDON DONALDSON C.B.E.	XI
EDITORIAL NOTE, 2ND EDITION	XIII

1. **THE CHURCH IN CORSTORPHINE: BEGINNINGS** — 1
    - The Parish Church — 3
    - Adam Forrester's Chapel — 5
    - The Collegiate Church — 9
    - The Tombs — 13
    - Papal Recognition — 18
    - Benefactors — 20
    - The Provosts — 21
    - The Provost's House — 25
    - The Prebendaries — 29
    - The "Dower House" — 32
    - The Chapter House: The Sacristy: The Seal — 35
    - The Hospital: The Alms House — 3
    - The Lamp Niche: The Lamp Acre — 38
    - The Bell Tower — 40
    - Niddrie's Aisle — 43
    - From the Outside: Sundials — 45
    - Treasures Within: The Font — 46
    - Grave Slabs — 46
    - Numerals — 48
    - The Reformation Settlement — 48

2. **THE REFORMED PARISH CHURCH** — 50
    - The Early Seventeenth Century — 53
    - Mr David Balsillie: The First Reconstruction — 54
    - Mr Robert Hunter — 57
    - Restoration to Revolution: 1662-89 — 59
    - Archibald Hamilton — 64

3. **THE EIGHTEENTH CENTURY** — 68
    - George Fordyce — 68
    - John Chiesly — 70
    - Thomas Sharp — 73
    - James Oliver — 73

4. **TO THE DISRUPTION** — 77
    - Dr David Scot — 77
    - David Horne — 78

OPPOSITE.
Looking 'doon the loan'
(Kirk Loan) c.1920. *(PB743)*

5. TOWARDS RESTORATION ... 81
   Robert K.D. Horne ... 81
   Dr James Dodds ... 82
   James Fergusson ... 83
   The Church Building ... 85
   The Windows ... 99
   The Manse ... 104
   The Sacrament of Communion ... 111
   The Teind Yard and Barn: Stipends ... 116

6. PARISH LIFE ... 120
   Cromwellian Times ... 120
   Defence of the Realm: 1660-1787 ... 127
   Quartering ... 127
   The Hearth Tax ... 133
   The Poll Tax ... 135
   Men and Supplies ... 137

7. EDUCATION ... 140
   To 1698: Schoolmaster's Land: The Lamp Acre ... 140
   John Cunningham ... 146
   Eighteenth Century Masters ... 150
   Daniel Ramsay ... 157
   To the 1872 Act ... 160
   The School Board ... 162
   Female Education ... 172
   Other Schools ... 177
   Playground and Street Names ... 179

8. LAW AND ORDER ... 181
   Justice Ayres ... 181
   Baron Courts: Saughton and Corstorphine ... 181
   Burlaw Courts ... 185
   Justices of the Peace ... 186
   Criminal Matters ... 188
   Black Market Poultry ... 189
   Captain John Swinton ... 189
   A Concealed Pregnancy ... 191
   The Murrayfield Murder ... 194
   Transportation: The Female Industrial Home ... 199
   The Kirk Session ... 201
   James Warden ... 204
   Fornication ... 205
   Selling Ale ... 208
   Profaning the Sabbath ... 211
   Theft and Housebreaking ... 214
   Slander and Strife ... 214
   National Collections ... 215
   Helping Others ... 216
   Caring for the Poor ... 217
   Witchcraft ... 222
   Foundlings ... 227
   Baptisms ... 231
   Marriages ... 236
   Funerals ... 240
   The Churchyard ... 245
   Craft Regulations ... 253
   Friendly Societies: Corstorphine and Saughton ... 254

APPENDIX 1: SERVANTS OF THE KIRK ... 258

APPENDIX 2: CURRENCY AND WEIGHTS AND MEASURES ... 265

INDEX ... 267

Acknowledgements

TO FIRST EDITION OF VOLUME 1

The information in this publication is based on primary and secondary sources. Though concerned with the western area of Edinburgh it is a lively detail in the wider backcloth of Scottish history. Parochial and national events inevitably intertwine.

The writer is grateful to the following institutions and their staffs who made two decades of research a pleasant task: the Scottish Record Office [now National Archives of Scotland] with its invaluable collections of family archives generously made available by their owners, church records, local authority records, sasines, testaments, maps; New Register House with its old parochial registers; the National Library of Scotland for the Liston papers; Edinburgh City Archives; Edinburgh Public Libraries; Corstorphine Trust for the Dickson papers; the Royal Commission on the Ancient and Historical Monuments of Scotland; the Society of Antiquaries of Scotland.

Thanks to fellow local historian, the late Mr Arnot Beveridge of Corstorphine, always happy to discuss and share points of mutual interest. And special thanks to the late Dr Ernest Cormack, local historian and beloved local physician, who presented the writer's tonic for the next two decades of her life when he said to her in 1968 that it was time someone researched and wrote a new version of Upton Selway's admirable Victorian work Corstorphine: *A Midlothian Village*.

A.S.C.

Acknowledgements

TO SECOND EDITION OF VOLUME 1

Illustrations are drawn from the Trust's own archives, indicated by the prefixes PB or S, with the exceptions noted below. Permission to publish from the holdings of the following is gratefully acknowledged:

The Trustees of the National Library of Scotland [NLS], *ii.*
The Royal Commission on the Ancient and Historical Monuments of Scotland [RCAHMS], *pp17, 36, 247.*
The National Archives of Scotland [NAS], *pp58, 79, 134, 136, 155, 192.*
The Society of Antiquaries of Scotland [SOAS], *p252.*
The Kirk Session of Corstorphine Old Parish Church for permission to photograph and publish items from the Church's Communion plate, *pp113, 232*, and an early Communion token, *p116.*
Messrs. Gillespie Macandrew W.S., *p155*

St Ninian's Church. An old drawing of the church by G. Upton Selway before the body of the kirk was enlarged. [GUS]

Occasional illustrations in the margins are taken from *A Mid-Lothian Village: Notes on the Village and Parish of Corstorphine* first published by G. Upton Selway [GUS] in 1890; from a series of line-drawing post-cards prepared for the Trust in 1971 by the late Ernest Weierter [EW]; and from line-drawings by Ron Green [RG], a member of the Trust's Executive Committee, whose co-operation in allowing these to be used is gratefully acknowledged.

Extract from letter received by Miss Cowper from the late Professor Emeritus Gordon Donaldson C.B.E., following publication of the First Edition of *Historic Corstorphine and Roundabout*, Volume 1, in 1991

10 March 1992

... [The book] is so packed with information. I can appreciate better than most the enormous amount of work you have clearly put in to extracting all those facts from the records. I not infrequently scold people who profess to lament the scarcity of record material in Scotland instead of using the vast amount which does exist, and your work is another example of the riches which can be quarried by those who are prepared to take the necessary trouble.

The picture of life which it presents is so enormously varied and lively that it should provide something of interest for almost everyone.

I was naturally especially interested in a volume which is mainly about the Church and associated activities. I have always been a friend to local history, partly because it is the foundation of national history – how can one generalise without knowing the details? – and partly because in local history one gets one's feet firmly on the ground and can come to conclusions with confidence.

You deserve warm congratulations ...

GORDON DONALDSON
H.M. Historiographer in Scotland

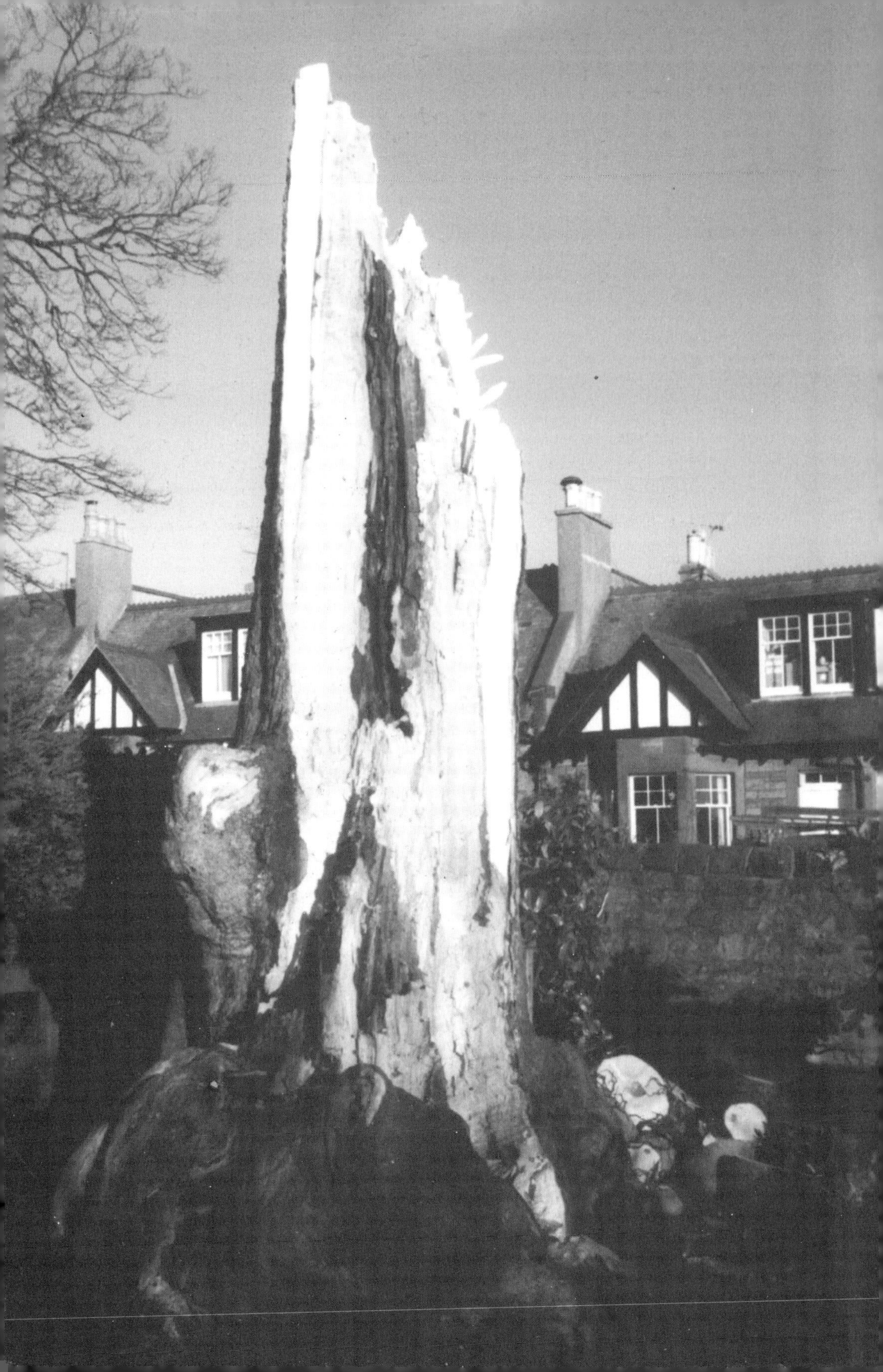

Editorial Note

TO SECOND EDITION OF VOLUME 1

In 1994 the Corstorphine Trust acquired from Miss Cowper the copyright in all four volumes of her finely detailed local history of Corstorphine and the surrounding area, in the full realisation that the series would constitute, for many years to come, the standard local history of our area from the earliest times to 1920. It is a testament to the quality of the 1st Edition that Volumes 1 and 2 have long since been sold out.

Miss Cowper later very kindly made her working index available to the Trust and this has proved invaluable both in its original form and as recast for this Edition. The Trust also gratefully acknowledges deposit for preservation in the Corstorphine Heritage Centre Archives of her extensive research papers compiled in the preparation of this and the remaining volumes. After cataloguing, these will be made available with the rest of the Trust's archives to future researchers.

The Trust's intention is to publish, as funds and circumstances permit, an attractive uniform 2nd Edition of all four volumes, professionally designed, with numerous illustrations and a full index to each. This volume represents the first step in the venture, and the Trust hopes that it is well received – and purchased! – by all who know and love Corstorphine and the area round about.

We have taken the opportunity to make some minor corrections to the text of the 1st Edition of Volume 1, and have added two appendices and an index. The first appendix lists the Servants of the Kirk; the second gives information about currency and weights and measures alluded to in the book, which we hope the general reader will find helpful.

We are grateful to Miss Cowper for valuable advice with respect to the photographs and captions. Otherwise, as joint editors, we take full responsibility for the book as it now appears, and for any errors or omissions.

OPPOSITE.
The stump of the famous Corstorphine Sycamore after the 400-year-old tree had been blown down by the great gale on 26 December 1998.

KEVIN AITCHISON AND ANDREW BROOM
MARCH 2003

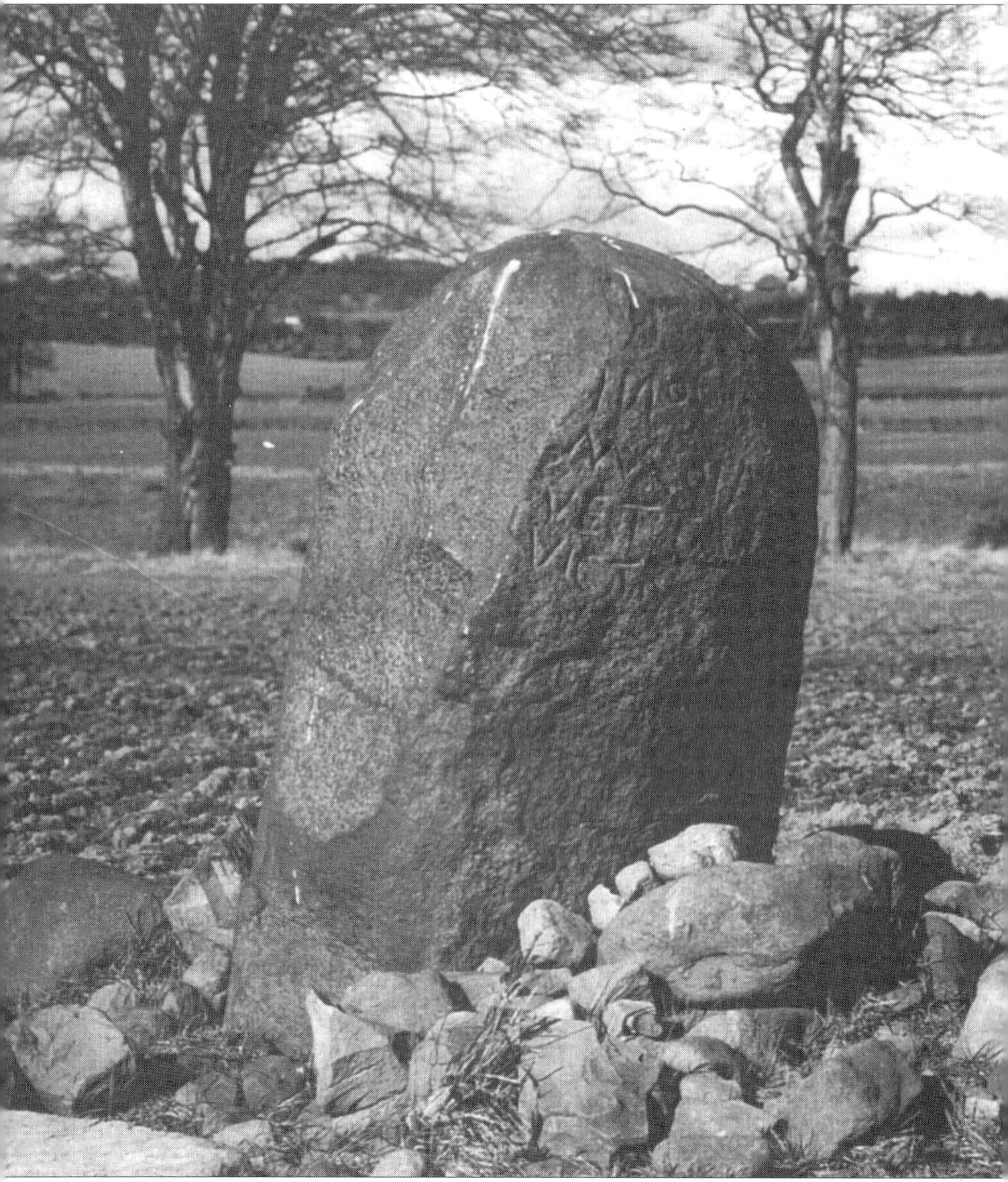

Chapter 1

THE CHURCH IN CORSTORPHINE: BEGINNINGS

At its southern end Kirk Loan, Corstorphine, turns in a curvilinear fashion towards the village High Street. The survival of this rounded ground close to the medieval church may be the last vestige of an early Christian burial site and chapel. Early enclosed Christian burial grounds were oval or circular in plan.

When the antiquary Edward Lhuyd in 1699 visited the Catstane, now within the area of Edinburgh Airport and comparatively near Corstorphine, the stone was seen to be in the centre of a low mound. When the farmland on which it stood was acquired for the airport the ground surrounding the stone had been largely flattened by years of agricultural cultivation.

The catstane, a block of whinstone, rises five feet above the ground in which it is embedded. It carries a Latin inscription ascribed to the late 5th century: IN OCT/ (V)MVLO IAC(E)T/VETTA F/VICTR meaning possibly that in this tomb lies Vetta daughter of Vitricius. When the airport ground was being prepared in 1977 for the main east-west runway, parallel rows of long cist burials were exposed, revealing an early Christian cemetery.

Dating the coming of Christianity to Lothian is debatable. The extent of the evangelising travels of Ninian in the 4th century has been disputed in recent years. Less controversial is the missionary work of the Northumbrian church in the 7th century. South-east Scotland from the Forth estuary to the Borders was, at this period, part of the territory controlled by the Angles of Northumbria.

Cuthbert was active in Melrose where he followed, as Prior, the Christian Boisil, whose name lives on in the place name St. Boswells. Between 651 and 661, according to tradition, Cuthbert preached in Perthshire, Fife, and the Lothians, teaching the practice of the Celtic Columban church of Iona.

OPPOSITE.
The catstane photographed in the 1950s. The farmland shown here is now within the boundary of Edinburgh Airport. The catstane, although in a restricted area, is still in its original position. *(PB45)*

It may be that when Cuthbert came to the loch beneath the deep, frowning glory of the rock of Edinburgh, fortified, possibly, a few years earlier by Edwin of Northumbria as his most northern outpost, he decided to build a cell or small *casa* for his missionaries to the surrounding countryside. More certain it is that the site of St. Cuthbert's Church, Edinburgh, is, if not the oldest, then one of the oldest ecclesiastical sites in Scotland. Dedications to St. Cuthbert in medieval times may be deliberate choice or may indicate earlier associations with him. Churches bearing his name in the Lothians include Colinton (Hailes), Kirknewton, Midcalder, and Dalmeny.

About 651 a monastic centre under the auspices of the Northumbrian churchman, Wilfrid, champion of Roman Christianity, was set up at Abercorn on the Forth estuary and no great distance from the Catstane and Corstorphine. Its purpose was to bring south-east Scotland under the Anglo-Roman church as opposed to the Celtic Columban church and to strengthen the Northumbrian hold on Pictland. The Bishop of Abercorn, Trumwine, styled himself Bishop of the Picts. The conflict between the two churches centred on the date of observing Easter. Finally, in 664, at Whitby, King Oswy of Northumbria, chose the Anglo-Roman church.

Trumwine's stay at Abercorn came to an abrupt end in 685. The crushing victory of the Picts at Nechtansmere in Angus over the Northumbrian Angles led by Ecfrith, son of Oswy, sent Trumwine scuttling back to Whitby and saved Scotland from being submerged in the English kingdom of Northumbria. The Northumbrian churchmen remaining loyal to the Celtic Columban church returned to their mother church at Iona.

By the 7th century when the political and religious struggles of Northumbria were having repercussions on Scotland, Christian burial grounds began to be associated with small rectangular chapels. From such origins probably evolved the parish church with its surrounding cemetery. In the Edinburgh area between the 7th and 11th centuries the work of the church of St. Cuthbert must have been carried on with great zeal for by the time of David I (c.1084–1153) it had great possessions in land and endowments.

There was a chapel at Corstorphine at this time belonging to Norman, the Sheriff of Berwick. It later appears as part of the church of St. Cuthbert. Then when David bestowed the church of St. Cuthbert on the Abbey of Holyrood the chapel of Corstorphine with two oxgates and six acres of land also went to Holyrood. Usually King David alone is given the honour of granting the chapel of Corstorphine to Holyrood but the chapel was also the gift of Norman, the Sheriff, – "sciatis me concessisse ... capellam meam de Crostorfin". The King later confirmed this gift. One of the witnesses to the royal charter was Norman the Sheriff.

By the next century, in the reign of Alexander II (1198–1249), the chapel appears again when the owner of Corstorphine – David, the King's Marshall – exchanged land with the Abbey of Holyrood. David le Mareschall got two acres belonging to the chapel as they lay between his lands: the Abbey got the meadow called "Hardmedwe" situated within the limits of "Salchton". "Hard" is a reminder of the existence of firm ground between the lochs of Gogar and Corstorphine.

The 1444 foundation charter of the collegiate church particularly notes that the church had been set up in a burial ground – "in cemiterio parochialis ecclesie de Corstorphine". The curve of the ground at the present war memorial in Kirk Loan is today the reminder of that early Christian cemetery.

THE PARISH CHURCH

Sometime between David le Mareschall's excambion and the coming of Adam Forrester in the second half of the 14th century the chapel at Corstorphine became the parish church dedicated to St. Mary. The territorial organisation of the Scottish church into parishes was the work of the 12th century Norman kings, sons of Queen Margaret, of whom David is perhaps the best known – "a sair sanct for the crown". It possibly was his gift of the chapel at Corstorphine to Holyrood Abbey in 1128 that led to the chapel becoming the parish church serving the community.

Dedications to Our Lady were popular in pre-Reformation Scotland. Even where a church was dedicated to another saint the preamble to the document pays tribute to the Blessed Virgin Mary. Holyrood Abbey had a joint dedication – St. Mary and the Holy Rood. Ratho, also connected with Holyrood Abbey, was dedicated to the Virgin. Gogar was another St. Mary dedication. From the Solway Firth to the Pentland Firth churches in medieval Scotland honoured the mother of Christ.

How Corstorphine parish church came to be dedicated to St. Mary is not known. It may have been because of the popularity of the cult or it may have been the personal choice of the lord of the manor. Before the Forresters the estate was owned by the More family who may have felt special devotion to Our Lady. Certainly in 1363 William More, Lord of Abercorn, endowed with his "land of Raylistone" (Ravelston) a chaplaincy at the altar of the Blessed Virgin in St. Giles' church, Edinburgh. In May 1617 when John Spottiswoode, Archbishop of St. Andrews, gave George Forrester a tack of nineteen years teinds of the parish kirk he styled the church "Our Lady Kirk of Corstorphine".

The parish church existed alongside the later collegiate church and served the needs of ordinary people while the collegiate church served the Forrester family. Of those who served in the parish church little is known. In 1446 Provost Bannatyne along with the Bishop of St. Andrews received a mandate from the Pope to deal with a complaint he had received. John Kers, "rector of the chapel at Corstorphine", was on Papal business when John Wyddirspon, perpetual vicar of Tranent, "caused him" to be attacked and imprisoned by certain laymen.

Moreover Wyddirspon, though excommunicated, went on celebrating mass "in contempt of the Keys". The Pope ordered Bannatyne and the Bishop to accuse Wyddirspon. If the facts were as stated he was to be deprived of his vicarage and Kers was to have it. The upshot was that Kers got the annates of the parish church of Tranent (£20 stg). In 1450 Kers became Abbot of Inchcolm.

Two donations made to the upkeep of the parish church were recorded in the Register of the Great Seal. In 1465 John Marshall, a chaplain in the collegiate church of Corstorphine, gave tenements under the Castle wall of Edinburgh to maintain a chaplain for the altar to the Holy Trinity. Marshall's endowment was confirmed again in 1510 along with another donation to the Holy Trinity altar granted by Alexander Forrester with the consent of his son Archibald. The Forrester gift provided for the chaplain's house and ground in Corstorphine and, in particular, the land called Gardener's croft.

In 1473 William de Camera, vicar of Kirkurd, gave the annual rents of property in Corstorphine village and in Edinburgh for the upkeep of a secular chaplain. He was to say mass at the altar of St. Anne for the souls of James II and James III, for their royal ancestors and for their posterity, for the deceased Sir Alexander Forrester, and for Archibald Forrester, for the donor's parents and for all the faithful dead. This ground in Corstorphine given by de Camera became known in the 18th century as Cock's Croft and now is part of St. Margaret's Park.

ADAM FORRESTER'S CHAPEL

As a medieval Christian Adam Forrester would be concerned to settle his burial place where prayers and masses could be said for the eternal welfare of his soul and for the well-being of his family. When he built his votive chapel is not known but his experience in the restoration of St. Giles' in 1399 after

Effigy of Sir Adam Forrester, d.1405, from his tomb in the south transept. (PB1476)

destructive English raids on his town may have inspired him to build his private chapel near his castle at Corstorphine.

Since Adam died in 1405 his chapel may have been built around 1400. He dedicated it to St. John the Baptist who has two anniversary dates. Usually a saint's day is the day of death but John the Baptist and Our Lady, alone of all the saints, were honoured in having the days of their birth recognised. The *nativitas Sancti Johannis* is 24th June.

Bannockburn was fought on 24th June 1314 when Robert the Bruce went into battle having called on St. John the Baptist, as well as St. Andrew, to help the Scots. The Baptist's other anniversary is 29th August, the Feast of the Decollation of St. John, a day to remember his beheading.

Adam endowed his chapel with an annual sum of £4 from the rents of property in Edinburgh. The Order of St. John of Jerusalem expected Adam to pay an annual sum of forty shillings out of the Templelands and Meadowfield in Corstorphine but he apparently failed to do so. The Chancellor of England was asked in 1404 to provide safe passage to Scotland for Friar Hildebrand Wooton to collect what Adam owed the Templars. There is no record of the friar reaching Corstorphine but it appears that the money went towards the finances of Adam's chapel. If his wish to have three chaplains was implemented then his widow and his son possibly added to Adam's personal endowment the income from the Templelands.

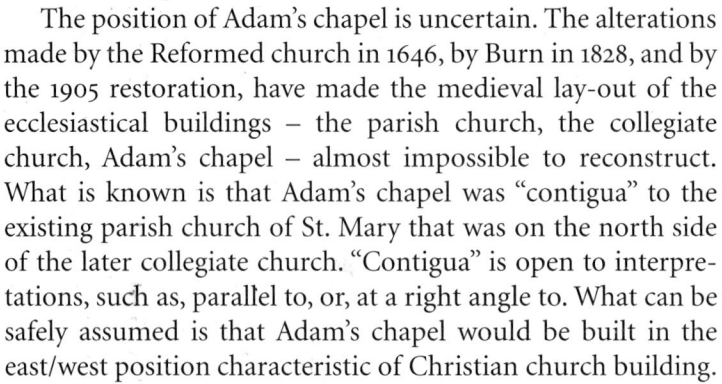

Tomb of Sir Adam Forrester in the Old Parish Church [GUS]

The position of Adam's chapel is uncertain. The alterations made by the Reformed church in 1646, by Burn in 1828, and by the 1905 restoration, have made the medieval lay-out of the ecclesiastical buildings – the parish church, the collegiate church, Adam's chapel – almost impossible to reconstruct. What is known is that Adam's chapel was "contigua" to the existing parish church of St. Mary that was on the north side of the later collegiate church. "Contigua" is open to interpretations, such as, parallel to, or, at a right angle to. What can be safely assumed is that Adam's chapel would be built in the east/west position characteristic of Christian church building.

There is also the possibility of Adam's chapel being incorporated into the later collegiate church structure. If so then there are three parts of the surviving church (now the Old Parish Church) which may have developed out of Adam's chapel. These are the chancel with its great east window, the nave, or the south aisle with its still existing east wall altar.

Since Adam was getting on in years by 1400, having been an established merchant in 1362, personal salvation would be primarily important and he may have contented himself with an adequate rather than a grandiose building. If he had been concerned with the imposing then, as a merchant and alderman of Edinburgh, he could have chosen interment in St. Giles'.

The chancel, greater in height than the nave, with its fine three lights window, belongs to the collegiate church period. The nave, lesser in height than the chancel, is a sizeable rectangular building and may have been Adam's chapel. The south aisle is a strong competitor for being Sir Adam's chapel on its own or along with the east part of the nave as its chancel. The three light window in the south aisle with its rectilineal tracery is late 14th / early 15th century work like the early perpendicular work in St. John's chapel in St. Giles' (1395).

The apparent similarity with the work at St. Giles' dedicated to the Baptist would seem to give the south aisle a prior claim to be Adam's chapel. Another though not generally accepted possibility is the medieval sacristy (now the vestry) described in 1838 as the confessional vault. But, no doubt, generations to come will continue to debate the point unless records as yet unfound come to light to clarify the issue.

The effigy in the south aisle has been attributed at different times to different people – Sir Adam, his great grandson Alexander, and Bernard Stewart, Lord of Aubigny. The three heraldic panels forming the table of the tomb cannot be used to identify the figure. The heraldry is Forrester and Sinclair of Orkney, which relates to Adam's son, Sir John who has his effigy, with that of his wife, elsewhere in the church.

The effigy shows an old man with wrinkled forehead. The armour and the detail are not earlier than about 1430. The helmet is the kind seen in manuscript illustrations around 1430. The little buckled triangle on the breast is not before 1420 and, perhaps, nearer 1450. The belt appears to be leather rather similar to that on an effigy at Coupar Angus. The trunk and limbs are clad in plate armour. The feet are in laminated sabbatons (shoes of leather covered with metal plates). There is a ring on the left index finger. The head, dressed in a bascinet (helmet pointed at crown) with camail (an attached mail fringe hanging down to cover the shoulders), is placed on an oblong cushion with a tassel at each corner. The armour is better suited to the period of Sir Alexander c.1460 than to that of Adam. The feet of the effigy rest on a dog.

A medieval altar surviving in the current vestry (former sacristy) of the Old Parish Church [GUS]

An interesting comment on this effigy was made by a visitor to the church in September 1799: "We found the door open and a wright at work … In another arched niche lies a solitary knight … with a most emaciated belly … a device of the artist to testify the repentance and devotion of the original, and perhaps to intimate that he ever imitated our Saviour in fasting forty days". The aged face and the shrunken body may be appropriate if the figure is old Adam. If it is the pilgrim-minded Alexander the leanness may indicate soul above physical appetite.

The visitor's observations in 1799 were not limited to the church for he noted: "On an old wall here grew *chelidonium majus* (celandine) which had probably escaped from some garden; for tho' a common weed in the country around London, it is scarcely native to Scotland". Celandine may have been uncommon then but in modern times as long as South Beechwood remained an open field the yellow spring flower grew in profusion along the path parallel to Balgreen Road.

Adam would he interred as near as possible to the altar of his chapel in order to gain the greatest merit for his soul. If his chapel were the nave then his grave would be at the east end close to where the chancel arch is. Burials were made in this area when the collegiate church was functioning for the 1443 Heriot stone was found at the 1905 Restoration under the wall that in post Reformation times blocked off the chancel from the nave.

If, however, Adam were the figure in the south aisle which may have been his chapel then he lies looking towards the surviving altar and credence where till the Reformation mass would be said.

Bernard Stewart was the third seigneur of Aubigny descended from Sir John Stewart of Darnley who for his military support of Charles VII was granted the lordship of Aubigny in 1422. Bernard was both a diplomat and a soldier. He commanded the French auxiliaries who helped Henry VII at Bosworth to defeat Richard III. The poet Dunbar described Bernard as "flower of gentleness". Louis XII sent him to Scotland in 1508 to renew the Auld Alliance.

Stewart's visit was an important state event. James IV presented him with seven horses with French saddles and held a tournament in honour of his visitor. Aubigny brought the King six horses. He took ill and died at Corstorphine Castle 11th June 1508.

On 2nd June the Lord High Treasurer's Accounts record that spur silver was paid to the "laddis of the Queir of Corstorphine". It was customary for anyone wearing spurs when entering a church to give money to the choir boys. Whose visit to Corstorphine Church occasioned a gift of spur silver – James IV or his representative? And was the visit made because Bernard Stewart was lying dying at the nearby castle? The royal Treasurer noted on 15th June a payment described as the "king's offerand at my Lord Owbigneis saule mes" but no place is indicated.

The tradition that Bernard Stewart is the effigy in the south aisle and that he was buried in Corstorphine persisted into this century. There is, in fact, no certainty about the burial of Stewart. He expressed the wish to be buried in the church of the Blackfriars in Edinburgh and this may well have been done. However the church of the Blackfriars was burned down in 1520 so that there is no record of burials there.

Appeal to the heraldic base of the tomb is of no help. It shows Forrester heraldry and it may not even be in its original position. Appeal to costume puts the figure about half a century before Stewart's death. The burial place of the Lord of Aubigny is one of history's unanswered problems. More certain is that he was one of the distinguished pre-Reformation worshippers in Corstorphine collegiate church. It may he that his deathbed at Corstorphine Castle brought King James to the church.

Bernard's heir was his cousin Robert Stewart, fourth son of the Earl of Lennox. The Stewarts of Aubigny came to an end in 1672 with the death of the sixth Duke of Lennox.

King James showed kindness to the villagers of Corstorphine when in March 1512 his Treasurer noted that money was given to poor "folkis at Corstorphin". Perhaps it was when news reached the village in the September of the following year that James had died on Flodden field that the poor folk remembered his kindness and of their charity prayed for his repose.

THE COLLEGIATE CHURCH

In early medieval times wealthy men supported monasteries but by the time of Adam and John Forrester their interests were turning to the establishment of family chapels. This

The Old Parish church from the south, c.1880. The doors shown in the porch and west side of the south transept have long since been filled in. (PB1451)

change of religious aspiration towards a private chapel came at the same time as the growth of the chantry concept. A chantry was a mass said for the welfare of a patron in life and for his soul after death and to effect this a chaplaincy was endowed.

In his prominent position as a statesman John may have felt that his father's chantry chapel was not sufficiently imposing or he may have thought that as an expression of his own piety bigger was better. Whatever his motive the next step for John was to build a collegiate church. The collegiate church was a grand chantry chapel, almost a small-scale cathedral. About forty collegiate churches were built in medieval Scotland. The buildings of thirty-one exist to-day either wholly or partially. Of these the earliest is St. Mary of the Rock at St. Andrews c.1250 and the latest is Stirling 1546.

The collegiate church was a college in the sense of a corporation of secular (not monastic) priests called prebendaries who were maintained from the revenue of lands or tenements granted by the founder and other benefactors, or from teinds annexed from some parish. The appropriation of parish funds such as teinds was greatly to the detriment of the parish church and the ordinary people who worshipped there and the consequently underpaid parish clergy. These sources of income for the collegiate priests were their prebends.

Choir boys were a feature of the collegiate church which did not exist in the parish church. Corstorphine choristers in the period 1566–72 were John Mason and Alexander Reid.

When James I returned to Scotland from his captivity in England Sir John Forrester got a charter in 1425 confirming Adam's foundation of three chaplains in the chapel of St. John the Baptist adjoining the parish church with the grant of an annual payment of £24. Of this endowment £20 was granted by King James from the fermes (rent equivalents) and rents of the burgh of Edinburgh and £4 from the annual rents in Edinburgh bestowed by Adam. This £20 was paid to the church at Corstorphine till about 1707 when a statute of limitation brought it to an end.

Sir John provided three acres of ground in the village for erecting houses for the chaplains and pasturage for three horses and three cows. In addition to prayers for the Forrester family the chaplains were also to pray for the King and for his Queen Joan Beaufort. Sir John was given the right of patronage in selecting his chaplains but their admission was the right of the bishop of St. Andrews. The right of patronage was materially advantageous as it allowed the founder patron to provide a collegiate living for his kinsmen. This possibly accounts for the Forrester arms on the grave slab of Robert Heriot, vicar of Gogar.

Margaret Forrester, Adam's widow, died about 1420, and in 1429 her son, Sir John, had from the King confirmation of a bequest Margaret had made in her lifetime to ensure the upkeep of Adam's chapel. Her bequest provided for two additional chaplains and for two choir boys and gave an endowment of £21-13-4 from property in Edinburgh and Leith as well as the Corstorphine Templelands and Meadowfield. Thus by 1429, when endowments and the framework of administration had been secured with the support of King James I, Adam's chapel was on its way to being transformed into a collegiate church.

Administrative control of a collegiate church was in the hands of a priest titled the Provost. Corstorphine is fortunate in having a tablet inscribed in Latin recording its first Provost:

Sundial incorporated into the Old Parish Church [GUS]

The stone tablet inscribed in Latin recording the name of the first provost of the Church in 1429, Nicholas Bannachtyne. (PB493)

"This Collegiate Church was commenced in the year of our Lord 1429, and that same year Master Nicholas Bannachtyne was provost of the said College, who, lying here below, died in the year 147–. Commemoration of him and his successors shall be celebrated and observed on the 14th day of June for which a yearly rent of £4 is set apart from the lands of Kirk Cramond. Pray for the Pope and for him."

The final sentence has been defaced and his date of death left uncompleted. He was alive in 1473.

How Sir John added to his father's chapel is a matter of conjecture. On the assumption that the chapel was used to form the nave of the new church then John added eastwards the chancel with a sacristy to the north. This would involve the breaking through of an archway (the line of the medieval arch is still visible) to join nave and chancel. In the chancel sedilia in the shape of arched and recessed wall benches were provided on the south side of the high altar for the clergy celebrating the mass. Over the sedilia survives an ornamental canopy of three ogival arched heads crocketed: three places for three chaplains. Adjoining the sedilia is the piscina with a bowl fashioned in eight radial flutes. The bowl originally projected from the wall but the projecting portion has been destroyed. It is combined with a credence shelf for the holy vessels.

The east window in the chancel has three lights and perpendicular tracery much restored. Before Burn in 1828 destroyed part of this window by driving an entrance doorway through the east end of the church and partly filling up the window it must have been a magnificent sight when the sun streaming through it lit up the tombs.

By the terms of the charter of 1425 confirming what Adam had set up the daily service at Corstorphine included the saying of the DIRIGE at Matins and Lauds: "dirigis Domine gressus meos". The chaplains also had the duty of the PLACEBO at Evensong. Both the *Dirige* and the *Placebo* are parts of the Office for the Dead.

Thanks to the skilful and sympathetic restoration work of George Henderson in 1905 the restoration of the east window has brought back to the spectator in the chancel a sense of past medieval religious glory – "the high-embowed roof" and "windows richly dight" that "bring all Heaven before mine eyes". Unfortunately there is no record of the medieval glass but as late as 1679 when the murdered Lord James was buried the spot chosen was beneath the east window then described as "great" – adjectival recognition of an important architectural feature.

THE TOMBS

The founder would naturally be concerned to have his tomb as close as possible to the high altar. Sometimes tombs were placed on the north wall of the sanctuary or in a transeptal aisle: others were free-standing before the altar. Medieval tombs were brilliant, some effigies coloured, and the tinctures of the heraldry adding to the splendour.

There are three tombs with effigies in recesses at Corstorphine. Two with male and female figures are on the north wall of the chancel, and one, a solitary male figure, is beneath the traceried window in the south aisle. The tomb with the two figures next to the chancel arch is taken to be that of Adam's son, Sir John, and one of his wives.

The armour dates to the first half 15th century: a close helmet with laminated chin piece, plate armour on body and limbs; laminated sabbatons on the feet. The hands are folded

Interior of the Church, looking east, after the 1905 restoration. Note the gas lighting and the relocation of the pulpit to its present location. *(PB67)*

on the breast over a shield shaped napkin with three hunting horns in relief. The feet rest on a lion.

The head of the female figure lies on two cushions. She has an enriched chaplet and wears a wimple pearled at the temples. Her neck is adorned with the fashionable 15th century chain and locket. A one-piece garment with sleeves is on the body and she has an embroidered belt and cloak. Her hands are crossed over a book, possibly a missal. On each finger she wears a ring. At her feet lies a small animal with an ornamental collar.

The continuous moulding of the arch of the recess is surmounted at its apex by a tilting helm, crested a dog's head, and below a canted shield with three hunting horns. The table of the tomb has five heraldic panels representing the Forrester family, and the families of two of Sir John's wives, St. Clair of Orkney and Stewart of Garlies. The table of the tomb with the solitary figures in the south aisle has three heraldic panels repeating the arms of Forrester and of St. Clair of Orkney and is apparently unrelated to this effigy.

Dr. Richardson, Inspector of Ancient Monuments, put forward an interesting solution to the positioning of these five and three heraldic panels. Sir John, as founder of the collegiate church, possibly had a free-standing tomb before the high altar below the great east window. As a free-standing

Tomb of Sir John Forrester (I), founder of the collegiate church in 1429, and his wife. *(PB1484)*

monument its table base could accommodate eight heraldic panels – the five presently on the north wall at the chancel arch and the three in the south aisle. Of the group of five there are two coats on one stone. This double stone could have formed the east end of the tomb facing the altar. The other six could be arranged three on the north side of the tomb and three on the south.

This would explain why in the south aisle the Forrester arms shown with the arms of the St. Clair of Orkney woman seem to have been wrongly cut heraldically. As seen to-day the male Forrester arms appear on the sinister when heraldically they should be on the dexter. But if this apparently wrongly cut stone was placed on the south side of a free-standing tomb situated at the entrance to the chancel and at a right angle to the altar the male arms would then come close to the altar – the highly desired position of the medieval man seeking eternal salvation through the mass.

It would also explain the obvious forcing of a tomb into the north wall at the chancel arch. For some unrecorded purpose Sir John's tomb, with its heraldic panels, may have been shifted from its free-standing position to be set into the north wall. The recess there could accommodate five panels but not eight. The other three panels would then have been used for the table supporting the effigy in the south aisle.

OPPOSITE.
Exterior of Church, and the tomb of Sir John Forrester (II), 1847, engraved by R.W. Billings. *(Courtesy RCAHMS, ref. EDD/58/85)*

Perhaps space was wanted before the high altar for liturgical purposes. A rood screen may have been erected necessitating floor space to be freed at the chancel area.

There were choir stalls because Provost Cairncross was inducted into his in 1525. Their installation in the previous century could have led to a re-arrangement. Space would also be needed for the choir lectern. Rearranging church furnishings is not an unknown exercise in present times. Sir John's death date is not known but his name appears in the Exchequer roll in 1448.

The recessed tomb on the east end of the north wall is a fine piece of stonework. It is understood to be the tomb of Sir John's son, the second John. The broad moulded arch has an almost triangular head. The projecting moulding above the arch is crocketed and terminates with shield carrying angels. The crown of the arch carries a tilting helm crested a dog's head. The head of the male has been destroyed. He wears plate armour and a cloak. The corselet, cuisses (thigh pieces), and jambards (leg pieces) are keel-shaped. Round his thighs an ornamented baldric carries a sword. The knee pieces are substantial. The spur chains at the ankles are decorated. The feet are in laminated sollerets (shoes). His hands are folded over a napkin on the breast.

The lady wears a chaplet and a wimple. The upper of the two cushions on which her head rests is placed diagonally on the lower with a rosette at each corner. Her flowing gown falls in folds and is caught at the waist by an ornamented belt. The trunk of the figure has a sideless cotehardie (body garment with buttons down front). Her cloak is fastened at the shoulders by a cord and her hands are crossed. Sleeved mittens cover the forearms.

The table base has three heraldic panels, two showing shields with Forrester hunting horns and between them a shield showing the arms of a Forrester man parted with what seems to be arms of a Wigmer woman. From the Wigmer heraldry both inside and outside the church it appears that some Forrester man married some Wigmer woman. The Wigmers were an important merchant burgess family in Edinburgh in the 14th and early 15th centuries. The heraldic shields have angel supporters which may be symbolic of a church benefactor as was the second John.

The tomb of the second John is impressive, almost surpassing his father's. It is unlikely that the second John

CORSTORPHINE CHURCH
AND TOMB
OF FORESTER

would have deliberately overshadowed his father's monument so it may be that the founder's tomb was indeed free-standing and not moved till a generation rose that had no personal recollection of him. The identification of the effigies is largely conjecture. Nevertheless the figures and the heraldry are in themselves fine works of the medieval mason.

They are not simply part of Corstorphine's history. They are an important part of Scotland's national and ecclesiastical heritage. This has been acknowledged most justly in the 1984 *Edinburgh* volume of the Penguin series *The Buildings of Scotland* where it is stated: "All the royal tombs at Holyrood have been destroyed so for monuments Corstorphine must take first place".

PAPAL RECOGNITION

Though founded in 1429, the date on the Bannachtyne stone, the Collegiate Church could not be accepted officially by the Bishop of St. Andrews. Sir John had to petition the Pope for recognition. Accordingly in 1436 Eugenius wrote to the Abbot of Holyrood to say that if the facts given by Forrester were correct then Holyrood could confirm Corstorphine as a collegiate church.

More money, however, was needed for such an institution and Sir John was ordered to make it available. This led to Pope Eugenius in 1440 acknowledging that Sir John had set up in the cemetery of the parish church of Corstorphine a college with an establishment of five priests, one of whom was the Provost, and two singing boys. He had also given an endowment of one hundred and twenty gold ducats yearly.

In 1436 Robert Heriot, canon of Glasgow, acting for the Provost and the Collegiate Church, asked the Pope for the whole annates of the parish church of Ratho (£40) to be united to Corstorphine when the incumbent resigned. The extra revenue from Ratho would provide for the daily performing of masses and the canonical hours with music and also for five additional priests. The Pope reduced the extra priests to four.

Finally in 1444 Eugenius issued a Papal Bull on the Institution of the Provostry and the Prebendaries of the Collegiate Church of Corstorphine. The establishment was the Provost, eight prebendaries, and two singing boys. The

Provost had the revenue of the church of Clerkington and the great teind sheaves of Ratho and Wasthall along with six merks.

The eight prebendaries had ten merks along with the great teind sheaves of Bonnington, Platt, Norton, Byres, Gogar, (H)addingstoun, Haltoun, and Dalmahoy: the prebendaries were designated by the names of these townships. The singing boys got twenty four bolls of usual victual and £3 yearly from the common purse, to be divided equally between them.

Money was also designated for church expenses, such as, bread and wine for the mass, altar lights, glass, waxes, chalices, books, and other church ornaments. These items witness to the liturgical splendour that once filled the church in Corstorphine. Tradition for long associated a golden cross with the church. An extension of this tradition tried to equate the placename Corstorphine with the Norman French idea of a *croix d'or fin*. The tale of a golden cross has been subjected to much scepticism but it deserves serious consideration. Since it is on record that Sir John gave a golden or gilt crucifix to the cathedral at Aberdeen it is not likely that he would have been less generous to his own collegiate church. At the Reformation the vestments and the silver of Corstorphine church like those of churches all over Scotland were, no doubt, either taken over privately by the gentry or sold and the money used for a variety of purposes.

The establishment of the collegiate church owed much to the support of Bishop Kennedy of St. Andrews who agreed to the union of Ratho to Corstorphine. As a token of gratitude, Sir John, with the sanction of Pope Nicholas V in 1450, founded a solemn mass with music to be said yearly after the feast of the translation of St. Thomas the Martyr during Kennedy's lifetime and after his death a requiem mass.

Sir John's petition in 1436 to Pope Eugenius to have Ratho united to Corstorphine is an example of medieval ecclesiastical "management". The Pope left the Abbot of Holyrood to transfer Ratho when the rector then in office resigned. The matter dragged on till 1440 when the Pope issued a Suspension. In this document he announced that he was promoting the rector of Ratho, Alexander de Lauedyr, to be bishop of Dunkeld. Thus legally the rector of Ratho was removed and Corstorphine got the benefits. But in 1450 William Lauder asked the Pope to restore what Ratho had lost as the parish was suffering from clerical deprivation. This led to Ratho regaining tithes not exceeding £8 yearly. Since William Lauder was the Lord of Hatton within the parish it would seem that his move was actuated more by financial considerations than by religious zeal. Ratho remained an unhappy association with Corstorphine till the 17th century when the benefices of the prebends were returned to it.

BENEFACTORS

Medieval religious belief encouraged men and women to become church benefactors. By so doing they were laying up for themselves credit in Heaven to compensate for earthly shortcomings. Thus in 1447 Thomas Broun granted the Collegiate Church of Corstorphine an annual sum of four merks from property in Edinburgh which Patrick Lamb occupied.

When John Philp Wood, at the close of the 18th century, was gathering material for a history of Corstorphine parish he noted a tablet on the west wall of the south aisle. The upper half was blank which made Wood wonder if an original stone had been removed or if the blank was a reversed stone. The lower portion had a Latin inscription recording that "the said Patrick gave in perpetuity, for the relief of the poor aforesaid, one year's return of forty pence in the said money from the entire lands of John March lying in the burgh aforesaid, according to the terms of the Charter issued there".

This tablet was also seen by General Hutton in May 1818 when he observed that the stone frame around the tablet had a decoration similar to that on the Bannachtyne stone. In 1839 the *New Statistical Account of Scotland* recorded that it was lying in the sacristy then used as the heating chamber for the kirk, Burn the architect having placed the stove there. This stone no longer exists. The forty pence were still being paid in 1512 when the sale of the property was noted in the Protocol Book of James Young as part of a tenement on the north side of the High Street of the Canongate. The transaction recorded that forty pence of annual rent had to be paid to a prebendary of Corstorphine. Presumably sometime after 1447 Patrick Lamb had taken over the property and continuing the gift to the church wished to have it recorded for posterity. Or it may be that some prebendary who got Patrick's money used it for the poor and set up a tablet to encourage others to do likewise.

In 1411 John de Barre, burgess of Edinburgh, being in financial difficulties, sold his property in Leith to John Brown, clerk to the Edinburgh burgesses. John Barre's wife was Mariotte Elder, daughter of John Elder in Corstorphine. The property had the burden of an annual payment to the Abbey of Holyrood and to St. Giles'. Then in 1475 Hugh Bar, burgess of Edinburgh, founded an additional chaplaincy at the altar of the Holy Trinity in Corstorphine Collegiate Church. The chaplain was to say daily mass for the souls of the King and Queen, the lords of the manor, the founder's wife and his mother and the faithful dead. He also had to speak to the people at the beginning of Lent urging them to remember the same persons by saying a Pater Noster and repeating the salutation of the angel to the Virgin Mary.

John Foular, notary, in July 1507 dealt with property on the south side of the High Street of Edinburgh which passed to Adam Bell and from which four merks had to be paid annually to the College of Corstorphine. Later Foular recorded on 2nd April 1534, that John Fischar, with the consent of his wife, Isobell Wyndzettis, had made over to sir Alexander Scott, Provost of Corstorphine, an annual rent of forty shillings from his property in Edinburgh.

This was for an anniversary to be celebrated yearly for the souls of Fischar and his wife. Another notary, James Young, in January 1513 arranged for part of a tenement on the north side of the Canongate to pass from John Quareour to David Balfour and his wife-to-be Elizabeth Quareour. Balfour had to pay forty pence annually of the sum due from the whole property to a prebendary of Corstorphine.

So it was that medieval man through the masses and prayers of the collegiate church met the challenge of death in a world beset by plague and warfare. Mindful of his own present and future he was also not forgetful of those who had gone before.

THE PROVOSTS

The Provost was responsible for organising the religious duties of the College. He was also answerable to the bishop of St. Andrews. A condition of his appointment was that he would reside where his college was. He was not to be absent at any time for more than fifteen days. The Provostry at

Corstorphine was dissolved by Acts of the Scottish Parliament in 1621, 1633, 1641. George, Lord Forrester, as patron of the church and heir to the revenues of the Collegiate Church, sold them to the owners of the estates from where they were derived.

NICHOLAS BANNACHTYNE (1429–73): The first Provost was a magister of St. Andrews University in 1426. He is remembered in a tablet sited on the east wall of the church (see photograph on page 12). The inscription records his mortification of a yearly rent of £4 from the lands of Kirk Cramond to he used to commemorate him and his successors on 14th June annually. This piece of Cramond ground once known as the Priests Acres later passed into the lands of the Inglis of Cramond family.

Bannachtyne was associated with the Bishop of St. Andrews in carrying out papal orders. In 1446 they dealt with a complaint involving the rector of the parish church of Corstorphine. Then in April 1462 the Provost and the Bishop of Glasgow were instructed to induct George de Graham as Provost of the Collegiate Church of Hamilton (Cadzow) which James Lord Hamilton had formed out of the parish church.

JAMES DOUGLAS (1479–80): graduate of St. Andrews University.

ALEXANDER CRAG (1503)

ROULL OF CORSTORPHINE (d. by 1507): William Dunbar, the great medieval Scots poet, in 1507 wrote *Lament for the Makaris*. His subject was the supremacy of death over all men. Each verse of Dunbar's Lament has the haunting refrain from the Office of the Dead : "Timor mortis conturbat me" (the fear of Death disquiets me). Among those named by Dunbar are:

"*He hes tane Roull of Aberdene
And gentill Roull of Corstorphin
Two bettir fellowis did no man se;
Timor mortis conturbat me.*"

Nothing certain is known of Corstorphine's "gentill Roull". In the winter of 1568 when plague beset Edinburgh George Bannatyne (c.1545–1608) made a collection of Scottish poetry, now preserved in the National Library of Scotland. He included a poem *The Cursing of sir John Rowlis* but whether this applies to Roull of Aberdeen or of Corstorphine is not known. The poem puts a curse on those who have stolen Roull's poultry and garden produce. David Irvine, 1861, in his *History of Scottish Poetry* commented: "if he was the vicar of Corstorphine his geese and apples must have been exposed to divers contingencies on account of their convenient distance from the metropolis."

The name Roull is preserved in Corstorphine Street names. Helen B. Cruickshank, poet and Corstorphine resident, wrote in her, *Octobiography* 1976: "one of my fantastic dreams is that the poems of the gentill Roull of Corstorphine may yet, like sections of a Roman road leading to Cramond, turn up in some unexpected quarter." To live on in history as "gentill" is no mean achievement.

ROBERT FORRESTER (1507) Master of Arts

JAMES MERCHAMSTON (1511–15): Rector of Hawick 1504; Later an Auditor in the Exchequer Court. When on court business for James IV in 1502 he brought a grey horse from Flanders. His town house was on the north side of the High Street of Edinburgh, possibly Monteith's Close.

ROBERT CAIRNCROSS (1525–28): Cairncross was inducted on 5th August 1525 to the Provostry. Other offices he held were: Chaplain to James V; Lord High Treasurer 1528; Lord of Session. In 1528 Cairncross became Abbot of Holyrood as a result of a wager with the King. He was appointed to the bishopric of Ross in 1538 which he held in conjunction with the Abbacy of Fearn till his death in 1545. In April 1542 when Bishop of Ross he got an annual rent from part of Over Barnton belonging to Robert Mowbray. On 2nd September 1536 he had his illegitimate children, John, Andrew, and Isabella formally legitimised.

Cairncross was buried at the cathedral of Fortrose in what is now the only surviving aisle of that noble church building in Ross-shire. When one of the tombs there was broken into by some workmen in 1797 it was reported that the inside of one stone coffin was plastered and painted white and decorated all round with red crosses. Relics inside the coffin included a bishop's crozier, and stole. If the red crosses had a significance other than religious then they, like canting heraldry, may have denoted that this was the coffin of Cairncross.

ALEXANDER SCOTT (1529–44): He was Depute to the Clerk Register, 1525-26; founded a chaplaincy at Irvine 1540;

was paid for his Exchequer "lauboris ditand the Rolls", 1539–41. In 1542 James V recognised Scott's long, faithful service to himself and to his father by assuring Scott of protection against the "unfriendis" who were making it difficult for him to "order his beneficc". James gave Scott full permission to use the revenues of ecclesiastical position as he wished, promising that if anyone molested him the offender would be punished.

JAMES SCOTT (1532–64): James was brother of Alexander, the preceding Provost; clerk to the Treasury; Lord of Session; Auditor 1551-59. He had a natural son, William, who got from him a "granoreum" in Leith 1551. This William also got in 1553 ten acres of Tollcross in the lordship of Dalry, and in 1553 he also got four acres of Orchardfield (now part of Edinburgh – Bread Street / Lothian Road/Spittal Street).

James was absent from Corstorphine in 1558 when a boy was sent to him at Balgonie, Fife, with a letter from the Queen. Alexander and James Scott were grandsons of Sir David Scott of Buccleuch. From James descended Sir John Scott of Scotstarvit.

WILLIAM SCOTT (1564–68): In the *Fasti* William is described as nephew of Provost James Scott. James, however, had a natural son William. Whatever the relationship the Scott family held the Provostry for forty years.

ROBERT DOUGLAS (1568–85): Though a post Reformation appointment Douglas enjoyed the life rent of the College revenues. He died at Clerkington in 1586. In his will he asked to be buried at Corstorphine College kirk. Douglas had a library of twelve scriptural and eight non-scriptural books. To the "lady of Corstorphing" he left his copy of "ane buik called Chaser" which she had borrowed from him. So a hundred years after Alexander Forrester went as a pilgrim to Canterbury a lady of the family sat in the castle reading Chaucer's immortal account of the pilgrims who went from the Tabard Inn "the holy blisful martyr for to seke". Perhaps Douglas was compensating her for having had to renounce her claim to her husband's library at the castle of Corstorphine.

ALEXANDER MAKGILL (1585–1628): Makgill was an advocate who held the emoluments of the Provostry *in commendam* (as a layman not performing religious duties). Neither he nor his wife attended the parish church so Mr Arthur, the minister, read from the pulpit the sentence of excommunication but not in its entirety in order to give them a chance to repent. Makgill appeared before the congregation on 1st February 1602 and satisfied the minister.

His wife remained obdurate but finally had to appear before the Presbytery of Edinburgh. There, on her knees, she admitted her sin of not attending church for eighteen months and promised to attend in future. Perhaps her real allegiance lay with the old church. In 1608 Makgill and Forrester were not on good terms for Harie Guidlet of Uphall stood as cautioner for George Forrester not to harm Makgill.

FLORENCE GARDNER (1632–59): Florence was a titular Provost. In a horning action raised by him in 1635 he got a decreet against the parishioners of Corstorphine concerning teinds and teind sheaves.

THE PROVOST'S HOUSE

The Provost had his own residence or manse. Presumably the original house was near the church. A new house which was built or started to be built by Provost Alexander Scott who died in 1544 survived till about 1885 when it was taken down to provide a site for the church hall at the east end of the High Street. Two of its skew putts were incorporated externally into the church hall roofing. One is inscribed: A S Poes. The other has a shield with Scott heraldry.

Dr. Sanderson, in her biography of Cardinal Beaton, notes the record in *The St. Andrew's Formulare*, ed. by Professor Gordon Donaldson, of Beaton authorising a visitation of Corstorphine Collegiate Church. This was requested by Alexander Forrester and his son, James, to whom the estate was made over in 1538. James complained of neglect of the fabric of the prebendal manses as well as non-residence of the clergy. Provost Alexander Scott's new Provostry was, doubtless, one result of the visitation. If the work was incomplete when Alexander died his brother James, as next Provost, possibly finished the work. This would account for Selway's suggestion that James c.1550 was the builder and for Alexander's skew putt. The house was occupied by the *in commendam* Provost Makgill till 1628 at least.

Though church property at the Reformation was largely taken over by the Crown the provostries, since they had originated in private religious foundations, were left with their patrons – in Corstorphine, the Forrester family. Florence Gardner, the titular Provost, may not have occupied the house as he had property elsewhere in the village.

George Forrester in 1621 asked Parliament to empower him to separate the Provostry from other church property. In 1634 the Provost – and Gardner as the nominee of Forrester would probably do as told – with the consent of Forrester and others dissolved the College. This was confirmed by Parliament in 1641.

While George Forrester was consolidating his position over church property his daughter, Margaret, in 1634 contracted to marry Alexander Tailziefer (Telfer) of Reidhews. In 1646 Florence Gardner "residenter" in Corstorphine granted sasine of the Provost's house to Telfer and Margaret Forrester which George Forrester confirmed.

Telfer was in financial difficulty in 1654 for Samuel Veitch, baron baillie of the Forresters, got a decree of apprising (a creditor obtaining ownership of a debtor's land) against Telfer for Reidhews and the Provost's House. The period for redemption of an apprising was seven years. Within that period James, Lord Forrester, "lawful superior" in 1657 drew up a disposition. This granted to Margaret, his sister-in-law, and her husband Telfer the Provost's house – "that tenement or great mansione house with close and yeard theirof lyand within the toune of Corstorphin and the north syde of the comone hieway betwixt the mansione house and yeard pertaining to the minister of Corstorphin on the west, the Churchyard on the eist, The Gleib of the minister on the north, and the public hieway on the south pairtes". The feu duty was three shillings and four pence.

Telfer was dead by 1659 when his widow was party to an antenuptial contract with John Shaw of Sornberg. A creditor of the Telfer estate was Patrick Telfer who took out Letters of Inhibition against Margaret Forrester and John Shaw to prevent them from alienating their lands till the debt was paid.

The next documented name connected with the house is Sir Robert Baird of Saughtonhall who was busy with repairs between 1689 and 1692. He bought the property in 1688. George Wilson, slater, undertook roof work, Sir Robert providing materials and the customary drink money. Particular mention is made of a run roof (sloping, narrow roof) to the turnpike (narrow, spiral staircase) which gives a little visual image of the house externally. The rigging (ridge) and two storm windows are noted in James Paterson's attestation of the work done by March 1692.

William Lourie, wright in Gorgie, was another of Sir Robert's tradesmen. However the man principally engaged on the work from 1689 to 1692 was Charles Gowans, mason. At November 1691 his account included "redling of rubbage at ye Lady's derection", souring lime (slaking), carrying sand, "slopping (striking out) hewing and putting up" seven windows, and building the close dyke on the east side.

There is also a charge for damage to adjoining property – repairing the breach in the minister's cellar and coal house. Another statement of work done indicates that the repairs and alterations were not finished by 1692. It seems that Gowans inhabited part, at least, of the house for he is charged with house rent. Baird also gave Mrs Gowans (Agnes Yorston) money to buy "shoon", a complimentary gesture to the lady of the house.

On 29th July 1728 Baird gave a tack of the house for fifteen years to John Whyte, mealmaker in Corstorphine, and Janet Midlemass his spouse. The property was then described as: "high and laigh with the yeard there-to ... fore closs ... bounded on east with the kirk yeard dyke and the minister's house on the west syde".

Whyte was to pay rent of £5 stg yearly but was not to pay till reimbursed for money due to him by Baird. The fabric of the building was a problem. Whyte had advanced money for roof work – timber (fir), thatch, lath – and for "casting the whole tenement". Liberty was given to take ale and other liquors for sale from anyone Whyte was pleased to deal with. So the Provost's house became a hostelry. Baird promised the roof would either be slated or covered with "wheat straw" except the turnpike stair and the "flankers" (side projections) which were to continue slated and pointed. In 1738 John Whyte paid the Kirk Session for permission to erect his father's gravestone which can be read in the kirkyard.

Baird, being short of money, was unable in 1736 to honour a bond of 1720. Decreets of Adjudication were taken against him in 1736 by Gilbert Clerk, a writer, and Mungo Rannie, brewer and baillie in Portsburgh, Edinburgh. In 1767 Gilbert Clerk sold the house to David Black, indweller in Corstorphine, who put the property to public roup in November 1767 at John's Coffee House, Edinburgh. The property was described as "that commodious inn or dwelling house with nine fire rooms, half an acre of garden with a good well" and a large court opposite the house on which buildings could be erected. No one came to the roup so the house was rouped again in December. However it does not appear to have been sold as in 1776 David Black disponed it in favour of Ann Lawson or Black in liferent and William Black in fee.

By 1790, according to J. P. Wood in his *Draft History of Corstorphine*, the Provost's House had become subdivided property. In 1796 Alexander Thomson, farmer Meadowhouse, bought the property which descended to his daughter Mrs Elizabeth Thomson or Dixon. On 16th May 1885 she sold to the Trustees for the heritors of Corstorphine who in August of the same year sold to the Rev. James Dodds and others, Trustees for the congregation of the Parish Church of Corstorphine.

When the Kirk Session bought the property their aim was to have a Mission and to use part of the ground for cemetery expansion. The Minister, Mr Dodds, pushed for the Mission Hall because he was unhappy about the heritors' proposal to reconstruct the Provost's House to provide cheap dwelling houses. He thought such houses would injure the amenity of the church grounds. The heritors were in advance of their times with their concept of Kirk care houses. However Victorian church support was great enough to justify a large church hall. Unfortunately the Provost's House was demolished to provide a hall site.

The Provost's House came back to the church after three centuries of secular possession and the church destroyed it albeit with the best of Christian intentions. J.C. Oliphant writing in 1892 – *Some Rambles Round Edinburgh* – lamented the loss of this ancient building: "It is only a few years since the house of the old provosts of the church, though still inhabited and in good condition, was destroyed for the sake of the materials, and that by the authorities of the church itself, from whom, if from anyone, better things might have been expected."

However the site remains with the kirk. Long may it be so, providing a much used, socially valuable small hall with other rooms, flanking the south entrance to the kirk and kirkyard. And for those who lift their eyes to the Heavens there are the sculptured skew putts of Provost Scott. In the church is the handsome carved reader's chair made from the oak beams taken down from the old house and fashioned lovingly by

John Darge, member of the church, joiner and draper, who lived in Gladstone Place in the village High Street. A hundred years on Mr Darge's chair, like the skew putts, links past and present in Corstorphine church history.

A recent photograph of the High Street, Church Hall with inserts showing the position of the 16th century 'skew Putts' incorporated from the Provost's House which formly stood on this site. *(PB2025)*

THE PREBENDARIES

The prebendaries were the chaplains responsible for saying mass and performing other religious services. The prebend was the prebendary's share of church revenues, usually rent from land and parish teinds. Some Corstorphine prebendaries have survived only in name. Where the name is prefixed by sir (dominus) the priest had no academic degree. Magister indicates a Master of Arts.

In the Collegiate Church of Corstorphine the teinds of Gogar and (H)addistoun were shared by two chaplains designated in documents as Half Gogar and Half Addistoun. Similarly treated were the two chaplains of Haltoun (Hatton) and Dalmahoy, the two of Bonington and Platt (Ratho Hall and Hillwood), and the two of Norton and Byres (Ratho Byres). In addition to their share of teinds the chaplains had ten merks yearly from the common purse. After the Reformation the prebends were dissolved but patronage continued for a while to create titular prebendaries.

DAVID SWINTON (1467): "mesne fruits" of Hatton and Dalmahoy; presented by the patron Sir Alexander Forrester.

ALEXANDER COLE (1472)

DOMINUS JOHN CURROR; WILL FORSTUR; ANDREW GAWINOK; JAC DE HALIS; ALEX STORY; HECTOR STORY; MALCOLM CHEPMAN (1477): Chepman had kirklands on the east of Kirk Loan.

PATRICK HAW (1496–1500): witness sasine Alexander Forrester to Gilbert Forrester of Drylaw of three oxgangs Corstorphine.

WILLIAM SIMSONE (1500): witness sasine

JOHN HOWISONE (1500): witness sasine

JOHN MERSCHEL (1510)

RICHARD BOTHWELL (1510): going to Pope Julius 22nd July 1510.

sir *THOMAS WILKIESON* (1525): President of Chapter House of the college; had a daughter, Christiane, dead by 1548 when her goods, by gift of escheat of bastards, were given by "Hir Grace" (Mary of Guise) to David Ramsay servitor to my Lord of Dunkeld.

MAGISTRI DUNCAN FORBES; JOHN PENNY; THOMAS SCOTT; THOMAS THOMSON; sir *JAMES RAMSAY; JOHN WILKIESON* (1539)

MAGISTER ALEXANDER GALLOWAY (1547): clerk Aberdeen; half Haltoun, Half Dalmahoy

MAGISTER GEORGE COK (1547): Half Haltoun, Half Dalmahoy

ROBERT MARJORIBANKS (1548): dead by November 1548

THOMAS MARJORIBANKS (1548): brother of and successor to Robert Marjoribanks; Half Haltoun, Half Dalmahoy

DOMINUS JOHN GREENLAW (1553–67): dead by 1567; Half Haltoun, Half Dalmahoy; a breviary printed at Lyons 1546 was bought in Paris by Greenlaw and later he gifted it to John Watson, Canon of Aberdeen. The title page has an illustration of the Image of Pity which Greenlaw spotted with red ink to represent Christ's wounds. The Image of Pity was popular in late medieval devotion to the Passion and is the central design of the Fetternear Banner, that treasure of Scottish medieval church needlework now housed in the Royal Museum of Scotland, Edinburgh. The Greenlaw Watson breviary formerly at Preshome Library is now in The National Library of Scotland.

ALEXANDER GILL (1562): Half Gogar, Half Addistoun

MAGISTER GEORGE LAUDER (1562): Half Norton, Half Byres

MAGISTER THOMAS MARJORIBANKS (1562–67): Half Bonington, Half Platt

JAMES GRAY (1562–87): advocate; Half Norton, Half Byres

MAGISTER JAMES WILKIE (1562–72): Half Dalmahoy, Half Haltoun

MAGISTER NINIANE BORTHWICK (1562–72): Half Gogar, Half Addistoun; minister Kirknewton, Lauder, and in 1514 at Westruther.

ROBERT DOUGLAS (1562–71): Half Bonington, Half Platt

PATRICK CREICH (1567): followed Greenlaw in Half Haltoun, Half Dalmahoy, parish minister Ratho

sir *ADAM LOWIS* (pre 1573): dead by 1573; Half Haltoun, Half Dalmahoy

GEORGE DOUGLAS (1573): son of William Douglas of Whittinghame; Half Haltoun, Half Dalmahoy

JOHN DOUGLAS (1584): son of Douglas of Whittinghame; followed George Douglas in Half Haltoun, Half Dalmahoy

CLEMENT KING (1589): Half Gogar, Half Addistoun

HEW McGILL (1617): caption against James Tweedy of Dreva and his son for money due McGill and his wife Jean Crauford

MAGISTER WIL ARTHUR (1618): titular; Half Haltoun, Half Dalmahoy, held jointly with James Inglis

JAMES INGLIS (1618–46): burgess Glasgow; Half Haltoun, Half Dalmahoy; described 1587 as "a prebendary of Corstorphine"

ROBERT SCOTT (1618–48): Half Haltoun, Half Dalmahoy

SIR JOHN DALMAHOY (1641): Half Haltoun, Half Dalmahoy, Half Bonington, Half Platt belonging to the King but assigned

JOHN YOUNG (1648): Half Bonington, Half Platt

BERNARD HUNTER (1648): Half Bonington, Half Platt

PATRICK DENNY (1648): Half Haltoun, Half Dalmahoy; notary

PATRICK VANCE (1676): Half Haltoun, Half Dalmahoy; Charles Maitland of Haltoun, Lord Treasurer Deputy, "undoubted patrone of the provostrie of ye Colledge Kirk of

Corstorphing" in so far as it included Ratho, made Patrick Vance, Keeper of the Tolbooth of Edinburgh, in July 1676 "prebender" with all its pertinents. Unfortunately history has not left an explanation of Maitland's transaction with Vance. It is, however, a last echo of the College Kirk of Corstorphine and its prebendaries.

THE "DOWER HOUSE"

When Sir John Forrester in 1425 began to form a collegiate church he assigned three acres of ground in the village for manses. In property sasines a brief indication of sites appears. Malcolm Chepman's kirkland lay on the east side of Kirk Loan in the area of Corstorphine House Avenue. Property in 1657 south of the church and beside the War Memorial, an area now grassed over, belonged to the prebendary of Half Norton and Half Ratho Byres.

An interesting other site exists in connection with the manse of Half Haltoun (Hatton) and Half Dalmahoy and the building presently known as the Dower House. But in the 19th century it was known as Gibson Lodge.

In 1587 James Inglis appears as prebendary of Corstorphine. King James in 1618 gave the church lands of Corstorphine to George Forrester including the prebend of Half Haltoun and Half Dalmahoy of which William Arthur and James Inglis, burgess of Glasgow, were titular holders. A deed of 1625 relating to Orchardfield, east of the Dower House, describes it as bounded on the west by the house of the prebendary of Half Haltoun and Half Dalmahoy – James Inglis.

Beatrix Ramsay, relict of John Livingstone, in 1646 acquired from George Forrester the house and garden with rig which had belonged to prebendary Inglis. Ownership of this property passed to Beatrix Ramsay's daughter, Christian, and her husband, Binny of Carlowrie. By 1719 it was owned by John Murray.

The Edinburgh lawyer, Samuel Mitchelson, in 1765 purchased the property sometime possessed by James Inglis, Beatrix Ramsay, and John Murray. Mitchelson made extensive alterations and additions. He built stables, coach houses, a barn and a gardener's house. It was, no doubt, in his time that the mansion was heightened by adding a storey. The surviving

18th century fireplace, the landscape in oils, and the panelling are possibly also Mitchelson's work. In 1766 his appeal against window tax failed: this may indicate his enlargement of the original building.

When Mitchelson left the village for a mansion he erected at Clermiston, the house in the High Street was bought by Dame Henrietta Watson, Lady Gibsone, widow of Sir John Gibsone of Pentland. Henrietta was there in 1792 but in her impecunious state she was unlikely to make any changes to the house. Thereafter Gibson Lodge passed to John Cowie and from him to Sir John Dick of Prestonfield. Then in 1872 it was bought by John Dickson of Saughton and Corstorphine. Finally the Dickson family in 1923 sold the property to Edinburgh Corporation.

Here then is a house and ground with a line of ownership from the prebendary James Inglis in 1587 to the City of Edinburgh in 1923. Gibson Lodge owes its name to Lady Gibsone. But where did Dower House originate? Probably it derives from J. P. Wood's *Draft History of Corstorphine Parish*, 1792, in which the author says when speaking of the stones of the old castle – "were carried away probably to build Mr Michelson's house which was the residence of the Lord Forresters". No authority is given for this Forrester connection.

Gibson's Lodge, c.1926, from Corstorphine High Street. Familiarly but inaccurately known in recent years as the Dower House, it is now the Corstorphine Heritage Centre and the headquarters of the Corstorphine Trust. *(PB229)*

Mitchelson may have used castle stones for the office buildings he erected and the castle may have provided the fine gateway to the house. Its moulded piers are surmounted by stone spheres held by wrought iron standards which rest on the pier capitals. Selway calls the property the Dower House but gives no authority for his statement. It is not noted in the *First* or *Second Statistical Accounts*. The Historical Monuments (Scotland) Commission quotes Selway. When John Dickson in 1869 purchased the lands and barony of Corstorphine the house was designated Gibson Lodge. It would seem that Wood and Selway are the only begetters of the "Dower House" tradition.

Since Beatrix Ramsay and her heirs owned the house from 1646 to 1702 it could hardly have been "built by one of the Lords Forrester as a dower house about 1660-70" (Selway). It came to George Forrester in 1618 as part of the collegiate church property and he sold it in 1646. In that space of time the only need, if ever there was a need, for a dower house would be when George's mother was widowed not later than 1618. She, however, had a life rent of the New Wark of the castle, and she remarried before 1625.

The house possessed by Inglis, the titular prebendary, was a prebendal manse for Half Haltoun and Half Dalmahoy. A tenant this century spoke of the entrance door being in the west wall. Despite alterations at upper levels the foundations and ground floor may be prebendal. Thomas *Lugton's The Old Ludgings of Glasgow 1901* has an illustration of the manse of Douglas which bears a similarity to the Corstorphine Dower House.

From the mid 19th century to 1923 the house was tenanted by generations of the Thomson family, highly respected market gardeners who worked the attached ten acres. The Thomsons in 1861 sub-let part of the house to Catherine Rose, a widow of 73 with two attendants, one a companion and the other a general servant. She had accommodation with four windows, possibly the first flat. She was the proprietrix of "Kilrawack" (Kilravock, Nairn). The Rose family was related to the Mackenzies of Belmont at the eastern limit of Corstorphine parish.

Fortunately what is basically a prebendal manse has survived with 18th century alterations. It is an attractive house in St. Margaret's Park. Though not so romantic, the name Gibson(e) Lodge has better documented support than the

Dower House. The time may now have come for the sake of historical accuracy to give the house another name.

Heritage House? Or, The Prebend? As this edition is published the medieval ecclesiastical site is entering a new life as The Corstorphine Heritage Centre.

THE CHAPTER HOUSE: THE SACRISTY: THE SEAL

The administrative committee in a collegiate church was the Chapter consisting of the Provost and the Prebendaries. The place for transacting business was the Chapter House. On 5th August 1525 Robert Cairncross was inducted into the Provostry of Corstorphine by the President of the Chapter, Sir Thomas Wilkieson. The induction took place in the Choir and in the Chapter House in the presence of Sir Alexander Forrester. Wilkieson assigned Cairncross his seat in the Chapter, doing so in the Chapter House.

The position of the Chapter House is not known but it may have been the upper storey of the sacristy which lies on the north side of the chancel and has corbels for two floors. The ground floor room has a medieval altar slab with five incised crosses symbolic of Christ's passion.

Line drawing of what is now the Corstorphine Heritage Centre (familiarly known, if inaccurately, as the Dower House) in St. Margaret's Park on the south side of the High Street. [RG]

This sacramental slab is a great spiritual treasure. Perhaps it was too premature in 1905 for it to be placed beside the Presbyterian Communion table. A generation yet to come, moved with the ecumenical spirit, may one day set this visible sacramental link with the past where the congregation can see it as did their medieval forebears at the celebration of the Last Supper: the same yesterday, to-day, and forever.

Adjoining the altar slab is a large stone basin which discharged its water content through the wall. Trial excavation c.1980 in the area outside the sacristy revealed part of a stone runnel.

The pointed barrel vault covered a garret above the upper floor. The sacristy in its original layout may have served both administrative and religious purposes. It has a strong claim to being the medieval Chapter House.

The seal of the Collegiate Church was appended to a tack made on 2nd September 1587 by James Gray, advocate "and prebendary" of Half Nortoun and Half Ratho Byres. He granted to his "kyndlie tenent" Thomas Young the teinds of

'Confessional Vault' by A. Archer, 1838. Now the vestry. The Communion slab and basin can still be seen. *(Courtesy RCAHMS, ref. EDD/58/84)*

Nortoun. The business was done "within the college kirk" of Corstorphine "with the consent of the Provost and remanent prebendaris".

Attached to the document was the seal of the College. The design showed St. John with rayed nimbus holding the Agnus Dei on his left arm and pointing to it with his right hand, a spray of foliage at each side of his feet and beneath the dove. On an inner escroll above his head: Ecce Agnus Dei. Legend (caps) : S. COMVNE ECCLE COLLEGIATE DE COSTROPHIN. Pointed oval 2 x 1¼ ins.

THE HOSPITAL: THE ALMS HOUSE

Attached to collegiate churches were hospitals for the poor, the sick and travellers. The Hospital at Corstorphine was in existence, at least, in 1538. One source of finance for the Hospital was an annual rent from tenants in the Over Bow of Edinburgh.

In 1568 John Wilson, John Hiltstoun, Janet Wishart, and Marion Gray, "beidmen and women of ye college of Corstorphin" raised an action against Catherine and Janet Hay and their husbands for non-payment since 1558 of the

THE CHURCH IN CORSTORPHINE: BEGINNINGS

The foot of Kirk Loan, probably pre-1914, looking to Saughton Road North. The houses on the right were demolished in 1928. The Alms House was part of this group of buildings. The first Corstorphine Public Library was added to the east (nearer) side of the Public Hall in 1903. (PB19)

annual rent from the Over Bow which was the patrimony of the Hospital.

The Hospital stood on the curvilinear ground south of the church, opposite the present Public Hall. A 17th century document notes "the houss and yeard pertaining to the Olimosioner of Corstorphing". The Hospital, later referred to as the Alms House, was where the bedesmen and bedeswomen lived who prayed for the departed Forresters and all faithful souls.

The Kirk Session in 1669 paid for roof repairs – thirty six shillings for five hundred divots "to help the Hospitall". By 1679 the Alms House was giving the Session concern for they considered it was ruinous. Moreover James Lord Forrester had taken possession of the yard. The feu-duty of Ferrybank house (part of the Templelands between St. Ninian's Road and Victor Park Terrace) in the 18th century included payment to the Hospital.

In 1810 the Heritors put the ground to public roup on a 99 years lease. John Cowie, victual dealer, was the highest bidder and he erected a house on the foundations of the Alms House. By 1816 Cowie was in financial straits and executed a trust disposition in favour of David Bain, accountant. Bain sold the lease and the house to Archibald Thomson. The Kirk Session, on behalf of the poor, exerted their right to the land and got an agreement for a yearly payment related to the price and value of twenty five and a half pecks of barley at the highest fiars prices in Midlothian.

By the mid 19th century the building was used by the Parochial Board to house the poor for which the Board paid rent to the owner, Mrs Thomson. The property in late Victorian times passed to Christopher Douglas Brown who had married into the Thomson family. Then it was bought by William Traquair Dickson. In 1924 it was sold to the City of Edinburgh.

Adjoining the Alms House were red pantiled cottages inhabited by Irish families attracted to work opportunities in Midlothian in the early 19th century. Local tradesmen this century used some of the buildings. Mr. Hume, the coal merchant, and Mr. Gray, the builder, had stabling, office and yard space. There was also a mortuary building. In 1928 the old houses were pulled down and grass was planted on the land that in medieval times belonged to the prebendaries.

Where once bedesmen and bedeswomen, within the shadow of the church, counted their beads there is now a green oasis, beautiful in Spring with flowering trees cared for by the city gardeners.

Site of the former Black Bull Inn, long since demolished and the site built on, at the sharp corner in the old village at the junction of the High Street with North Saughton Road, known as Irish Corner because of the large numbers of Irish labourers living here in the 19th Century. [GUS]

THE LAMP NICHE: THE LAMP ACRE

Lamp Acre as a field or a place name occurs but rarely on either side of the Cheviots. In the indexes to the Register of the Great Seal there appears a lamp acre in Peebles-shire 1643. In medieval times Corstorphine and the adjoining parish of Gogar each had a Lamp Acre. That at Gogar is recorded as providing the money to maintain a lamp in the church there dedicated to St. Mary.

For lack of documentation the origin and the purpose of the Corstorphine Lamp Acre cannot be so readily or so exactly defined as that of Gogar.

It must, of course, have been to maintain a light of some sort. Light would be particularly relevant in a church dedicated, as Corstorphine was, to the Baptist. The Baptist's anniversary day in June, being close to the summer solstice, inevitably attracted to it the more primitive customs of sun-worship and kindling fires.

THE LAMP

THERE SHONE OF OLD FROM THIS CHANCEL GABLE A LAMP SERVING TO GUIDE WAYFARERS THROUGH THE MARSH STRETCHING EASTWARDS FROM THE CHURCH. IT WAS MAINTAINED BY THE ENDOWMENT OF THE "LAMPACRE"

ON 2ND APRIL, 1958, THE LAMP WAS SET IN PLACE AND LIGHTED AGAIN TO THE GLORY OF GOD AND IN PRAYERFUL, HONOURED REMEMBRANCE OF

SIR JOHN FORRESTER OF CORSTORPHINE
flor 1394–1448
CHAMBERLAIN OF SCOTLAND

WHO BUILT AND ENDOWED THIS COLLEGIATE CHURCH IN 1429.

"LET YOUR LIGHT SO SHINE BEFORE MEN THAT THEY MAY SEE YOUR GOOD WORKS, AND GLORIFY YOUR FATHER WHICH IS IN HEAVEN"

Carrying blazing torches through corn fields on St. John's Eve to protect crops was once an Inverness-shire ritual. As late as July 1589 the Session of St. Cuthbert's Edinburgh made Isobel Lauriston do public repentance for taking part in bonfire celebrations at Saughton "on midsummer's even" and James Lauriston was censured for having children at the bonfire.

Light, in the form of a lamp, was part of the furnishings in churches dedicated to the Baptist. In 1505 King James on midsummer's eve at Perth made an "offerand to Sanct John's lycht at Sanct Johnis cors, ridand throw the toun".

Tradition has no hesitation in linking a lamp at Corstorphine with the niche on the outside of the east gable of the church and with the local geography of the medieval village surrounded by marsh and loch to the east, west and south. The lamp was to be a guiding light for travellers.

Medieval Corstorphine was no backwater. The Forresters brought distinguished visitors to their castle. The Collegiate Church with its Hospital doubtless brought the pilgrim, staff in hand, whether journeying south to a shrine such as the Cross Kirk at Peebles, or going north by mountain tracks to St. Duthac's at Tain.

LEFT.
The east gable of the Church showing the niche above the window holding the lamp presented by Corstorphine Rotary Club in 1958. (See also photo on page 143) (PB661)

RIGHT.
Plaque in the chancel of the Church narrating the history of the lamp. (PB636)

That Corstorphine was a 16th century landmark is illustrated in John Major's commentary on the text: "Whosoever shall compel thee to go a mile, go with him twain". Major elucidates it thus: "If thou art in Leith and anyone will force thee to go up to Edinburgh then shalt thou say, 'Nai, domine, usque ad Corstorphine ... (even unto Corstorphine)."

The gable niche poses questions. Was it originally intended for a statue? Was it later used to house a lamp? The Rev. James Oliver in the *Statistical Account* put forward two explanations: "Some say that it was in honour of the Virgin before whose statue it was lighted up; others, with more probability think that it served as a beacon to direct travellers."

The niche strongly resembles a statue niche. If it ever housed a figure then it would possibly be that of St. John the Baptist. The close-by parish church would have a statue of St. Mary to whom it was dedicated. Mr Oliver knew that it had held a lamp: "It is not long since the pulley for supporting it was taken down." (c.1793). Could the truth lie in a combination of tradition and fact – a statue of St. John with, at night, a lamp, offering a point of devotion as well as a guiding light?

The Lamp Acre appears in recorded history in 1642 when in a charter of the lands of Dalry to Thomas Mudy it is excluded as being mortified to the Provostry of Corstorphine. Possibly George Forrester got the Lamp Acre in 1618 when King James granted him the collegiate church.

From this period onwards the Lamp Acre became educational, not church, history. The niche remained empty from Mr Oliver's time till 1958. The Corstorphine Rotary Club had the happy idea to restore light to the east gable niche. A service dedicating the new light was held on 2nd April 1958.

So once more when darkness falls across the rooftops of Corstorphine the parish kirk sends forth its light. No longer required to guide wayfarers over the marsh ground the light burns, symbolic of the Light of the World as well as John the Baptist to whom the kirk was dedicated five and a half centuries ago.

THE BELL TOWER

The main entrance to the church is by the plain porch on the west side, basically what was erected in the mid 17th century when the old parish church was taken down and its stones used for alterations and additions to the collegiate building which by then had become the reformed parish church. Externally, above the porch window, there are two heraldic shields with Wigmer and Forrester arms.

From the porch, entry to the church is by stepping down, and passing under an arch, formerly the west window, and then progressing through the tower area into the nave. The stepping down into the church is symbolic of stepping into Jordan as did those who were baptised by John the Baptist.

Externally the tower has a squat but attractive octagonal stone spire divided into three tiers by battlemented bands. Mr Simpson, the school-master in the early 19th century, described the spire as terminating "in a Cardinal's cap". It has been suggested that the three tiers are symbolic of the Holy Trinity. Tower and spire are only 50 feet in height. There are small windows in the main faces and the pinnacles at the corners are decorated with leafy knobs.

Entrance to the tower is by a small turnpike. The stair is lit by narrow lights and the jambs and lintel show evidence of the 15th century work. The chamber at first floor level was converted in 1905 into a gallery opening into the nave. Above on the second floor is the bell chamber.

The bell measures twenty one inches from sound bow to crown and has a diameter of two feet across the skirt. The shoulder carries the inscription: "Sir James Forrester gifted me to this kirk anno 1577 and the heretors (sic) of Corstorphine me reneued anno 1728 R M fecit Edr".

Above the inscription is an enrichment of figures and trees and below is a band of conventional ornament. There are two annulets on the crown, three annular mouldings on the waist and one on the sound bow. Maintenance of the bell featured in the accounts in 1712. The floor of the bellhouse needed repairs. Leather was bought "to hang the tongue" and money was expended on "righting her". A fresh "tow" (rope) was got. Oil was a recurring cost. In 1721 a "rocking tree" and oil cost twelve shillings.

Then on 25th February 1728 the Session Clerk entered in the Session minute book that as "the great bell in the steeple was rent some months ago and was now of no use" the Session had asked the minister to speak to the heritors "that they might cause cast and renew the bell."

Then on 5th May the Session was informed that "the Founders had the bell in their work house in the Castle Hill of

The second (and current) bell of the church, being a recast in 1728 of the first bell gifted by Sir James Forrester in 1577. *(PB1466)*

Edinburgh" and that it "would be ready to he returned in a short time." Finally on 6th June it was recorded that "the New Bell" was now hung in the steeple.

According to the Founders' account the old bell was three hundred and two pounds weight which the heritors agreed to sell to the Founders at ten shillings per pound and allowed them "ten per cent of drawback" of the old metal. "The Payable Mettal" was two hundred and seventy two pounds weight. At ten shillings per pound the price of the old bell was one hundred and thirty six pounds Scots.

"The new Bell is Three hundred and Eighty four pound weight at Twenty Shilling per pound and the Wheel to the Bell was Twenty four Pounds Scots. The Whole of the Charge of the New Bell was Four hundred and thirty six pound Scots. Exceeding the price of the Old Bell is Three hundred Pounds

Scots which sum the Heritors have payed in to the Founders conform to their several Valuations."

The heritors, landowners in the parish, paid according to the valuation of their estates:

Sir James Dick	£103-9-8
Sir Robert Myreton of Gogar	£84-10-6
Mr Watson of Saughton	£71-2-10
Ravelston	£29-7-0
John Dickie of Corstorphine Hill	£11-10-0

The account was paid to David Hodge coppersmith in Edinburgh and Trustee to the Founding Society. The bell founder may have been either Robert Meikle or Robert Maxwell, founders in Edinburgh.

This is the bell that still rings over the old village – 1577, 1728, to-day – fulfilling one of the church's age-old functions as the public recorder of time on a Sabbath morning. When the bell rang out lang syne the villagers knew it was time to get ready and set off for the kirk: to the ungodly in ale houses it was a warning, not necessarily heeded, of judgement to come.

The ringing of the bell regulated the order of service. When there was a reader he conducted a preliminary service of reading public prayers and Scripture passages. This usually lasted an hour. Sometimes school pupils read the Catechism. Then at the ringing of the third bell the minister came into the church for prayers and preaching. The third bell was a sign to sinners making public repentance by standing at the kirk door to come inside to the place of repentance.

The great bell was also tolled at funerals. For this a fee was charged, the bellman getting part and the rest going to the Poors Box.

NIDDRIE'S AISLE

Another piece of the historical jigsaw is that the South aisle of the Collegiate church was also known as Niddrie's Aisle. Adam Forrester in 1370 got two carucates of land in "villa de Nudreff" resigned by William de Setoun. When Adam's grandson Henry in 1450 witnessed a charter he styled himself "of Niddry".

Between 1490 and 1515 John Forrester of "Nudry" engaged in land transactions, and his brother Henry, also styled of

Niddry, passed the lands of Malcomston to James Wardlaw of Riccarton in 1500. The brothers in 1494 were granted remission for being art and part in the killing of William Dundas and Malcom Duncan Dundas. John in 1504 alleged he had a tack of the Mains of Winchburgh from George Lord Setoun and so evicted the tenant, John Young, who got Sir Alexander Bruce of "Erlishall" to raise an action against Forrester. In 1506 witnesses to a deed were John Forrester of Niddry and his brother Archibald.

When James Forrester of Corstorphine in 1582 got Longhermiston and Currie one of the witnesses to the document was Alexander Forrester of West Niddrie. John Forrester portioner West Niddrie and burgess of Edinburgh in 1610 had to find caution not to harm John Brown in Gorgie Mill.

A footnote in the Diocesan Registers of Glasgow asserts that the Forresters of Corstorphine owned the castle of West Niddry later purchased from them by George, IV Lord Setoun. This claim is open to question. The Setons owned Niddry (Winchburgh) in the early 12th century and in 1634 acquired the Forrester 52 acres of West Niddry that featured in the Glasgow rentals.

The land was known as Niddrie – Forrester since it was possessed by Henry Forrester. The West in West Niddrie was to denote the Linlithgowshire Niddry. The Niddry Forresters had property in Corstorphine. A tenement of ground on the north side of the High Street in 1646 belonged to Alexander Forrester of West Niddry. When this area was bought in 1864 by John Paterson from Sir William H.D. Cunyngham its eastern boundary was Manse Road.

When the Watsons of Saughton in 1683 were involved in getting documentary evidence of their right to burial in the vault at the entrance to the South aisle the location is given as "Niddrie's Ile". So still at the close of the 17th century the Forrester of Niddrie connection with the church was recognised.

The heraldry on the outside of the South or Niddrie's aisle is Forrester and Wigmer. On each side of the window with its perpendicular tracery is a shield each with Forrester arms impaling Wigmer. Centred above the window is a Forrester shield. Heraldically the arms on the shields have been cut in reverse and the crest is also reversed as if the mason had worked from a seal matrix.

FROM THE OUTSIDE: SUNDIALS

Externally the church has retained its medieval appearance with its slabbed roof, partly original and partly restored. The medieval still stands the test of time. The buttresses would originally have pinnacles but these were replaced with cubic simulated sundials, probably by Burn in the early 19th century. One is original and possibly gave the restorer the idea to repeat the shape.

A sundial was a natural embellishment on the outside of a village church. Like the church bell the sundial provided a time-keeper to regulate life in the community. As early as Saxon times vertical sundials appeared on churches. That splendid example of Anglo-Saxon art, the cross at Bewcastle, dating from the 7th or 8th century, has a sundial cut on it.

Later dials, usually on south facing walls, were simply rough circles cut into the stone with scratched lines radiating from a central hole. These have been thought to be mass dials to indicate to parishioners the time of Mass. They may, however, have been used to time other services and were probably Norman in origin. A dial of this type is on the wall of the Carmelite chapel at South Queensferry, now St. Mary's Episcopal church.

The present position of the true Corstorphine sundial at the top of a buttress raises doubts as to whether it is in its original place, or has become the victim of "Fate, Time, Occasion, Chance and Change" as has so much in this historic church.

The Priests' door into the chancel is modern but in its original place. At its entrance from the graveyard a large oblong stone has been used as paving. It has the look of a flat gravestone and might prove, if turned, to be another link with history. It cuts across the burial ground of the Paterson family who in 1905 at the request of Rev. Fergusson agreed to this path to the priests door being made on condition that its use was limited to the minister. Not immediately visible, but there, are the remains of gargoyle water spouts behind the chancel and transept buttresses.

A stone that now appears to have vanished was noted by Mr Simpson, the dominie: "On the top of the north aisle is place a stone bearing four faces cut out of the solid and all looking in different directions". It was found at the rebuilding in 1829 behind the steeple and could only be seen by getting on to the roof. It was thought to be a key stone. The masons cleaned it and replaced it at the north aisle. Mr Simpson was of the opinion that it represented the four evangelists.

TREASURES WITHIN:
THE FONT: GRAVE SLABS: NUMERALS

THE FONT

The free stone font in the South aisle came from the chapel at Gogar. It is circular – diameter of bowl 2ft 4ins, diameter of orifice 1ft 10ins – with mouldings at lip and base. The inside is rough so it may have had a lining. Possibly it is early 14th century. For long it lay neglected at the gate of Gogar churchyard but the revival of the church there in 1891 saved it. Then when Gogar church closed in 1954 the font was brought to Corstorphine where it continues to play its part at baptismal services.

Gogar Church, not now used for services. Currently let to a cabinet-maker as his workshop, a few hundred yards west of the underpass, and to north of the main Glasgow road – not visible from the road. [GUS]

GRAVE SLABS

At the East ingoing of the Priests door in the chancel is the Heriot grave stone beautifully lettered: "Here lies Master Robert Heriot, Bachelor of Philosophy, late Rector of Gogar, who died on the 10th day of June in the year of our Lord 1443". The inscription is in Latin and the stone is cut with Forrester arms and a communion chalice. At the 1828 alterations it was dug up under the wall then dividing chancel from nave.

West of the Priests door is Alexander Tod's stone with Latin inscription: "Here lies Alexander Tod, late son of Thomas Tod, knight, who died on the 20th day of September in the year of our Lord 1489. Pray for his soul". Archibald Forrester's second wife was Agnes Tod and Alexander was her brother. Their father, Sir Thomas, was Provost of Edinburgh in 1448.

East of the Priests door is a sepulchral floriated slab of the Calvary type – a cross on a base with steps – with an incised sword. This stone has no date or inscription. Dating is conjectural but decorated crosses tend to be 14th century. This may be the stone referred to in the *New Statistical Account* in 1839 as being then at Corstorphine Hill House. In undated notes

Mr Simpson left on record that he gave Mr Keith (the then owner of the mansion that is now the Zoo House) "last year a stone with no reading" but with "a sword and some devices" which made the schoolmaster think it was a Templar stone. It was found at the entrance into an arched vault in the body of church before the pulpit when tradesmen were excavating in 1829.

Mr Simpson also noted that in the church were found many bones and rotten wood and that another stone had been taken by him to form "a cover to my well". These notes are tantalising. If only Mr Simpson had realised that these stones were historic treasures which the church should have preserved. However the gift to Mr Keith appears to have come home. The fact that it was found at a vault "before the pulpit" (then at the South West corner of the North aisle) links it with the Watson vault at the entrance to the Forrester-Niddrie aisle (South aisle).

It certainly was not a Watson stone as the Watsons did not bury there till the 17th century. This creates speculation that the floriated slab may be a Forrester-Niddrie memorial. The fate of Mr Simpson's well cover is yet to come to light: it may be somewhere beneath the extended school buildings in the High Street.

Inserted in the west wall of the south aisle is the magnificent heraldic grave slab with iron rings originally recumbent in the Watson burial vault at the entrance to the aisle. It commemorates James Watson of Saughton who died in 1620 and his wife Jean Douglas. The marginal inscription is from Ezekiel 37 on the resurrection of dry bones.

The Adam Forrester stone now in the porch but once on the external wall of the porch may be the gravestone of a child – Adam's grandchild. All that was visible to the naked eye was: "Hic iacet Adam Forstar". Modern photography has now provided a fuller: "Hic iacet Adam Fo (r) s (tar)/ Filius D (omi) ni Ioa (nn) is/ Forstar m(ilitis)".

In the porch is a small stone with an incised sword and floriated cross characteristic of a medieval military grave. Incised slabs were usually for burials within the church where they formed part of the paving: relief slabs were for outside burials. Cross slab stones were the subject of an early Scottish law which ran: "Esteem every sepulchre or gravestone sacred, and adorn it with the sign of the cross which take care you do not so much as tread on". Another stone in the porch has

The ancient baptismal font from the old church of Gogar, transferred to Corstorphine Old Parish Church in 1956. (PB2021)

Roman lettering only partially readable. It may refer to Adam's wife Margaret: "(M)a(r)gareta Da … Domini Iohannis … eodem e Dom … csto in(i)…"

ARABIC NUMERALS

On the West wall of the Priests door opposite the Heriot stone three dates have been cut. 1429 – the year of founding the College – and 1455 are the earliest examples in Scotland of Arabic numerals. The date 1455 may be connected with the death of the founder Sir John.

The third date 1769 seems not to be of special significance. However that year masons were busy laying paving stones in the church. The Priests door, not then being part of the building set aside for the parish church, would not be sacrosanct. Perhaps a mason's apprentice seeing the other dates tried his hand at stone cutting.

THE REFORMATION SETTLEMENT

In August 1560 the Scots Parliament cancelled Papal authority in Scotland, prohibited the Latin service of the Mass, and adopted the reformed Confession of Faith. Religious houses gave way to the parish ministry. Ministers had power to preach and to administer the Sacraments. Exhorters were limited to preaching and readers to reading the "common prayers" from a service book as well as reading Bible lessons and homilies. By 1572 the reader was allowed to baptise and to marry and the office of exhorter fell into disuse. Church property became Crown property but not the provostries and certain endowments as these had been established privately.

Ratho, like Gogar, in medieval times had its church dedicated to St. Mary with a nearby Our Lady's Well. In 1444 the Collegiate Church of Corstorphine was given by the Pope the teinds and the patronage of Ratho. This resulted in the four prebends connected with Ratho – Dalmahoy, Haltoun, Bonnington, Platt – being given to Corstorphine. In the same year Clerkington was assigned to Corstorphine: in 1574 Mr Thomas Majoribanks, prebendary of Corstorphine, became the reader at Clerkington.

When George Forrester in 1618 got a charter of novodamus of the lands and barony of Corstorphine he also got the patronage of the kirk. In 1621 the kirk, parsonage, and vicarage of Corstorphine with the manse, glebe, and teinds which of old had belonged to the Abbacy of Holyrood were dissolved and erected into a distinct parsonage of Corstorphine. The four prebends were united to Corstorphine but a sum of money was allotted to the minister of Ratho.

Then in 1633 the four prebends which meant the teind sheaves of Ratho were taken from Corstorphine and restored to Ratho because the existing arrangement was "prejudiciall" to Ratho. Finally in 1641 the separation of Clerkington from Corstorphine was confirmed. George Forrester as patron and heir to the founder of the medieval revenues sold them to the owners of the estates with which they were associated. The patronage of Half Dalmahoy, Half Haltoun, Half Bonington, and Half Platt, formerly belonging to Alexander Dalmahoy was ratified to Sir John Dalmahoy. This patronage and the teinds of Ratho in 1671 passed to Charles Maitland of Haltoun (Hatton).

Gogar Church c.1918, not visible from the main Glasgow Road but situated almost opposite the entrance to the former Gogarburn Hospital. The church is currently used as a cabinet maker's workshop. *(PB2026)*

Chapter 2

THE REFORMED PARISH CHURCH

While the rule of the old church was coming to an end in Corstorphine the way of the reformed church was beginning. The parish church, as a possession of the Abbey of Holyrood, was served in the 15th century by a canon of Holyrood. On the eve of the Reformation in 1560 there is no evidence of anyone serving the parish church but in 1561 it had a reader – Mungo Wood "parson and vicar of Gogar". Walter Cowper was reader 1567-69 and Mr Robert Pont was minister in 1574. Pont's son, Timothy, was the celebrated mapmaker. The Synod of Lothian and Tweeddale in 1589 arranged for the minister of Ratho to deal with Corstorphine baptisms and marriages until provision could be made for Corstorphine.

In March 1587 Sir James Forrester and the parishioners reminded the Presbytery of Edinburgh that the parish church of Corstorphine was "of old foundit and erectit be auld fundationis ane paroche kirk". Later that month Sir James was instructed to produce his evidence of Corstorphine being a long established parish church. On 19th March Sir James came to the Presbytery "producing sundry foundations with Bulls and other rights" which were duly "sychtit" and then "it is fund that the Kirk of Corstorphine is of old a paroche kirk".

Andrew Forrester was minister 1590-98. In February 1591 the Presbytery instructed Sir James to come to them to explain why he had not given Mr Forrester the two prebends he had promised him. Even after a fourth summons Sir James did not appear but John Coise who had delivered the last notice explained that the laird was "diseasit of ane sair arme". However James appeared on 4th April and promised to remember the minister when a prebend fell vacant.

Some of the Presbytery questioned James Forrester's right to dispose of prebends which led him to say that he would produce the foundation documents of the collegiate church. When Sir James was further questioned about ordering the minister "in ane unseemly maner" to "flitt fra ye houss" he countered with a promise that he would give another manse and yard.

On 6th June 1591 a presbyterial visitation led by Mr David Lindsay and Mr John Hale was able to report that they found nothing "sclanderous" but everything in good order. They also considered the position of Gogar Kirk where the congregation was "so small" that they advised uniting it to Corstorphine. At the end of August Mr Forrester, the minister, appealed to the Presbytery to designate his glebe.

The Synod of Lothian in 1592 was concerned to prevent the Bishop of Orkney, Adam Bothwell, commendator of Holyrood, from interfering with the teinds of Corstorphine. The Synod also arranged in 1593 with James Forrester for the union of the kirk at Clerkington with the kirk at Temple. Clerkington, now Rosebery, was part of the parish of Temple.

In 1593 the collegiate church building became the reformed parish church. Mr Forrester's position was still unsatisfactory in 1595 when a Presbytery deputation went to the Abbot of Holyrood about provision for the minister. In 1597 the Presbytery granted a testimonial to Mr Forrester testifying to the soundness of his doctrine and the honesty of his life.

1598 was a year of presbyterial visits. In July James Forrester was not present at the church so when the visitors came they went to see him about better provision for the minister at Ratho. On 4th August Gogar was visited. John Coise, the reader there, was removed when the Presbytery arrived so that they could ask the congregation what they thought of him. They said he was honest but did not live at Gogar and they could not insist on residence as he was not their minister. They also reported that he had let the kirkland. The Commissioners ordered Coise to limit his work to prayers and catechising, the articles of belief and the commandments. There were no elders as there was no minister. The people promised to repair the broken kirkyard dykes if a minister was appointed.

The congregation was so small that union with Corstorphine was put forward to the Presbytery. The Laird of Corstorphine favoured union and also asked that "ye tounis of Sauchton and Sauchtonhall wt Brumhouses myt be also united to thame".

On 22nd August the Presbytery men came to Corstorphine. They found both buildings in a sad state of disrepair. They reported "ye queir of ye paroch kirk ruynous" and decided to speak to the Abbot of Holyrood about its repair. In the collegiate church they "fand ye glass windowis down yr upon thai concludit to speik to ye Provost of Corstorphin to glass ye same and ye laird promisit to wyre ye said windows".

Clearly Forrester loyalty was to the building founded by the family. So the ancient parish church called Our Lady Kirk of Corstorphine was left to fall down while the reformed parish church, housed in the medieval collegiate church, started its life in the building which is to-day known as the Old Parish Church.

When enquiry was made into Mr Forrester's conduct the visitors heard of "soundness of doctrine, honestie in lyf, wyfe and familie". The elders, however, were found wanting: a number were slack in church attendance on the Sabbath for which "thai wer shairplie rebukit" and then promised to do better in future. The Session book which was found in order, has unhappily, disappeared.

Corstorphine was found to have no schoolmaster. Half the kirkyard dykes were broken down but the Laird said he would repair if the people shared the cost with him. The Presbytery was asked to speak to the Abbot of Holyrood about providing for the minister. There was also a case of discipline. Robert Haistie brought a complaint against William Young for "dinging" him. The Laird said he would deal with William in the baron court and pass him to the Presbytery to discipline him.

Old Parish Church from the west. [RG]

When the Presbytery considered the report they decided to speak to the heritors of Gogar after the harvest and tell them to provide a minister or accept a merger with Corstorphine.

By September 1598 Andrew Forrester had gone to another charge leaving the vacancy unfilled. Forrester went to Dunfermline where in 1612 there was a complaint that he had allowed a crucifix to be painted on the chancellor's desk in the church. In 1616 Forrester absconded with the Poors Box money.

James Allan, Alexander Crafurd, and Mungo Crafurd went to the Presbytery to ask for a minister for Corstorphine. In January 1599 the presbytery had a petition from Henry Forrester and the parishioners saying they had been impressed by William Arthur whom they would like to be their minister. The Presbytery, disturbed by the small congregation and the lack of money at Gogar, wrote to the heritors – the Laird of Smeatoun, Logan of Coitfield, and Mr John Layng – and a temporary union was accepted. After the Presbytery decided to admit William Arthur to Corstorphine the people, though having nothing against his life and doctrine, became upset for they felt he was too learned a man for them.

Nevertheless Mr Arthur was admitted to Corstorphine on 8th June 1599. No one from Gogar appeared at the service. They felt, and rightly so, that Gogar was a parish of old and should have its own minister. The Presbytery then ordered Mr Arthur to preach Sunday about at Corstorphine and Gogar and the people of both parishes were to attend.

Financing the kirk at Corstorphine was the main concern of the year 1600. Since it was a kirk attached to the Abbey of Holyrood the Abbot was asked what provision he was prepared to make. The reply was that he had given a tack of the teinds of Corstorphine to the Laird, Henry Forrester, on condition that he maintained the choir and reserved to the minister the manse and glebe. Henry Forrester resisted the pressure exerted by Mr Arthur to compel him to use Gogar kirk.

By July 1600 the Corstorphine people, having tired of alternate services at Gogar and Corstorphine, got the Privy Council to exempt them from attending at Gogar. In September 1602 the Gogar folk submitted to coming to Corstorphine till they "provydit for thameselves". Unfortunately Gogar was never able to finance a church and their historic chapel became a ruin. The burial ground continued to be used well into the twentieth century. Corstorphine at the close of the 19th century built a church at Gogar. It incorporated the ruined walls of the old chapel. The Victorian church lasted till 1954 when history repeated itself and lack of people forced its closure.

The parish kirk of Corstorphine in the 17th century served a civil purpose for when occasion arose it was used as a place of imprisonment. The tower appears to have served this purpose. Mr Arthur left Corstorphine in 1607 when he was translated to St. Cuthbert's, Edinburgh, where, doubtless, his academic superiority would be better appreciated than it evidently was by the toilers of the good earth in Midlothian.

THE EARLY SEVENTEENTH CENTURY

The Scottish church of the 17th century was a national united church with two systems of organisation alternating in control – the Presbyterian and the Episcopal. The ministries in Corstorphine of Robert Rutherford, M.A., and Robert Lindsay, M.A., covered the first quarter of the century under a moderate Episcopalian rule.

Mr Rutherford came to Corstorphine in 1607 when King James's scheme to unite Scotland and England, put forward in 1604, was destroyed by a hostile English Parliament. So the place name "Borders" remains with us though James wanted to re-name the area "middle shires" to remove an implied separation of his kingdoms.

Rutherford died on 25th April 1616 leaving behind him his wife, Christian Dick, and his children Catherine, Isobell, Margaret, and Agnes. His possessions included the crops on his glebe – oats, pease, beir – and his library worth £100 Scots. James Crauford in Gogar owed him rent for the use of the Gogar glebe. Rutherford owed James Ramsay the rent of the house he occupied in Corstorphine so either there was no manse or what was available was not acceptable to Rutherford. His servants had to be paid their year's wages, Agnes Jonstoun and Margaret Lowrie £8 each and Janet Kincaid £6.

Robert Lindsay and his wife, Elizabeth Abercrombie, spent ten years 1616-26 in Corstorphine. They occupied a house owned by Nicoll Edward for which they paid rent. No doubt they discussed the General Assembly at Perth 1618 when the Five Articles, including kneeling at Communion and confirmation by bishops, were introduced. When Lindsay died his wife claimed the stipend due to him by the Provost and the baillies of Edinburgh for Gogar kirk as well as the stipend owed by George Forrester for Corstorphine kirk. Lindsay owed money to Florence Gardner and to John Eleis "keeper of the kirk" at Corstorphine, possibly of the Eleis of Stenhouse family.

MR DAVID BALSILLIE, M.A.: THE FIRST RECONSTRUCTION

David Balsillie's ministry in Corstorphine 1626–53 witnessed political and ecclesiastical changes of great national importance. In June 1633 Charles I came North to be crowned in the chapel of Holyrood with pomp and circumstance reminiscent of the old church. Following his return to London he created a diocese of Edinburgh to which Corstorphine was united and in October 1633 he gave orders about the "apparel of kirkmen".

THE REFORMED PARISH CHURCH

The east gable of the Old Parish Church c.1880, as reconstructed by William Burn in 1828. Note the niche for the lamp above the window. (PB1450)

Then in July 1637 the use of the Scottish Prayer Book (taught incorrectly to generations of Scottish children as Laud's Liturgy) led to the demonstration in St. Giles' church forever associated in popular mythology with Jenny Geddes, the Edinburgh greengrocer, whose legitimate claim to fame is making a bonfire to celebrate the Restoration of Charles II.

This was followed by the signing of the National Covenant in February 1638 as a protest against innovation in worship and the King's church policy. George Forrester of Corstorphine was a signatory. By the end of the year the Glasgow Assembly rejected episcopal government. When civil war broke out in England the Covenanters allied with the English Puritans in the Solemn League and Covenant of 1643.

In the midst of this national upheaval David Balsillie went about the affairs of his parish. In February 1630 the Commissioners for the Surrenders of Superiorities and Teinds listened to the Laird of Corstorphine and James Foulis, son to George of Ravelston, speak "anent the farre distance of the lands of Sauchton and Ravelstoun frae the parish kirk of St. Cuthbert's and the nearness of the said roumes" to the kirk of Corstorphine. The Commissioners unanimously agreed to unite these districts to Corstorphine.

Balsillie appealed to have his stipend increased from the

funds of the Bishopric of Edinburgh and for his good services was given an increase of 100 merks per year. The order from the Privy Council in December 1635 that the parish of Corstorphine was to contribute to the relief of plague stricken families "in the toun of Nether Cramond" would be organised by the minister and the elders.

On 4th January 1646 he met with his elders and deacons and a fresh Session record book was started. It is the earliest surviving Kirk Session minute book for the parish, now preserved in the Scottish Record Office.

On that historic, for Corstorphine, day 4th January 1646 plague which had afflicted the country in 1645 was the principal item of business.

George Cochrane and Florence Gardner reported that "they had in ye time of trouble" distributed money to the poor. Sebastian Parke, the clerk, had listed the names of those assisted in the previous minute book, now lost.

Standards of morality were of concern to the Session so in March Thomas and Marion Paterson had to confess "their fault, under promise of marriage", at the place of repentance in the kirk.

The great event in Balsillie's ministry was the reconstruction of the collegiate church building to accommodate the reformed parish church. The 12th century parish church of St. Mary was taken down and its stone used for the adapted building. At the close of 1646, after the expenses of the alterations had been paid by the heritors and the church, the Session balanced their books by examining the Box. On 1st November "ye box was sighted and found therein two hundredth and eight libs."

The Box was an important item in church furnishings. To safeguard its contents it had usually two locks and two keys which were kept by the treasurer and by another member of the Session. In 1667 Robert Alexander and Robert Grahame were jointly responsible for the Box. Generally the minister was not allowed to handle the Box although it might be kept in the manse as a safe place. Boxes varied in size, some small with a slit for inserting money, others large chests. The opening of the Box was an occasion. It was done before the Session and the minister.

In 1845 the schoolmaster, Mr Simpson, had in his possession a box of the type with a slit in the lid and with a broad belt to attach the box to the person when carrying it between the church and the home of its keeper the Session Clerk who was also the teacher. After the Poor Law Act 1845 provision for the poor passed to Parochial Boards and the box fell into disuse. By 1890 there was no trace of the Corstorphine box.

David Balsillie was married to Margaret Cranstoun and they had, at least, one son and five daughters. Bethia married William Monro of Culcraggie in 1658. Helen was married twice, firstly to George Marshall, tailor, and secondly to John Forrest, chirurgeon. She had an interest in lands at Nether Gogar which she sold to Sir John Cowper 1677. Margaret seems to have been an unfortunate for in 1673 when she was added to the roll of poor she agreed to leave her goods and gear on her death to the kirk as a return for help.

Since Corstorphine was part of the rich farm lands of Midlothian agricultural factors affected the lives of the people and the work of the kirk. In June 1652 the villagers were ordered to attend a service of public humiliation for the current drought threatening famine and starvation.

Balsillie retired in December 1653 owing to ill health. By that time he had endured witch trials among his people and the misery of military occupation of the village and kirk by Cromwellian troops. David Balsillie's lines had fallen in eventful times.

Example of an old Communion Cup [GUS]

MR ROBERT HUNTER M.A.

On 11th June 1654 the Kirk Session unanimously decided to call Mr Robert Hunter, Master of Arts, to be their minister. So on 9th July they instructed Richard Murray to ride to Hamilton to "speir at" Mr Hunter who was then with the "Lady Duchess" of Hamilton if he would come to Corstorphine kirk. The new minister was installed on 11th April 1655.

By August that year unseasonable weather and excessive rains brought rot to the crops. In May 1656 the weekday sermon was cancelled for it was the time of the "beir seed" and farmers were anxious for a good crop after the previous season. In Edinburgh the Canongate parish in 1656 tried to get Mr Hunter to come to them but he chose to remain at Corstorphine "being convinced of the goode providence of God in leading him hither".

There is a very brief record of the Session meeting on Tuesday 29th April 1656 – "nothing to be marked". Yet on that

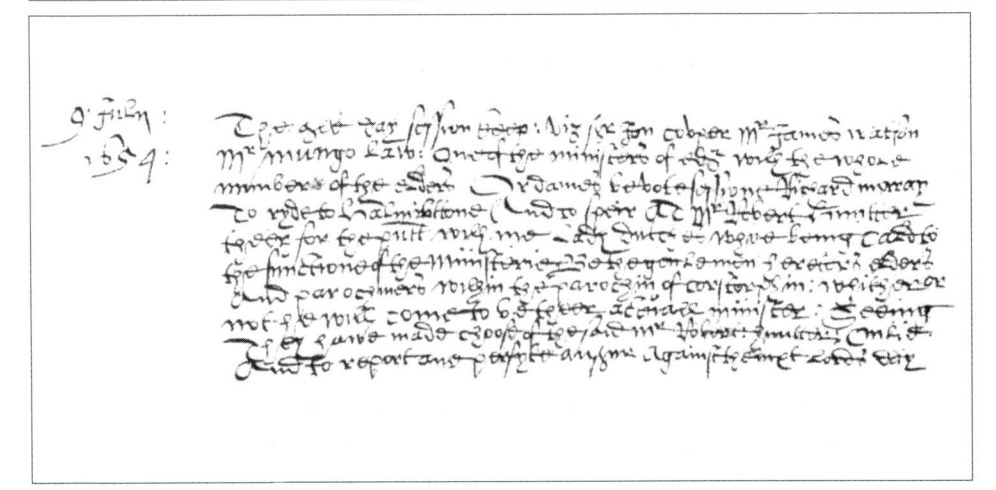

Extract entry from Corstorphine Kirk Session minutes, 9th July 1654, recording the instruction to Richard Murray to go to Hamilton to invite Mr Robert Hunter to be Minister of Corstorphine. (*Courtesy* NAS, *ref* CH2/124/1)

day Anne, Duchess of Hamilton, whose life story has been so vividly re-created by Dr Rosalind K. Marshall in *The Days of Duchess Anne*, was married to the Earl of Selkirk at the kirk of Corstorphine. The marriage is not recorded in the church marriage register.

Lord William Douglas, Earl of Selkirk, was reared as a Roman Catholic while the Duchess was a Protestant. On the day before the marriage he signed a statement at Edinburgh that he was not a Papist. Mr Hunter's period with the Duchess was when the Palace at Hamilton was occupied by Cromwell's man, Colonel Ingoldsby. The Duchess's friendship with Robert Hunter, added to the matter of Selkirk's religion, probably led to the marriage ceremony at the country village of Corstorphine rather than in an Edinburgh church.

During his ministry Mr Hunter had to adjust his services to meet the needs of the land. In 1655 he suspended the weekday sermon when seed had to be sown and when crops had to be harvested. Heavy rains in 1658 destroyed the corn and brought sickness to the people.

When Charles II was restored in 1660 the bishops were re-introduced and congregations lost the right to choose their minister. Anyone previously appointed by a congregation, as Robert Hunter had been, was ordered to be readmitted by the bishop of the diocese. This was not acceptable to Mr Hunter who was then in 1662 deprived of his church for non-conformity. About a third of ministers in Scotland were of like mind. Unhappily the Kirk Session record books between August 1658 and May 1665 are missing so that there is no local detail of Mr Hunter's demission.

RESTORATION TO REVOLUTION: 1662–89

Mr Hunter left Corstorphine in 1662. Charles II on his restoration to the throne filled the Scottish Parliament with those who would do as he wished. From 1663 to 1667 the Earl of Rothes, behind whom the driving force was Lauderdale, controlled Scotland. The 1663 Act, known as the "Bishops Drag Net" against "separation and disobedience to ecclesiastical authority", imposed heavy fines on absentees from parish churches. The ejection of ministers and the imposition of "King's Curates" aggravated the religious tension. At Corstorphine William Ogstone was minister for 1664. Then on 13th March 1665 Thomas Mowbray took over but by May the following year he was dead.

Mrs Mowbray was left with a daughter and a son who was born posthumously. The minister's earthly goods were his horse, a cow and its calf, his household plenishings and his clothes. Stipend was owing to him as well as money he had lent to Florence Liston in Gogar. James Alexander and Elizabeth Robertson, his servants, were due wages. There was an account from Hew Neilson, apothecary, for medicines supplied in "the time of his sickness". He arranged for his brother, John Mowbray, minister at Uphall, to settle his affairs.

The repressive measures of Rothes led to a rising of Covenanters who were intercepted by the "Muscovite", Tam Dalyell of the Binns, at Rullion Green and were routed on 15 November 1666. Lay patronage, abolished in 1649, was restored by Charles II in 1662. The presentation by James Forrester of Archibald Chisholm in accordance with Episcopalian practice was ratified by the Bishop of Edinburgh when on 7th December 1666 Chisholm took charge at Corstorphine.

From 1668 Lauderdale was responsible for the government of Scotland. Chisholm's ministry ended with his death in Spring 1670. Chisholm's wife, Margaret Coult, was the daughter of the minister at Inveresk who gave her a tocher (dowry) of 3,000 merks in 1666. They had two children. Chisholm had a long illness. In 1672 Mrs Chisholm appealed to the Privy Council to get the vacant stipend and was awarded 500 merks.

When James Binning, advocate, paid £29 Scots as "pecunial mulk" for fornication a rex dollar [about £3 Scots. *See* Appendix 2] was given out of his fine to Alexander Chisholm, baillie of Dunblane, as repayment for expenditure by Thomas Mowbray while at Corstorphine. Chisholm married Mowbray's widow.

John Pringle took charge in July 1670. His patron was Lord Forrester and his presentation was ratified by the Bishop of Edinburgh. Lord Forrester requested Pringle in September to instruct the elders to list absentees from church "in contempt of ye present government yrof ". An Act in 1670 imposed penalties, including the death penalty, for preachers at conventicles (unauthorised meetings for worship) and fines for those attending.

Poor health dogged Pringle and, after his death in September 1670, John Duff, student of divinity, at the desire of Lord Forrester and the people, served the parish till July 1671. But he received no stipend from the heritors so he had to petition the Privy Council who granted him an allowance.

On 9th May 1672 George Henry was appointed. Like Pringle and Chisholm before him his patron was Lord Forrester, and the Bishop of Edinburgh confirmed his appointment. Pressure of work was not accepted as an excuse for avoiding the minister's examination of the religious state of his flock for in Spring 1674 he announced that he would examine on the Sabbath days "because of ye throng of ye labour on ye week dayes".

Lauderdale in 1674 proclaimed a pardon for those who attended field preachings. This says Kirkton, in his history of the Church of Scotland, was "looked at by the common people rather as an encouragement for the time coming than as a remission for what was past ... Scotland broke loose with conventicles of all sorts in houses, fields, and vacant churches."

In Edinburgh the Covenanters held a conventicle in the Magdalen Chapel for which the city was fined £100 stg. The Laird of Cramond, Inglis, was fined for listening to Covenanting sermons in his church. And the Covenanting women were active in 1674 when they tried to seize Archbishop Sharpe as he passed through Parliament Close to a Privy Council meeting but they were foiled by Rothes.

Despite James Forrester's attempts to make his villagers conform Corstorphine became a place for conventicles where the meetings took place "in the toune and hilles". The leader was Patrick Glasse who was before the Privy Council in 1674 for trying to prevent Alexander Gadderer, minister, going to preach at Girvan. That same year Thomas Weddell, spurrier,

THE REFORMED PARISH CHURCH 61

The 'low village' looking south over the Glebe. The new church hall (middle right) was completed in 1886. The new Public Hall was erected by the Corstorphine Public Hall Company in 1892. The hall can be seen in the middle distance. *(PB1153)*

burgess of Edinburgh, was in trouble for attending a conventicle at Corstorphine. Mr Henry announced from the pulpit that he intended to preach every Thursday except at seed time and harvest.

Patrick Glasse was before the Privy Council in 1675. The previous year, in the month of May, when it was known that Mr Henry was to preach at the vacant kirk of Cramond, Glasse invited a Mr Riddell to preach in Corstorphine kirk. Riddell arrived accompanied by "a multitude of persons from Edinburgh and elsewhere". Glasse offered the beadle money to open the kirk doors. Mr Henry and his servants who had not left for Cramond decided to occupy the kirk and were threatened by the intruders. But Glasse was "frustrat … by the love and kyndnes of the parochiners who guarded the person of the minister safely to the pulpitt".

Glasse then took Riddell and the crowd to his house where they held a conventicle. The Privy Council fined Glasse £200 Scots and he had to find caution for 5,000 merks against not repeating the offence.

Mr Henry in 1676 was concerned with the poor attendance at church and instructed the elders to make a "more narrow

The Corstorphine Sycamore in all its Spring glory, c.1960. (PB3)

search". Later he had to speak to Harry Aikman, Florence Liston, John Rob, and Marion Spence, noted as church absentees. That year, from the money collected at the marriage of Barbara Cowper of Gogar and Thomas Robertson, Mr Henry paid £15 for a new church Bible. He also bought from church funds a new pulpit cloth with fringes. The minister was empowered in 1678 to buy wood to repair church seats and forms.

In 1677 Alexander Lowrie in the Marchall of Gogar was called to the Session for having his child baptised by a nonconformist minister "contrary to ye established government of ye church". Sir John Cowper of Gogar and Mr Henry, however, failed to get Lowrie to name the minister concerned. Later Lowrie submitted to the Session, promising to attend church and never again to have a child baptised by a noniconformist. His signature to that undertaking in the Session book resembles strongly the handwriting of the clerk. Lowrie was fined six rex dollars.

Among those "missed" from church in 1679 were the daughter of Thomas Young in the Goyle and George Young in Saughton. The covenanting ill-feeling towards Archbishop

Sharpe came to a head on 3rd May 1679 when on Magus Muir in Fife his coach was stopped by a group including John Balfour of Kinloch and David Hackston of Rathillet and the Archbishop was murdered. Balfour escaped to Holland to join the Prince of Orange. A fine marble monument in the parish church of St. Andrews, Fife, marks the grave of Sharpe. In Corstorphine on 29th August 1679 Lord James Forrester was killed at the sycamore tree. Mr Henry's ministry was a time of violence, local and national. Church expenditure in 1681 included payments for "sackcloth for delinquents".

In 1680 and in 1681 Mr Henry called for the names of absentees. The Session 1682 declared that absentees from the church and from "ye Examine" would not be given "ye church benefitt". The Session records break off in 1685.

From other sources it is clear that the minister had a difficult time with no support from the Forrester laird. In 1688 Mr Henry complained that Torwoodhead (William Forrester) had told his tenants not to attend the parish church but rather go to a meeting house. Moreover Forrester had kept the villagers from bringing the minister his coals and from labouring the glebe for him as was customary.

Forrester's explanation for his animosity to Henry was that in 1679 the minister had refused to pray for the Duke of York, later James VII, because he was a Papist. Contemporary opinion was that Forrester's real reason for being hostile to Mr Henry was that the minister was pressing Forrester for repayment of a loan which was, in fact, the truth.

There was possibly another factor. By 1688 Forrester may have seen the writing on the wall for episcopacy. Whether sympathetic to it or not he must have known about the Torwood (Forrester land) incident of September 1680 when the Covenanter Donald Cargill imitated what Richard Cameron had done at Sanquhar the previous June. Cargill gathered the people at Torwood and then "excommunicated and delivered to Satan" Charles II, the Duke of York, Lauderdale, Dalyell of the Binns, and renounced allegiance to the throne. Cargill preached at Torwood in a square field near the William Wallace oak tree.

When the Revolution came in 1689 George Henry refused to read the proclamation and to pray for William of Orange and Mary, his wife. Accordingly he was deprived of his benefice and the kirk of Corstorphine was declared vacant.

Henry's petition to the Privy Council in 1691 put on record

Example of old
Communion tokens [GUS]

his financial dealings with the Forrester family. When Henry came to Corstorphine in 1672 he was compelled by James Forrester to give a bond for 1,000 merks to the widow of the previous minister, Archibald Chisholm, as a debt on the manse building. Henry had a receipt for his payment of the money. He complained that he had lain out of this money for twenty years and had little hope of getting repayment from the Forrester family. He pointed out that since he was put out of the church there had been no minister appointed. Accordingly he asked for the two years vacant stipend. He was awarded payment for 1689–90. So ended George Henry's residence in Corstorphine.

No more were the parishioners to be entertained as they once were on a Sunday morning when a cow wandered into the churchyard. Mr Henry, incensed at the sight of the animal among the graves, ran "at her like a bull dog, and, throwing his Bible at her, wished that all the plagues and curses contained in the book might befall her and her master that did not keep her better at home".

Mr Henry's affairs, however, continued to concern the Kirk Session for some years to come. Apparently he took with him £200 Scots belonging to the Poor Fund to hold until the heritors paid what was due to him. In 1696 the Baron baillie, Duncan Robertson, was asked to get the Edinburgh baillies to instruct Henry to repay. In 1697 a decreet was got to enforce payment. Then in July 1697 the Session agreed to raise Letters of Horning (penal execution against debtors) against Mr Henry. Eventually Mr Henry paid £14 to the kirk.

William of Orange and Mary were received as King and Queen in Scotland in April 1689. The Scottish bishops supported James VII who had fled to France. In 1690 William by statute restored Presbyterianism in church government.

Robert Law from 1689–91 was the parish minister. The Session minutes from February 1685 to April 1692, if written, have not survived thus depriving posterity of a picture of local life during Mr Law's ministry.

ARCHIBALD HAMILTON

Archibald Hamilton was one of a family of ministers. His father, minister at Wigtown, removed in 1663 to Bangor in Ireland, having been accused before the Privacy Council in

1662 of disloyalty to the Restoration government and consequently deprived. His brother, John, a Presbyterian minister at Cumber, Co. Down, came to Scotland in 1689 to be minister at Cramond. Later he had the second charge at Greyfriars, Edinburgh. His brother, Henry, was minister at Currie in 1691.

Archibald came to Corstorphine in 1692 and was apparently not impressed with the previous administration for within the first month of his arrival he stirred the Session into promulgating seven acts aimed at controlling parish affairs.

He was concerned to have a list of the poor and to organise the Poors Fund. There was reluctance among some of the elders to stand at the church door to collect the poors money so an act was passed in the Session stating that any elder who did not appear "at the ringing of the second bell" was to be fined six shillings Scots for each absence.

Villagers who did not attend the afternoon service were to be rounded up and to do this three elders with the kirk officer were to "search houses and especially change houses". The importance of Session meetings as the means of parish management was stressed by an order that elders failing to attend would be fined if their excuse was not "relevant". Fortunately for George Young he was able to say that he had been at his aunt's funeral in Edinburgh. Alexander Anderson's explanation was that he had been at the West Kirk of Edinburgh hearing the sermon for it was Communion day there.

Heads of households were instructed not to take in servants or others without first ensuring that they had "a sufficient testimony of their former behaviour" from the parish from which they had come. Marriage proclamations had been done in a "disorderly" fashion so, in future, the minister was to be consulted first before names were publicly announced.

Then there was the problem of incomers without means who in time would need financial assistance. To prevent this, the Session forbade the giving of a house to anyone likely to become a burden on parish funds. Distribution of the poors money came under strict control when it was limited to those listed by the Session as recognised poor persons.

Strong action was to be taken against beggars in accordance with the national attitude to vagrants. They were to be apprehended, imprisoned, and fed on bread and water for a month by which time arrangements should have been completed to pass them to their native parishes. However four shillings were given to a poor Irishman making his way home: probably the Session were glad to get him out of the parish and the minister, having an Irish background, may have felt it a duty to help the traveller.

Despite the vigilance of the church, cases of fornication continued to keep the writers of the minutes busy and led to yet another act of Session in 1693. Anyone guilty of adultery or fornication was to be imprisoned till able to find "bond and caution" for the offence under a penalty of £100 for adultery and £40 Scots for fornication. Even sin was graded financially. Sessional acts, however, did not intimidate everyone for Elizabeth Wallace was reported for saying that the Session "had given out an act for hanging of a dog and he was unhanged as yet". The lady had a sense of humour not appreciated by the Session.

On 8th February 1695 Mr Hamilton had a fast day on account of the death of Queen Mary, wife of the man who in Scotland was William II and in England William III. In July that year the minister announced his intention to hold the weekly sermon on Thursdays and "did seriously exhort" the elders to attend to be a "good example to others".

Corstorphine bairns were apparently not overawed by the kirk for the Session had to order "the kirk officer to punish all children whom he finds breaking the Sabbath". Strict Sunday observance was dear to Mr Hamilton.

Next year the major social problems were drunkenness and swearing. The Session's determination to keep the parishioners on the straight and narrow way was extended in 1697 from inspecting behaviour in the village to going "through the landward of this parish to see yr be any disorders". The first elder to undertake this work was George Girdwood in Saughton.

Possibly the biggest scandal during Mr Hamilton's ministry was the drunken behaviour of the schoolmaster, John Cunningham, who in 1698 on his way home from Edinburgh "went tottering west". Over the summer of 1702 the minister, with permission from the Presbytery, was away "about his necessary affairs abroad": possibly he was in Ireland.

Over the period 1698–1707 the schoolmasters who also acted as Session Clerks had not been conscientious about keeping the minutes of Session meetings so when William Wood was appointed he was asked to transcribe the relevant notes and bring the register up to date.

On 1st May 1707 England and Scotland were incorporated into the United Kingdom of Great Britain. One of the effects of the Union was to bring the coinage of both countries into one system. The Session took action on this at their meeting on 3rd April when they were told "that the English money such as sixpences, shillings, half crowns and crowns are to be reduced to the value with England and that there hath been a proclamation … to give it to the Bank … so that none may be the losers by it; it is therefore ordered that all these species of money, that may be found in the poors box, be taken out and exchanged".

The minutes break off in August 1708. Archibald Hamilton died on 30th April 1709. When the minutes resumed on 7th July 1709 with deliberations about a successor Mr Hamilton was described as "our worthy and dear Minister". When the Prime Minister, Neville Chamberlain, spoke to the General Assembly of the Church of Scotland in May 1939 he said: "Like many Englishmen, I have a Scottish connection. One of my maternal ancestors, a certain Archibald Hamilton, was the minister of a Presbyterian church in Corstorphine, and his bones lie there to this day". Where Mr Hamilton was buried is not known.

Old Parish Church from the south. [RG]

Chapter 3

THE EIGHTEENTH CENTURY

GEORGE FORDYCE

On 29th July 1709 George Fordyce, probationer, son of the minister at Rafford, was called to Corstorphine. It was a great social day for the heritors. The account of what they owed James Warden for entertainment "at ye election" reveals how grand an occasion it was.

There was the hire of three coaches to bring the heritors to the village. After deciding to appoint Mr Fordyce the heritors turned their attention to the flesh pots of food and drink. Placed before them were two breasts of beef, two legs of mutton, two geese, five ducks, fourteen hens, a dove pie, wheat loaves, seven dozen rolls, onions and "turneeps". To wash it down were six pints of wine, five pints of brandy, twelve gallons of ale and eight ounces of sugar.

The room where they dined was filled with smoke from the tobacco and pipes supplied. The horses that had brought the coaches were not forgotten for their "meat" cost £3–12–0. The total cost was £112–01–0 Scots. Like every other financial business involving heritors the cost was proportional to their estate valuations. The owner of the barony, Dickson of Sornebeg, paid £38–13–0 and Watson of Saughton £34–0–0.

On 18th October 1709 the induction took place and George was to serve the parish till his death on 30th August 1767. At once work was undertaken on repairing and renovating the church and the manse. Sin varies little from generation to generation so that George Fordyce and the Session had before them regularly the fornicators, the drunken, and the Sabbath breakers. Irregular marriages and foundling children were additional causes of upset. Mr Fordyce was anxious to set up prayer societies throughout the parish in 1712. The elders were instructed to speak to the heads of families about this proposal but nothing seems to have come of it.

In 1720 Sir Francis Grant, Lord Cullen, Senator of the College of Justice, took a lease of the castle mansion for a summer residence. His wife, Sarah Fordyce, was a sister of the minister. Lord Cullen was of the Ballintomb family in Moray and first of the Monymusk Grants. He became an elder in Corstorphine kirk and later acted as ruling elder to the Presbytery and the Synod. He continued in these offices till his death in 1726. When the Gogar parishioners asked for the hours of worship on winter Sundays to be adjusted to suit weather conditions it took Mr Fordyce a few years to appreciate the reasonableness of their request.

Mr Fordyce was no respecter of persons. When Trotter of Mortonhall assaulted a servant girl who had been a foundling in Corstorphine the minister was prepared to take legal action to get justice for the girl. For the first year of his ministry (1710) church collections amounted to £212–13–0 Scots. Other monies came from the hire of mortcloths £16–14–0, marriage money £18–00–00, and sinners fines £10–00–00. The total income was £257–7–0 Scots. In his last year, 1766, the income of £910–12–0 included £12–0–0 marriage fees and £106–8–0 from mortcloths.

Like other kirks the collections for the Poors Box attracted unacceptable coinage, "bad copper". This was obsolete or debased money. Though the Corstorphine records do not name the coins there would almost certainly be the doit, a Dutch coin popular in Stewart times in Scotland and equal to one twelfth of an English penny. The only way of dealing with bad copper was to sell it to smiths and coppersmiths. In 1732 there was £7 of bad copper in the box. Again in 1737 a total of £4–8–0 Scots was sold and realised 15 shillings Scots.

Mr Fordyce's stipend in 1727 included £15–13–0 Scots, the cash equivalent of what the lands of Saughton owed him in bear and meal. Generally the Corstorphine ministers took their victual stipend without commuting it.

Mr Fordyce had two daughters. Anne married John Dickie, W. S. who owned the estate of Corstorphine Hill. Sarah became the wife of David Moubray, minister at Currie and later Liberton. George Fordyce had a brother, Thomas, a writer, who was factor at Aytoun in Berwickshire. Thomas was buried in 1755 in Greyfriars churchyard, Edinburgh, "at the foot of McClellan's ground", possibly Sir Samuel McClelland, Lord Provost of Edinburgh, who died in 1709.

The Old Parish Church from the west prior to the major restoration of 1905. Today's main door in the porch had yet to be introduced. *(PB160)*

JOHN CHIESLY

The Patronage Act of 1712 gave the laird the privilege of appointing the parish minister. Sir Alexander Dick of Prestonfield and Corstorphine, laird and patron, appointed John Chiesly from St. Monans, Fife, in 1768. Watson of Saughton questioned whether the patronage right belonged to Dick or to "Lady Forrester spouse to George Cockburn of Ormiston". Dick was influenced by Mr Alexander of Clermiston who was indebted to Chiesly for helping him when he stood for MP in the Anstruther burghs.

Mr Chiesly began his ministry at Corstorphine by examining the state of the Poors Fund and seeing if a higher rate of interest could be got on the capital. Then church renovations were considered. Such Session minutes as have survived from 1768 to 1784 are little more than bald statements about the collections and the poors money. Sinners seem to have disappeared from the Corstorphine scene. Perhaps Mr Chiesly had a mind above village scandal or perhaps the schoolmaster clerk, Alexander Bannatyne, preferred brevity to time-consuming discipline records.

In 1776 Mr Chiesly placed himself before the public eye by attacking, in the Synod of Lothian and Tweeddale, the appointment, by the Presbytery of Edinburgh, of Dr Webster to introduce Mr Balfour of Lecropt to be the minister at Lady Glenorchy's chapel, Edinburgh. Lady Glenorchy in 1773 built a chapel in the valley between the old and the new towns of Edinburgh where Platform No.1, Waverley Station, now stands.

Chiesly's objection, supported by Mr Robertson of Ratho, halted Lady Glenorchy's plans. The objection was that the chapel was private property, not an established church. The General Assembly of 1777 spent two and a half days debating the issue and in the end left it to the Presbytery of Edinburgh to ensure that any minister appointed would conform to the established church standards. Mr Balfour was unable to accept as the Presbytery of Dunblane refused to relieve him of Lecropt. Eventually the Rev. Thomas Snell Jones from England was accepted by the Presbytery and admitted to the chapel where he worked till his death in 1837.

When Lady Glenorchy died in 1786 she was buried in her Edinburgh chapel. In 1844 the building was demolished to make room for the railway. Hugh Miller vividly described the fog shrouded morning when Lady Glenorchy's body was disinterred and removed to the family vault at St. John's Episcopal Church, Princes Street. Later it was interred below the Communion table in the Holy Trinity Church, Roxburgh Place, Edinburgh, to which the chapel congregation shifted. Then in 1971 because of moving population the Roxburgh Place church decided to remove to Wester Hailes. Now Lady Glenorchy's remains rest under the Communion table of Holy Trinity Church, Wester Hailes.

Lady Glenorchy's Edinburgh home was Barnton estate which she sold, shortly before her death, to the Edinburgh banker, William Ramsay. In 1895 it passed to the Royal Burgess Golfing Society of Edinburgh. The old house was re-erected stone by stone on the other side of the Atlantic.

Mr Chiesly little realised when he stirred up trouble for Willielma Maxwell, Viscountess Glenorchy, that he was opposing a woman whose work in founding churches in

Scotland and in England would long be remembered when his name had faded.

Not far from Wester Hailes, at the junction of Calder Road and Wester Hailes Road, is the church of St. Nicholas planned in the summer of 1939 and carried on in hutted buildings till 1957 when the present permanent building was completed. £51,000 to help costs was raised by the children of Scotland so that the church was given the name of St. Nicholas. The site of this church is another link with John Chiesly of Corstorphine.

In 1781 the General Assembly sanctioned the use of paraphrases in church services. When Chiesly announced a paraphrase from the pulpit at Corstorphine a section of the congregation objected and left the church. They went to the southern boundary of the parish to Larbour Farm on the south side of Calder Road where the old Thieves Road (Wester Hailes Road) branched off towards Colinton and Currie. There they set up their secession church. The stile which they used to get into the steading from the Thieves Road survived till c.1945 and was known as the Seceders Steps. The stile was almost opposite, but a little to the north of, the farm cottages on the west side of the road. The cottages were pulled down when the Calder housing estate was built post 1945. When the Corstorphine folk applied to the Secession Church for recognition of their Larbour church they complained not just about the paraphrases but also about "their want of due administration of the gospel" at Corstorphine.

By 1783 the dissenters, joined by others from Colinton, formed a church at Slateford. The building, though no longer a church, still stands through the pend on the Lanark Road opposite the junction to Longstone.

The farmer at Larbour converted the simple secession oblong church with its outside stair into a barn. No reason appears for the Seceders choosing to set up their meeting place at Sighthill. However, forty years earlier two families at Sighthill and Saughton were associated with the Secession church of Adam Gib at Bristo Place, Edinburgh. It may be that there was in the Larbour area a sympathy towards seceders. The modern St. Nicholas Church occupies approximately the site of the Secession Church of the 1780's.

John Chiesly came to Corstorphine under the patronage of the estate owner. Two years after his death the heritors had not paid his widow the arrears of stipend due him. To safeguard herself she recorded each debtor and the amount due, thus giving them an immortality little to their credit. According to J.P. Wood Mr Chiesly was "not much regretted by his parishioners".

THOMAS SHARP

Thomas Sharp had a brief ministry. He came from Hawick in March 1789 and died at Corstorphine in July 1791. His appointment was a matter of controversy. Sir William Dick, as patron, presented Mr Sharp but a large number of parishioners did not want him. The Presbytery were reluctant to go forward with his admission but the Synod of Lothian supported him and the Presbytery of Jedburgh were willing to allow his transfer. Sharp before entering the ministry was a tutor to the Dick family.

JAMES OLIVER

Sir William Dick presented James Oliver, minister at Ancrum, to Corstorphine kirk on 5th July 1792. Mr Oliver's first task was to reconstitute the Session which had not met for some time. The only elder who had continued to have a concern for the church was David Johnston, the brewer. However Mr Oliver found John Comb in Gogar Mains, James Nimmo in Sighthill, Robert Watt in Ravelston, and John Foreman in Corstorphine willing to act as elders: the Session then began to put church affairs in order.

Mr Johnston asked to be relieved of his office of kirk treasurer as he had served for some years. He presented his accounts for 1791–93. The Session then ordered their clerk to record their gratitude to Mr Johnston for his "faithful discharge of his office" to which Mr Oliver added that, though no Session records had been kept since 1784 Mr Johnston's book of accounts was kept meticulously. In maintaining the Poors Fund Mr Johnston had personally supplied £22–7–8½ which was duly refunded.

In 1793 Mr Oliver responded to Sir John Sinclair's request to compile an account of the parish for the historic *Statistical Account of Scotland*. In so doing the minister left posterity a picture of Corstorphine in the last decade of the 18th century. He knew of the tradition of the golden cross: for the derivation of the placename he preferred Gaelic origins. The May and June beauty of the sycamore "in a close belonging to Sir William Dick" (an alley / Dovecot Road) obviously delighted him. He noted that the pulley for the lamp on the east gable of the church had "not long since" been dismantled. Population was 1037 : males 484; females 553. He attributed a decline in population to the mineral well going out of use.

Occupations were listed as were religious denominations. Agriculture was the mainstay of the parish. There were seventeen farms. In Edinburgh there was a ready market for potatoes, especially Red Nebs, and also for Corstorphine cream, a dish similar to rennet or yoghurt. The parish had two threshing mills. Wages of ploughmen were "not extravagantly high". Masons and carpenters could command more because, as Mr Oliver thought, their skills were in demand in the developing new town of Edinburgh.

The remains of the old castle moat were still visible. The minister did not favour talk of a canal through the parish. One of his objections was that goods from the West would cease to come by horse which would be detrimental to Corstorphine trade in hay, oats, pease, and beans. While admitting that he was "not much conversant in subjects of political economy" he did not hesitate to discuss the pros and cons of agriculture versus manufactures.

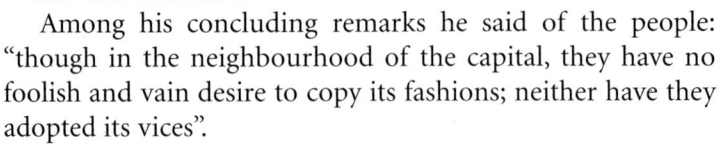

Among his concluding remarks he said of the people: "though in the neighbourhood of the capital, they have no foolish and vain desire to copy its fashions; neither have they adopted its vices".

There is a strange irony in an observation made by Mr Oliver in the *Statistical Account*. Writing in 1793 he said: "The grasping hand of avarice, never satisfied, exacts from children employed in manufactures, tasks unsuited to their years. Since the manufacturing rage hath commenced, the waste of the human species would not be easy to compute. Children bear the confinement with impatience, unjustly deprived of the hours which, in the season of youth, should be devoted to play, they often are tempted to embrace the opportunity of making their escape."

Yet, in 1796, he and the Session met in April to settle the future of two orphan boys, William Finlay and David Ramage, whose education and maintenance had been paid for from the church funds. Finlay and Ramage were aged eight or nine. Consequently they were considered fit for work.

View of the 17th century Dovecot in Dovecot Road, now cared for by *Historic Scotland* [GUS]

At New Lanark, David Dale, a Glasgow weaver and importer of fine yarn for linen weavers, had in 1784 built a large mill beside the waters of the Clyde. He built a village to accommodate his workers. Children worked from 6am to 7pm for six days a week. There was a break of half an hour at 9am for breakfast and an hour at 2pm for dinner. Breakfast and supper consisted of oatmeal porridge with milk. Dinner was barley broth made from fresh beef. The beef was given to one half of the children while the other half got cheese. Underclothing was changed once a week.

Education was provided but it took place in the evenings from 7.30pm to 9pm after the children had worked in the factory for thirteen hours. They slept in dormitories with three sharing a bed.

The Session of Corstorphine were told that the boys would get a practical training and be educated in reading and religion. Mr Dale would require "no recompense but their own labour for a certain period of years". The proposition was attractive to the Session for it would relieve them of the financial burden of supporting the boys.

Mr Oliver contacted Mr Dale's Edinburgh agent, Mr Henderson, a merchant with an office in the West Bow of Edinburgh. It was agreed that the boys would be "conveyed at Mr Dale's expense to New Lanark and remain there for a period of six years". Shortly after on a June morning Finlay and Ramage left Corstorphine for New Lanark clutching the Session's parting gift – a Bible for each lad.

Three years later, 1799, Mr Oliver signed indenture papers binding the orphan, John Geddes, to New Lanark for eight years. He, too, got a Bible as a parting gift. It is one of the ironies of history that those who were pillars of the kirk were largely blind to the virtual enslavement in mills of children who, as Tom Johnston so justly said, "toiled for a master's profit". The only comfort in the story of the Corstorphine orphans is that New Lanark was the most humanely organised mill of the period.

Severe winters in 1796–97 and the ensuing hardship led Mr Oliver to appeal to the heritors for assistance with the Poors Fund. Accordingly Sir Alexander Dick, Charles Watson of Saughton, Ramsay of Barnton, Keith of Corstorphine Hill, Dundas of Beechwood and Belmont, and Robinson of Clermiston agreed to he assessed at eight shillings for each plough gate of land they possessed.

The Session minutes were not kept after 1807 and the parish registers were irregularly written. Mr Oliver died in 1814. Among his papers were "loose sheets" and "slips of paper" relating to church finance. Mr Oliver apparently undertook to be kirk treasurer, 1806. Thereafter till 1814 there were no active elders or Session Clerk. When matters were reviewed after Mr Oliver's death the Poors Fund was at a low ebb, a contributory factor being the reduced opportunities for church door collections "from the circumstances of the congregation meeting only once a fortnight".

Mr Oliver's apparent neglect of church affairs from 1807 till his death may have been owing to domestic pressures. Up till then he had shown an active interest in the parish and the village, subscribing to the Friendly Society and attending the Sunday afternoon cock fighting at the toun's end. His wife, Eliza Hamilton, died in 1809 "much and justly regretted". Stephen, his eldest son, died 1812 aged nineteen. Ramsay, the schoolmaster and Session Clerk, by 1810 was in trouble with the law over payments to wives of militia men.

When Mr Oliver died in March 1814 members of the Presbytery of Edinburgh attended his funeral on the 15th. Thereafter they held a meeting at Corstorphine to appoint interim preachers. This would seem to imply that Mr Oliver was interred in the kirkyard he knew so well. If a stone ever marked his grave it has disappeared. By August 1814 a successor was presented by the laird.

Tomb in the Old Parish Church of Sir John Forrester (1). [GUS]

Chapter 4

TO THE DISRUPTION

DR DAVID SCOT

David Scot was the son of a ploughman at Carrington. His father, a Scotsman in the theological mould of David Deans, sold his cow to enable him to publish in 1778 a refutation of Arianism under the signature of "Penicuik Ploughman". This was aimed against dissenters such as Adam Gib.

After village school and Edinburgh University David Scot was licensed as a minister but failed to get a church. He then studied medicine obtaining his M.D. His bent, however, lay towards oriental languages in which he made his reputation. He taught young gentlemen preparing for service with the East India Company.

This led to his friendship with Sir John Majoribanks. In 1812 Scot tried for the Chair of Hebrew in Edinburgh University but a contemporary and distinguished philologist, Dr Murray, was appointed. Two years later Majoribanks used his influence with Sir Robert Keith Dick to have Scot presented to Corstorphine.

During his ministry Dr Scot continued lecturing and writing on oriental languages. He had a kindred spirit in Dr Morehead, an Episcopalian clergyman from Edinburgh who had a summer residence opposite the foot of Clermiston Road. Both men passed happy hours with classical literature.

Whether the author of *Discourses on some Important Subjects of Natural and Revealed Religion*, introduced by a *Short View of the Best Specimens of Pulpit Eloquence given to the World in Ancient and Modern Times* was the best choice for a congregation composed largely of agricultural labourers is a moot point. Scot's academic frame of mind and his unwillingness to live in the manse, preferring to stay in Edinburgh, and coming out only on Sundays to preach, probably made his ministry less effective than what Corstorphine needed. Eventually, however, at the insistence of the heritors he came to live at the manse. The social work of the church in caring

TOP.
Rev David Scott MD, Minister 1814-1833. *(PB914)*

BELOW.
Rev David Horne, Minister 1833–1863. *(PB915)*

for the poor continued. In 1818 when a man broke into the garden at Ravelston and was fined a pound which he had to give to the church the money was given to Robert Clelland with a family in distress. Dr Scot regularly contributed to the Friendly Society in Corstorphine.

The outstanding event of Dr Scot's ministry was the decision to renew the church building. An octagon was proposed in 1826 but, fortunately, did not materialise. The architect, Burn, in 1828 produced a plan which, the heritors accepted. The final year of David Scot at Corstorphine, 1832, found the village upset with fears – fear of the body snatchers and fear of the cholera epidemic sweeping through Edinburgh and surrounding areas.

Late in life Dr Scot found his real vocation when in 1832 he was appointed to the Chair of Hebrew in St. Mary's College, St. Andrews. When attending a meeting of the British Association in Edinburgh he was seized with a dropsical complaint and died on 18th September 1834. Dr Scot's body was brought to be buried in Corstorphine. His tombstone is immediately on the right after entering the churchyard from Kirk Loan.

DAVID HORNE

When David Horne was studying for the church he also acted as tutor to the family of Sir Robert Keith Dick of Prestonfield. Mr Horne's first parish was Yester, 1831, where his only child was baptised Robert Keith Dick Horne. Horne succeeded Dr Scot for Dick of Prestonfield was the patron.

Alterations were done to the manse and further renovations to the church. A new pulpit Bible was got and a psalm book for the precentor. William Ramsay Watson of Saughton and New Saughton died in 1841 and left a legacy of £2,000 to the poor but his executors delayed payment until the Court of Session in 1844 ordered it to be paid to the church. One of Mr Horne's contributions to the social life of the village was setting up a parish library.

The great event of his ministry, however, was also a national event – the Disruption of 1843. Patronage was one of the contributory factors to the Disruption. In 1834 the Church of Scotland passed the Veto Act to prevent ministers being intruded on unwilling congregations. The civil courts declared that the Church had no such power and upheld calls made by patrons even when the people refused the person nominated. This eventually led to confrontation between the established state church authority and the ministers who declared for spiritual independence.

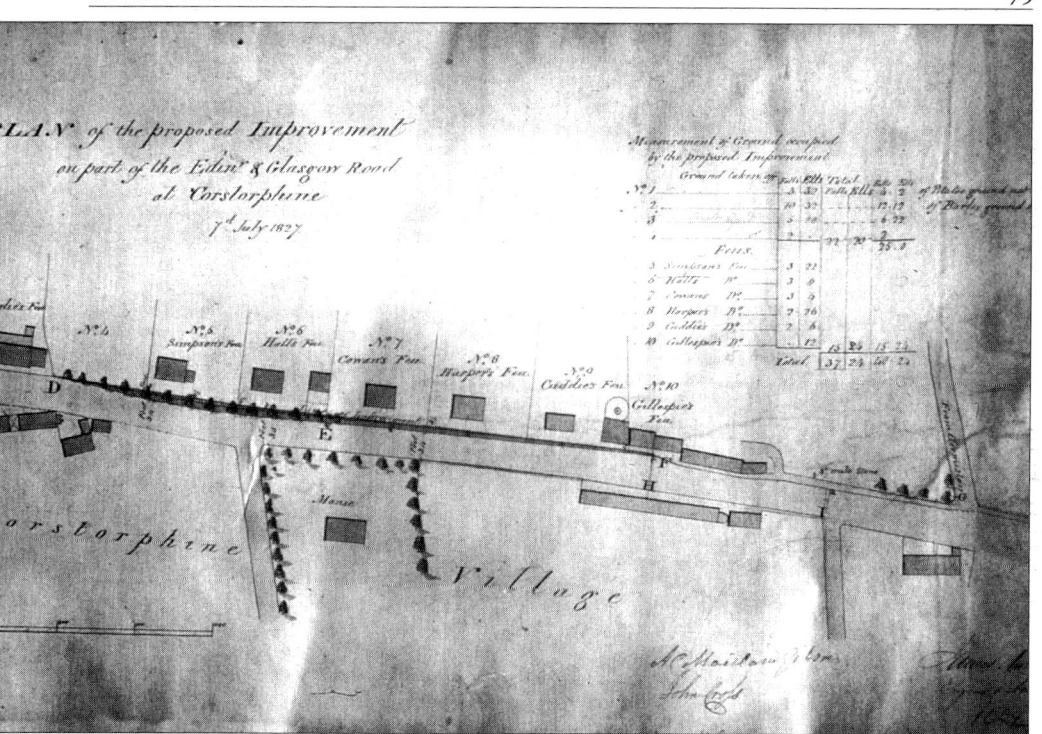

About 2.30 on the afternoon of 12th May 1843 the crowd that had gathered outside St. Andrew's Church, George Street, Edinburgh, saw the arrival of the Lord High Commissioner to begin the meeting of the General Assembly of the Church of Scotland. Dr Welsh, the retiring moderator, after the opening prayer instead of going on to constitute the Assembly protested against further proceedings. He laid the statement of grievances against the Established Church on the table and then left the building. Dr Chalmers followed him and others joined in till the church was left half empty. In a column four deep the breakaway ministers walked to Tanfield Hall, Canonmills, and held there the first Assembly of the Free Church of Scotland.

Leaving the state church involved giving up one's livelihood and leaving the manse, a scene of heart break feelingly depicted by George Harvey in his painting *Quitting the manse*. It was not an easy decision for a man with a wife and family

The main Edinburgh–Glasgow road (now St John's Road) in 1827. Simpson's Feu and Hall's Feu opposite the top of Manse Road became, in 1844, the site of Corstorphine Free Church (now St Ninian's). The Harp Hotel was built on Harper's Feu. Sadly, the name 'Harp' was discarded by the hotel's owners after the 2002 refurbishment. (*Courtesy* NAS, *ref.* RHP 10293) to make. At the time of the Veto Act Mr Horne supported it both from the pulpit and at public meetings. He organised a meeting, held in the parish church, in support of non-intrusion, at which Dr Candlish of Edinburgh spoke.

When, however, the time for action came in 1842 Mr Horne changed his stance. Those of his congregation who supported the Disruption were left to fend for themselves. And this they did. On 28th May 1843, two weeks after the Disruption, a minister and thirty six people met in the old schoolroom opposite the north end of Manse Road adjoining the ground on which later the Free Church was built. Its story is the story of St. Ninian's Church.

Mr Horne owed his position to a patron. His son carried the patron's name. The second Horne, in due course, followed his father into the pulpit at Corstorphine. The younger Horne was ordained 23rd July 1863.

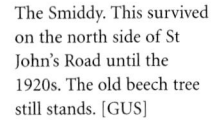

The Smiddy. This survived on the north side of St John's Road until the 1920s. The old beech tree still stands. [GUS]

Chapter 5

TOWARDS RESTORATION

ROBERT KEITH DICK HORNE

Patronage was not abolished till 1874. Robert Keith Dick Horne was for a while tutor to the family of John Inglis, Lord Glencorse, Lord President of the Court of Session. The Inglis family was associated with Tibbermore near Perth: the younger Horne's first church assistantship was at Redgorton.

R.K.D. Horne was responsible for the recovery of the old hour glass belonging to the church; it had been missing for a long number of years. A former beadle had paid a stone-cutter working at a tombstone by giving him the hour glass. Mr Horne traced the glass to its new owner and got it back. The original glass was 17th century Florentine but breakage in the 18th century led to replacement. The original ran for half an hour being usually turned once for the old hour long sermon. Now the glass runs for fifteen minutes. Gone are the days when the people laid down their heads in the pews as the minister laid down the heads of his discourse in the pulpit.

In 1876 the Presbytery of Edinburgh were petitioned by a group of parishioners to visit the parish. Since no reason was

Rev Robert Keith Dick Horne, Minister 1863–1881. *(PB916)*

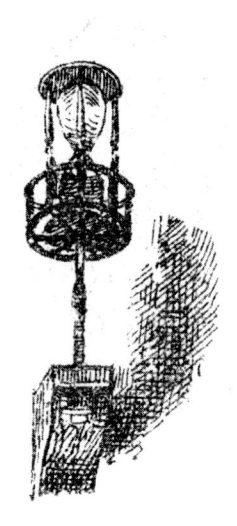

A representation of the old hour glass in the Old Parish Church. [GUS]

given the Presbytery declined to act. Six months later a fresh petition supported by the owner of the estate and legal representation compelled the Presbytery to act. Three months later, in July 1877, Mr Horne agreed to form a Kirk Session which was in action by June 1878. This situation explains the poverty of mid 19th century church records.

By 1880 Mr Horne's health caused him to ask for leave of absence. Then in 1881 he suggested that an assistant and successor should be appointed. Further deliberations led to R.K.D. Horne resigning. In August 1881 Dr Dodds was called to Corstorphine.

DR JAMES DODDS

Dr Dodds came from a city church, St. George's Glasgow, to a village church where time had almost stood still for a century. In Corstorphine the precentor led the Sabbath praise with his tuning fork. Gradually Dr Dodds introduced changes. In 1883 it was decided to get a harmonium, Next year, Mr Fleming, the precentor, retired and Joseph Hibbs took charge of church music. The old practice of collection plates at the church door before service was replaced with bags for collections inside the church during the service.

When the church hall was built on the site of the demolished Provost's or Kirkstyle House the harmonium was transferred to the hall. The Sunday School met in the hall for which Thomas Middlemas, watchmaker, gifted the timepiece. A pipe organ, supplied by Conacher of Huddersfield, was erected in the church. To accommodate it the pulpit was removed and a reading desk introduced. Church funds in 1891 supplied £5 towards the cost of the choir's annual trip.

By 1892 the Session began to realise that the building alterations of 1828 left much to be desired, but church restoration was to be the work of Dr Dodds' successor, Mr Fergusson, who came as assistant in 1895. Blackhall in 1899 with a population of 250 was a village at the junction of three parishes – Cramond, Corstorphine, and Dean. The greater part of Blackhall lay in Corstorphine: only six houses were in Cramond. The Trustees for the Craigcrook Mortification had just then feued ground in the area for sixteen villas and for tenements.

Church services were held in the Gartshore Hall where the preaching was shared by the assistant from Dean Church and the minister from Davidsons Mains Free Church. The Cramond minister was anxious to get a regular forenoon service as the "class of people settling about Blackhall will not come out to an evening service".

The folk at Dean were then considering a new building so did not wish any further financial commitment. Corstorphine agreed to share with Cramond the feu duty for a building site for only three years as Corstorphine, too, was thinking of extension. In 1903 Blackhall got St. Columba's Church designed by P. MacGregor Chalmers.

Dr Dodds suffered in his later years from poor health but in 1906 attained his fiftieth year in the ministry when the church presented him with a silver casket and silver salver. The Presbytery of Edinburgh in noting the jubilee of Dr Dodds made special mention of his successful efforts to "recover some of the early volumes" of records. This was, indeed, a great service to Scottish church history and to Scottish social history for it is in the records of the Session that the historian finds the source material for the life and work of the ordinary man and woman.

For the Scottish History Society Dr Dodds edited the *Diary of William Cunningham of Craigends.* Dr Dodds died on 17th January 1907.

Rev James Dodds DD, Minister 1881–1907. *(PB928)*

JAMES FERGUSSON

James Fergusson was minister at St. Columba's, London in 1893 when Dr Dodds chanced to hear the young preacher. He was so impressed that, when the service ended, he offered Mr Fergusson the assistantship at Corstorphine.

During his ministry at Corstorphine his powerful preaching inspired all who sat under him. Among the many gifts presented as tokens of appreciation of his parochial work were the Kirk Loan entrance gate with the Forrester horns in wrought metal, the brass reading desk for the Communion table, and the south gate with its hammered iron work.

Mr Fergusson's keen interest in education led to his being Chairman of the School Board and after Corstorphine became part of Edinburgh he was made Vice-Chairman of the Education Authority. To the Royal Flying Corps at Turnhouse and to the local branch of the British Legion he acted as chaplain. He was Right Worshipful Master of the Lodge of St.

Example of heraldic device featuring on the Forrester coat of arms

Rev James Fergusson TD, Minister 1895–1926. *(PB930)*

John, Corstorphine, and chaplain to the Grand Lodge of Scotland 1917–18. In 1925 he became clerk to the Presbytery of Edinburgh.

It was Mr Fergusson's practice to spend the month of September each year in London when he preached at St. Columba's. And it was there that the end came for him in September 1926. His last sermon was inspired by that noble passage in the gospel of St. John giving assurance that "in my Father's house are many mansions".

On the front panels of the tower gallery of Corstorphine kirk James Fergusson's congregation inscribed their tribute to his service in beautiful Renaissance lettering cut by the master carver Alexander Carrick:

> "To the Glory of God and in memory of the Reverend
> James Fergusson, who served this parish 1895–1926.
> An eloquent preacher and a man greatly beloved;
> through his zeal and devotion this church
> was restored in 1905."

The 1905 restoration was Mr Fergusson's crowning glory. He gave back to Corstorphine its historic medieval collegiate church. In so doing he did an even better thing: he gave to Scotland a priceless treasure of restored Christian architecture.

THE CHURCH BUILDING

The great event for Scotland as a nation in 1646 was the surrender of Charles I to the Scottish army. Locally in Corstorphine the great event was the demolition of the 12th century parish church of St. Mary and the altering of the collegiate church building to suit the needs of a reformed parish church.

The Session record 3rd May 1646 runs:

> "Mr James Watson and George Cochran were ordained to revise ye compts and depursments of moneye for taking downe and putting upe of ye pend betwixt ye Kirk and ye Quire, ffor stanes, lyme, sand for yt effect; for timber to be ye coomesyle and scaffolding for masons and workemens wages; as also for taking downe of ye old paroch kirk, putting upe ye new Isle; for lyme, timber to be cooples, dales to be sarking, nailes, wages to masones and wrights and others workmen their servants and for their drink allowed to them who brought home lyme, sand, stanes, timber, slaites; as also for glase windowes wyre tirle-leisses. Was found be them yt ye expenses extended near to XIIIc [1,300] merkis".

Later alterations have made it difficult to reconstruct exactly what was done. Certainly the "pend" (archway) between the "kirk" (nave being used as parish church) and the "quire" (choir/chancel) was dismantled ("taking downe") but it was also reconstructed by being blocked off ("putting upe") and for that stones, lime and sand were needed.

The people retained the nave but the chancel, where at the altar mass had been said, had no part in the reformed church. The features associated with the Popish church (piscina, sedilia) were thus screened from the sight of reformed worshippers. The chancel ("quire") then became the private burial place of the Forresters: the last to be interred there was James in 1679 before the east window.

The Old Parish Church from the north-east, as sketched by James Skene of Rubislaw, c.1817. It shows the lairds lofts. Robert Southey, the poet, commented in 1819, while en route to Linlithgow, on the 'odd' church which looked like three or four put together. *(PB1448)*

The Skene drawings c.1817 depict the floor of the chancel in a sad state of neglect, the earth being thrown up in heaps. It was small wonder that Burn, the architect, in 1849 asked if the representatives of the Forrester family had any "right or interest in the Forrester aisle and monuments". Sir R.K. Dick Cunyngham, then laird, thought that the "ancestors of the present proprietor" had got everything connected with the Forrester family. The Earl of Verulam, however, asserted himself and made provision for the preservation of the tombs.

Skene also depicted the blocked up arch with two doors set into it at ground level, giving access to the nave / parish church. A stairway is shown leading up against the walled arch to a door into the laird's loft. This loft looked up the nave to the pulpit. Above and high up, on either side of the loft door, were two windows placed below a sloping roof. The loft not only projected into the parish kirk but it also had its own roof within the arch on the chancel side. This might have been the "coomesyle" though the "coomesyle" of the accounts may refer to the wooden frame used by masons when building up the arch.

This work on the chancel arch may explain the pushed-in appearance of the Forrester tomb adjoining the archway. The line of the original medieval arch is still visible on the west side. Below the loft staircase between the two ground level doorways Skene drew a bench with two ladies seated. This seat strongly resembles the seat in St. Conan's Church, Loch Awe, which Walter Campbell of Innischonain, a collector of antiquities, got from Corstorphine when he started to create St. Conan's in 1907. A group of three are chatting opposite the sedilia and at the priest's door entrance a gentleman is lifting his hat to two ladies. The impression given is that of the chancel having become a social foyer for the congregation before going into the service.

Since in the 18th century everyday community affairs were discussed on Sunday mornings when the people foregathered, usually in the churchyard, it may have been that Corstorphine folk were able to enjoy a sheltered village parliament in the Forrester chancel.

The taking down of the old parish church of St. Mary is not surprising when it is remembered that a hundred years previously the Forrester family had appealed to Cardinal Beaton to get something done about the neglect of church property at Corstorphine. The masons in 1646 possibly reused some of the stone in the erection of the present porch.

The building of a new aisle to the north was an architectural balancing act to form with the medieval south aisle a new north – south transept. It has been suggested that this "new Ile" was built on the site of St. Mary's of which the only documentary description is that it was "contigua" to Adam Forrester's chapel.

Did the 1646 masons take down a St. Mary's that stood parallel to the nave of the collegiate church? Or did they demolish a St. Mary's situated parallel but nearer the tower end of the collegiate church? In either case ground would then be available on which to erect a new north aisle to complete the transept in the collegiate building. Was St. Mary's physically an obstacle or was the reformed church using it as an economical quarry for stone?

Another piece of the puzzle may be in the Session record for 1735. Charles Bruce, glazier Edinburgh, "having lately built a house on the east end of Corstorphine Hill" (Belmont) asked permission to build a seat for himself and his family by "taking down a stone wall built under a pend or arch in the East sidewall of the North Ile ... which arch appears to have been designed for an entry to the kirk formerly".

Bruce's seat came to the east side of the Baird of Saughtonhall loft so he undertook to support and "keep up the jeasts" (floorbeams) of the loft "in all time coming". Another condition was that his seat was not to come "further within the church than two inches within the face of the pend on the inside thereof".

Bruce and the Session concluded that the infilled arch was previously a doorway but could there be other possibilities? Could it have been an arched west entrance to St. Mary's which was simply blocked up in 1646 to form part of the east side of the new north aisle? If so, then the old parish church was parallel to the collegiate building. Or could the blocked arch have been the arched east end of St. Mary's? Nothing is known of the form of the east end of the old parish church. When Henry Forrester in 1597 got a tack of the teinds it was on condition that he maintained the "quire" of the parish church but which parish church – the reformed collegiate or the still standing St. Mary's?

The possibilities are many: the certainties are few. The building costs of the 1646 alterations were 1300 merks (£200 Scots) to which John Cowper of Gogar, James Eleis of Stenhouse along with his mother-in-law, James Watson of Saughton, James Gibbiesone, and Robert Scott contributed. The balance of costs was to be paid from the church Box. As late as 1684 when funds in the Box were low the minister and the Session took legal action to recover what was due to the Box since "ye building of ye North Isle, cuting ye penn".

When certain persons in 1693 objected to Alexander Alexander wanting to set up a seat "under the pend of the wester vault" the Session gave him a place on the west side of the north aisle behind Thomas Baillie.

Baird of Saughtonhall applied to build a loft in the north aisle in 1694. At that time he owned the Provost's House. There was no objection from Chalmers of Gogar but Watson of Saughton objected. However the Session did not think that Watson's objection was valid. Baird had a document supporting him signed by Forrester and other heritors.

The Session allowed him to build his loft to extend from

Skew puts. These architectural features from the Provost's House (demolished) beside the Old Parish Church are incorporated into the present church hall built on the same site. [GUS]

the north gable forward to the cover of the "laigh seat" belonging to "the laird of Stennopmilnes" who was by that time Watson of Saughton. Skene's drawing of the exterior of the church in 1817 shows the outside stair to the Saughtonhall loft as well as the ground level extension for seating Bruce of Brucehill (later Belmont). This clutter of extensions gave the old kirk the appearance of bits and pieces haphazardly stuck together.

One certainty about the new north aisle was that, unlike the medieval building, the roof was slated. This led to concern about its condition in 1667. Lime and sand were got by Robert Graham for pointing and Robert Alexander arranged to pay the slater. The "pecunial mulct" or fine imposed on Captain George Buchan of the King's Guard for fornication with Janet Drummond was used to pay the expenses of repairing the arch and the roof of the north aisle.

In 1656 the minister reported to the Session that Lord Forrester intended "to deface the fabricke of the kirk by the removeall of the seattes in his Loft and leaveing the said Loft void of fixed seattes".

Moreover he was going "to cutt off a great pairt of the kirk by putting up a division for keepeing of his buriall place". A wright was already at work so the Session decided that Forrester should be asked to do nothing harmful to the kirk and that the Presbytery should be informed of what was happening.

Despite a promise to do no more Forrester, two weeks later, on a Saturday in person with some servants "pulled downe all the seats of his Loft". There is no indication why he did this. It may have been to limit the usage of the Loft or he may have wanted space for something more splendid in the way of individual chairs.

His idea to protect the Forrester burial place by setting up a "divisione" may have been to confine people coming into church, as they did by way of the chancel, to a corridor or narrow passageway. This would prevent them walking over burial ground. Nothing, however, was done.

In 1657 further renovations were carried out. Offerings at this time were collected at the church door by elders who had a little seat there. Some of the congregation had their seats "before" the west door. This position was draughty so the Session arranged to have doors put on the porch, the cost being borne by the discipline fines. That same year the place of public repentance, a wooden platform on high supports, was replaced. Cromwell's soldiers in 1650 had used the original for firewood.

Seating was important, It carried status even in a reformed church where all were supposedly equal in the sight of the Almighty. In 1656 Foulis of Ravelston and James Haldan of Saughton complained about not having seating allocated to them. Lord Forrester in 1668 gave the elders for their exclusive use the "long seat" formerly possessed by the Baillie of Corstorphine, John Swinton, who had been put to death for murdering his wife. At the same time Haldan of Langsaughton was allowed to set up a seat "at ye pulpit dore". This seat was claimed in 1679 by David Watson of Saughton possibly because it was near the area of the Watson burial vault. Villagers who had not seats sat on the kirk forms. These forms were also available for hire for secular purposes such as wedding parties. If only Corstorphine had had a Breugel what pictures might have survived of social scenes where villagers seated on kirk forms enjoyed baked meats. Whether the result of religious or other use the kirk forms were constantly needing the attention of the wright. Robert Adamson worked on the kirk forms in 1675, 1678, and 1680. In 1693 James Adamson claimed the Session for non-payment of work done from 1688 in maintaining forms.

The south aisle, anciently the Niddrie Forrester aisle, was allocated by Lord Forrester 1668 to "any honest man" who wanted to erect a pew.

Later formal divisions of the church for seating were made. One such took place in December 1681 when John Lord Bishop of Edinburgh with others visited the kirk. Ruthven, son of James Forrester, claimed the Forrester loft and burial place as well as the south aisle. With this claim the visiting group agreed but Ruthven had to consent to giving Foulis of Ravelston the east side of the south aisle with permission to make a door on the east wall if such was desired. Foulis was also allowed to extend his seat three feet north "without the pend" but the seat was not to have a headpiece so that the view of the worshippers would not be spoiled.

The west side of the aisle was given to James Eleis of Stenhopmiln with a passage of at least three feet between his seat and Ravelston's seat to allow easy entrance and easy access to the Communion table. This seat was not to come beyond the pend of the aisle. The minister was given two pews on the west side of the north aisle towards the "little door". They were immediately in front of Gogar's floor level seating but at least half a foot lower in height.

David Watson of Saughton was placed at the east wall of the North aisle below the breast of Gogar's seating. Watson's seating was to be kept within the north portion of the church. Feuars could build seats on the south wall of the building. No seats were to be erected on the north wall as the north half of the floor area was to be kept for the Communion table.

The south aisle in 1683 was the scene of dispute between Watson of Saughton and Sir John Foulis of Ravelston. Watson had an interest in the south aisle for entrance to it came close to the area of his family burial vault. By 1683 he also had a seating interest through giving financial assistance to Eleis of Stenhouse whose kirk seat was in the south aisle. When Mr Fordyce was admitted to the church the fabric was examined and the bell house floor was found to need fifteen planks. Cratch [a substance used for filling up joints] and lime were got for the roof and the windows received some attention.

Because there were heritors who still lacked seating areas, some of them met in 1710 to make a fresh division of the church. Sir Robert Dickson who had bought the Corstorphine estate, retained the easter aisle, and Sir Archibald Primrose of Ravelston kept the Ravelston half of the south aisle. Watson, by then proprietor of Stenhouse, had the other half of the south aisle and built his own private access door in the west wall.

Myrton of Gogar in this 1710 division took the lower part of the north aisle and Baird of Saughtonhall kept his loft above Gogar. The minister's seat was on the left of the pulpit between the pend of the north aisle and the pulpit. This places the 18th century pulpit almost diagonally opposite its present position which was adopted at the 1905 restoration. The Session was given the area from the pulpit forward to the choir where the sacrament tables once stood. In 1712 the heritors were called to consider the need for "a speedy reparation" of "several breaches in the roof" and other fabric defects. A man was paid to cut "bushes" growing on the roof and to clean out the water spouts. The mason work was done by John Cleghorn.

As usual the heritors did not like having to pay the accounts. Gogar said that Sir Robert Dickson should pay for the whole of the easter aisle for it was his burial place "being no part of the body of the church". Gogar also thought that since Sir James Baird had been in the habit of maintaining the north aisle since he built his loft he should continue to do so. As for the remaining repairs Gogar was willing to pay in proportion to the valuation of his lands.

Sir James Baird hastened to point out that any previous costs he had met were voluntary payments. Moreover since Gogar had got the whole floor level of the aisle for himself Baird felt he should pay only a proportional share. Gogar continued the dispute. Baird's final offer was to pay a fourth part which was equal to his share of the area. The other heritors agreed but Gogar took the matter to the Presbytery. The Presbytery gave the judgement of Solomon in deciding that Baird should repair as far as his loft extended.

The tradesmen reported that the roof of the whole church needed pointing with cratch and that a whole course of flags in the easter aisle was missing. The foundation of the church required securing with lime and stone. Before the masons did the pointing work the Beadle was paid for "redding" the area in which they were to be working. Thomas Forrest, glazier, undertook the glasswork. Having examined the roof of the north aisle John Watson, slater, Edinburgh, advised stripping it and re-slating and the heritors agreed.

When James Clelland, baillie and merchant in Edinburgh, came to live in Corstorphine he asked in 1713 for a seat in the easter aisle between the door of Saughton's old seat and the door of Mrs Heriot's seat. When he renewed his request in 1729 pointing out that he was proprietor of the property belonging to Ranken of Orchardhead (Dunsmuir) he proposed to make some adjustments between Dickie's seat and the seat of Saughton tenants. The Session agreed on condition that access to the Communion table was not interfered with.

Again in 1721 the Beadle had to cut "ash trees" growing in the roof spouts. In 1725 trees had to be burned out of the steeple. It is not surprising that in 1721 the stool of repentance had to be repaired; it was probably the most used piece of church furniture.

John Dickie in 1729 petitioned the Session for the seat he had acquired from David Heriot, advocate, when he bought the lands of Corstorphine Hill. Heriot's wife was Katherine Primrose and the Heriot seat was on the south side of the east end of the kirk next to Ravelston's seat. Dickie wanted to repair and enlarge the Heriot seat into a pew. The Session agreed but stipulated that the seat was not to come out into the area of the kirk where it might narrow the passageway to the Communion table. The pulpit steps were mended in 1730.

The door of the choir was enlarged in March 1735 and the slated roof was pointed. When Mr Chiesly came in December 1768 the Session's suggestion of paving the area of the church was approved by the laird, Sir Alexander Dick. Alexander Peacock, mason, Edinburgh, was consulted on the cost of pavement laying. Alexander Punton, wright, was asked to prepare a seating plan.

Thereafter local men were employed. Francis Mitchel, mason, was to pave at fivepence per square foot. Thomas Samuel and William Imrie, wrights, were to arrange seating at three shillings per square yard. Hinges, hooks, eyes, and stay bands were to be paid for in addition. More overall the work was to be subjected to examination by skilled tradesmen. When the work was duly passed as satisfactory the men were paid.

The seating of the church then led to the letting of seats. Those under Sir Alexander Dick's loft were not popular because it was not good for hearing. Those that were let cost £4–10–0 yearly and payment was to be in advance. This affected the Beadle financially. George Sclate had enjoyed "a considerable perquisite" for the chairs that stood in the church but these were no longer needed. Sclate was "far advanced" in years so the Session agreed to pension him off with ten shillings sterling but were careful to record that this was not to create a precedent.

Extensive repairs in the summer of 1781 hindered the dispensing of the June Communion but Mr Chiesly intimated that weather permitting he would preach "without doors". The Watson seat in the south aisle was repaired by Thomas Samuel 1770 and in 1784 John Samuel laid "sleepers" (beams) and built supports to strengthen it.

Capt. Stuart of East Craigs who had erected a seat in the "baptism room" was asked in 1793 to pay "compensation" or rent to the Session. Stuart said that he understood that having paid for the setting up he had no further liability. But the Session was concerned with loss of income to the Poors Box as seat rents went to support the poor. Finally in 1795 Capt Stuart agreed to pay ten shillings yearly. In lieu of paying arrears Stuart agreed to the seat becoming church property for the benefit of the poor when the time came that he no longer needed it.

The pulpit floor was repaired in 1800. John Samuel in 1821 was employed to clean the walls and the roof of the church.

Next year 1822 Thomas Mackie of Corstorphine Hill called the attention of the heritors to the decay of the church seats. By 1825 it was agreed that new seating was urgent. Mr Thomas Brown, architect, who had drawn up a seating plan in 1817 was asked to consider "the propriety of lathing and plastering walls". It was also decided to speak to Sir James Gardiner Baird about his loft. In 1826 Mr Tait, architect, was called in to amend the plan put forward by Burn, the architect.

The heritors then considered taking down the centre of the church, retaining the unoccupied eastern portion and the tower, and using as much of the west wall as would be needed to form the side of an octagon which would enclose the body of a new church. The unused north east aisle was to he removed. At the same time the Session Clerk who was also the schoolmaster, Mr Simpson, was told to prevent any burials within the projected area of the possible new church.

Fortunately nothing came of the octagon. In April 1828 the plan by William Burn for altering and repairing was accepted. The best that can be said of it is that it removed the 18th century external additions.

Robert Southey on his way to Linlithgow in 1819 noted in the journal of his *Tour of Scotland*: "There is an odd kirk (at Corstorphine I believe) which looked like three or four little ones put together." Enough of the historic church was left on which in 1905 a restoration could be made of the medieval building.

The principal changes involved using the chancel as the main entrance, and doubling the width of the nave by giving it a northern extension. This meant cutting the great east window to form a wide entrance doorway (see photograph on page 55). So till the end of the century the congregation walked over the grave of James Lord Forrester beneath the window. Another change by Burn meant a reconstruction of the north aisle.

Across the double width nave Burn built a gallery which was entered from a stairway in the entrance chancel. The sacristy on the north of the chancel became a heating chamber. During the alterations Burn removed several of the medieval bosses with Forrester heraldry: some survive today. They were built into property at Juniper Green (corner Lanark Road / Baberton Avenue) and also set into the frontage of Hermiston House now part of Heriot Watt University. Beyond recovery is the stone that was sold for road metal.

Various estimates were given for the work – Andrew Ferries £2060, Charles McGibbon £1870, James Fairgrieve £1283, and the one that the heritors accepted – Grieve, Denholm, Forrester and Mackenzie £1609 along with James Knox's slating estimate of £75.

Increased seating was the main purpose of the Burn alterations. Sir James Baird gave up his interest in a seat as the family no longer had property in Corstorphine. The seats which Burn provided were judged "exceedingly uncomfortable" because there were no backs. It was then decided to have square boxes of uniform height. Buchan's estimate for painting the new seating was £39–10–8.

Repairs in 1835, according to notes left by John Lunn, the Edinburgh builder, included a new pulpit, windows, plastering and whitewashing. John Reid, wright at Belmont, was in charge. Mr Lunn worked on floor repairs in 1836. The old flooring and joisting were replaced with Arbroath pavement.

The church officer had some difficulty controlling the heating so on the advice of the Session Clerk a thermometer was bought. Heating again caused concern in 1844 when Mr Aitken, ironmonger, Hanover Street, Edinburgh, provided a stove for £31. This was placed at the new east entrance door where the elders had been complaining of the cold. The installation of the stove required a drain to carry water from the furnace pit. The minister observed that this was "a good opportunity" to consider the drainage of the churchyard and the village "both of which certainly stand much in need of it".

As Corstorphine grew in population and as housing developed in the second half of the 19th century the question of accommodation for worshippers again became a pressing matter. In August 1892 the Session received a letter from James Hope of Belmont with "accompanying plan by Messrs Kinnear and Peddie for the restoration and enlargement of the church". In reply the Session expressed their satisfaction that the plans provided "for the removal of certain objectionable features introduced by Mr Burn in 1828 and for the restoration of the older portions of the church to their original form". Three years later James Fergusson came as Dr Dodds assistant and successor and with him a new chapter opened in the history of Corstorphine kirk. By 1905 the alterations of 1828 were replaced by sympathetic restoration work that brought back the medieval spirit of the church.

Mr George Henderson of Hay, Henderson and Tarbolton,

Mr George Henderson, architect of the 1905 restoration. *(PB1029)*

architects, was responsible. Mr Henderson had wide experience in Australia and in Scotland. He worked in Edinburgh on old Coates House, Craiglockhart Church, and St. Paul's Episcopal Church. He was also engaged on the tower of St. Andrew's, Peebles, and the nave of St. Mary's, Haddington. Abroad the cathedral at Bermuda was designed and built by him. Sadly he did not live to see Corstorphine opened but the church paid him a well deserved tribute. Built into the east wall of the chancel to the right of the great window is the Bannachtyne stone provided by the first Provost who for forty years guided the young collegiate church. As a companion tablet to the left of the window the congregation placed the memorial to George Henderson, the architect who gave back to Corstorphine its historic church building. It is particularly apt that the memorials to these two men of vision spanning the centuries in the story of Corstorphine kirk should he placed side by side.

The firms employed included J. Millar and Sons (masons); Stuart Granolithic Stone Co. Ltd. (roof work); Henderson and Wilson (oak seats and doors); J. and T. Scott (pulpit); Birnie Rhind (reading desk); Ballantyne and Sons along with N. Bryson (stained glass); Lister of Corstorphine (plumber work). No alteration was made to the exterior except using granolithic roof slabs on the nave, the north aisle, and the transept. This was to harmonise with original stonework on the chancel, the sacristy, and the south transept. The plaster work done by Burn was removed. The east entrance created by Burn was taken away and the window restored where it had been cut. An entrance was formed in the west porch through the tower.

The sacristy was rescued from its 1828 fate as a coal hole and lumber room. It was reconstituted as the vestry with its ancient altar slab and piscina preserved. The area of the tower above the arched entrance was made into the only gallery. The north extension of the nave was separated from the medieval nave by an arcade of three arches carried on two massive stone pillars with foliated caps which also serve to uphold the heavy roof. Stone slabs were used to pave the floor.

The pulpit was placed at the arch crossing the south transept. Formerly it had been set at the south west corner of the north aisle looking towards the chancel arch. The 1905 position on the south wall was in keeping with the practice in many reformed churches. The stone base of the pulpit, a

"THIS TABLET ALONG WITH THE WEST WINDOW IN THE TOWER IS ERECTED IN GRATEFUL MEMORY OF GEORGE HENDERSON ARCHITECT WHO DESIGNED AND CARRIED OUT THE RESTORATION OF THIS CHURCH & WHO DIED MARCH 24th 1905 JUST BEFORE THE WORK WAS COMPLETED THE MEMORY OF THE JUST IS BLESSED"

Memorial stone in the Church commemorating Mr Henderson's achievement. *(PB2030)*

replica in Riga oak of Wycliffe's pulpit at Lutterworth, is inscribed: "Preach the Word". Andrew Dryborough of Gogar Park gifted the pulpit.

A new organ was got from the Edinburgh organ builders, Hamilton, as space in the restored church could not accommodate the old organ. The oak organ case was designed by the architects. The total cost of the restoration was £6702–13–10.

Among the many individual efforts to raise money for the restoration was the Jumble Sale organised by the Men's and Women's Guilds. This was held in Tynecastle Church Hall, Gorgie, on 3rd June 1905. Hugh Kerr provided his pony and trap to transport items collected by Mrs Lethbridge.

For the opening of the restored church the ladies of the congregation presented Mr Fergusson with a new pulpit robe. "Believing in supporting local tradesmen the ladies successfully resisted the blandishments of robe makers from Edinburgh and commissioned the local tailor, John Wallace, to do the work."

William Traquair Dickson, W.S., of Corstorphine, took a keen personal interest in the history of the church. It may be that some surviving, unsigned and undated notes are information he gleaned from local tradition. The informants were John Gillespie, smith, age 70, William Samuel, mason, 60, Archibald Thomson, wright, 60, John Cuddie, gardener, 80,

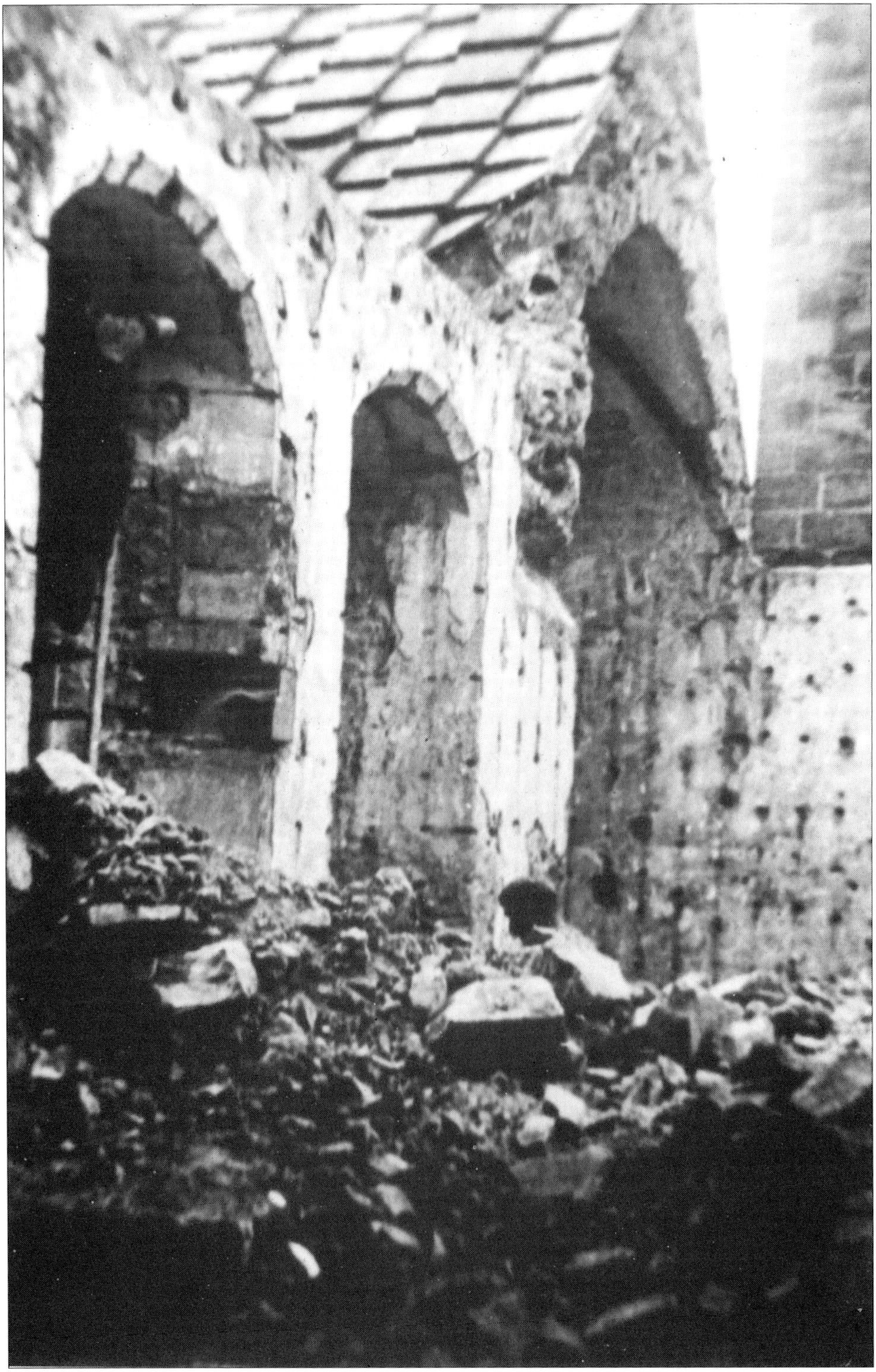

and Robert Smith, the bellman. They were questioned about the church at the 1828 repairs. As far as these men knew the Bannachtyne stone was in its original position. The church door had been on the south-east "a little beyond the buttress" but there was no remaining mark because the "ribbits" (hewn stone at side of door) had been removed and ashlar put in. No one remembered a vault – presumably the Watson one – below the pulpit in its pre 1905 position. The informants knew William Mossman, a mason at the 1828 work. There had been a door in the Saughton aisle. Mr Samuel added a tantalising detail when he said that there had been an inscription on the wall of the minister's seat which had been plastered over but he could not tell what it was about.

Despite the alterations over the centuries the church still carries marks that go back to the era of the founders. A mason on a job cut his mark on the stone with which he was working. Consequently if error occurred in the construction the workman responsible was readily identified.

When Adam Forrester was appointed to oversee the rebuilding of the five chapels at St. Giles' after the destructive raids of Richard II in 1385 the masons employed were John Primrose, John Squire, and John of Scone. At St. Giles' a nave pillar and the surround of the east door at the Thistle Chapel carry masons marks which also appear at Corstorphine on the south transept window exterior mullions, the chancel piscina, the vestry entrance, and the moulding of the east-most Forrester tomb in the chancel.

Since John Primrose was retained to work at St. Giles' after the restoration there of the chapels, it may be that his fellow craftsmen, John Squire and John of Scone, came out to Corstorphine to work for the Forrester family.

OPPOSITE.
The 1905 restoration in progress showing the arch of the south transept (under the flagged roof). The present pulpit is on the wall above the workman's head. *(PB1069)*

THE WINDOWS

Like so many other features of the medieval collegiate church the glass of the windows is unrecorded. However maintenance of windows in the 17th century, like the kirk forms, was a recurring item in the accounts. Thomas Jamison, glasswright in Edinburgh, worked on windows in 1669. Repairs in 1682 raised the question of liability for costs. The Session paid for the part of the building used for the services of the kirk. The great east window, however, in the burial place of the Forresters, and the

Modern view of the nave and south transept (Baptistry) c.1956. The pulpit has been transferred from the west wall to the south wall, seats now face south, the gallery has been removed, and the original stone exposed. *(PB977)*

other windows in the choir and in the Forrester loft, were considered Forrester family responsibility. Accordingly the baillie for the estate was appointed to speak to the curators of Edward Ruthven, the son of James Forrester's second marriage.

Mr Heriot whose property was near the present Corstorphine Inn in the High Street raised the matter of glazing windows in 1698. Apparently Thomas Baillie had said that the work would be done but the Session recorded that they were "displeased" with Thomas for speaking out of turn. They stressed that the Poors Box was not to be used to defray such expenses. The estimate furnished by Alexander Burton, glazier, was passed to the laird and other heritors for their attention. At this time Heriot made a reasonable suggestion to the Session but it was not accepted. He wanted ten merks to be laid aside annually to form a window repair fund.

Had Heriot's plan been followed the 18th century window accounts would have been less burdensome. The greatest window destruction was the 1828 cutting of the east window by Burn to make a church entrance doorway. In 1835 new windows were put elsewhere in the building. Most of the present stained glass dates from 1905. The east window in the chancel depicts Christ and the two disciples at Emmaus. This is particularly appropriate to the area where in medieval times the mass was celebrated and where now in Presbyterian times the Communion is served. For both ages and for both faiths the inscription has equal aptness: "He was known to them in the breaking of bread".

In the tracery above the east window are two shields. One shows the Lamb with the flag, symbolic of John the Baptist. The other has the pelican that feeds its young from the blood of its breast, symbolic of Christ and His Church. These windows, executed by Ballantine and Son, are a memorial to John Dickson, superior of Corstorphine, and his wife Elizabeth Anne Traquair.

On the south wall of the chancel are two windows. The portrayal of John the Baptist and of the Good Shepherd was

Compare the above pre-restoration sketch (made sometime between 1828 and 1905) with the view on the facing page from exactly the same viewpoint. *(PB1764)*

Windows depicting the Parable of the Sower and the Reaper *(Matthew Ch13, 14–30)* in the south side of the nave. Ballantine & Son, Edinburgh 1905. *(s796)*

gifted by Mrs John Herdman of Hazelbank (now Distillers PLC, Ellersly Road). The artist for this window was Nathaniel Bryson, 8 Leith Street Terrace (now St. James shopping centre). The other window showing Christ carrying His cross and attended by mourning women was erected to John Macmillan of Corstorphine Hill House and his first wife.

The sacristy / vestry off the chancel has a window of two lights depicting the Presentation in the Temple with Simeon's words: "Lord, now lettest Thou Thy Servant depart in peace". The small window above the altar slab depicts the fields of the parish and is a tribute to past generations of land workers.

The south wall of the nave has three two-light windows

The north aisle window, the oldest surviving (1898), depicts the 'Works of Mercy' *(Matthew Ch25, 35–40)*. Ballantine & Gardiner, Edinburgh. *(s836)*

illustrating the teaching of Christ: the Sermon on the Mount; the Last Command; and the Sower sowing the seed with angels reaping. On the north side of the widened nave are three two-light windows: the adoration of the Magi; the Call of the disciples; and the Garden of Gethsemane, all illustrating the life of Christ. One of these windows is a tribute to the well loved village physician Dr Matthew. The themes were suggested by Dr MacGregor of St. Cuthbert's, Edinburgh.

In the north aisle Dr Thomas N. Johnston of Corstorphine House and his sister, Mrs Adamson, placed a window to their parents. Here are six scenes of works of Mercy done by Ballantine and Gardiner, 1898.

The fine tracery window in the south aisle originally carried a Munich painted glass representation of Christ weeping over Jerusalem, the raising of Lazarus, and the parable of the Talents. This was installed by the old Corstorphine family of Girdwood in 1861 to the memory of John Girdwood.

A window by Gordon Webster replaced the Girdwood window in 1970. The theme of the new window is Baptism which is fitting, for the south aisle is now used as the baptistry. Webster who died in 1987 was one of a group of artists who in this century created Scottish ecclesiastical stained glass of outstanding quality. His skill was in his sense of colour and his use of hand blown glass so that his windows have great brilliance. Among the many windows he designed are those in Dunblane Cathedral, Dornoch Cathedral, and the war memorial window of Glasgow Cathedral.

The window in the tower gallery carrying the arms of the Knights of St. John of Jerusalem was dedicated to the 1905 architect, George Henderson. At the base of the tower is a window to Scotland's patron saint, St. Andrew. On the south wall of the porch Christ is shown as the Light of the World. Above the entrance door is a semi-circle inscribed:

"Abide with us, O Lord, for it is toward evening and the day is far spent".

THE MANSE

At the time of the Reformation the principal residence for the clergy was the Provost's House built c.1540–44 by Provost Alexander Scott. It was occupied for some time afterwards by clerical representatives. Provost Alexander Makgill held the house *in commendam* from about 1585 to 1628. Where the early ministers of the Reformed church lived is uncertain. Rutherford, the minister who died in 1616, paid rent for a house in the village. His successor, who died in 1626, occupied Nicoll Edward's house.

In 1646 Florence Gardner, titular Provost, granted sasine of the Provost's House to Margaret Forrester and her husband, Telfer of Redheughs, so that the Provost's House then passed into secular possession. That same year the Session, in discussing provision for a schoolmaster, noted that Lord Forrester had given a teacher's house which was situated with "ye minister's manse on ye east".

Thus it seems that a manse had been provided by 1646 and possibly after 1628. Being west of the Provost's House and east of the schoolhouse which was known to belong to the Provostry, the manse would be a building that was part of the collegiate church complex, possibly in poor condition.

Whether the Rev. David Balsillie who came in 1626 and stayed till 1655 occupied the manse or not is not on record. But he did in 1632 provide himself with substantial property at the corner where now Saughton Road North turns into High Street, the block called Oakland. He may have lived here till the manse was made available. Balsillie retired in 1653. In December 1655 when Robert Hunter was minister the Session approved the payment of £83 for timber for the manse. Apparently a manse was then under construction. This £83 appears again in a copy of a statement drawn up and signed by Hunter in 1665 regarding expenditure of £900 on building the manse.

Hunter made this statement to justify payments he had made from church funds: the Session accepted it "does hereby discharge him for now and ever". The heritors signed – Forrester, Sir John Cowper, and James Haldan. The minister shrewdly pointed out that the bills for timber and workmen were, more or less, the same as the total of what the heritors had failed to pay.

Possibly Mr Henry, the minister, who produced in 1673 Hunter's document when church funds were under discussion, did so to remind the heritors of their obligation to the upkeep of the manse. He may also have been concerned about the Act of 1663 on the subject of manse provision and maintenance which set out the liability of the heritors and the minister. Where a competent manse did not exist the heritors were to build one. Where a manse was satisfactory it was to be "upholden by the incumbent ministers during their possession". When the heritors were relieved of upholding the building it was declared a "free manse".

Where Mr Hunter's manse was located is not clear but it possibly was at the south end of Glebe Road where the present U.F. Church is. By 1699 it needed extensive repairs. Mr Hamilton, the minister then, presented the heritors with an account for repairs. Two masons worked for two days at fourteen shillings per day. A barrowman (labourer) was employed for two days. Work was done on the brewhouse, the byre, and the old back cellar. Materials included lime, trees

Laburnum Cottages. Old houses now demolished which used to line St John's Road on the south side, near the junction with Glebe Road, later replaced by shops. [EW]

(beams), dails (planks), flooring nails, and garron nails (large spike nails). A wright was also employed. A thatcher and his man used sixteen threaves (24 sheaves) of thack and three thousand divots (thin flat rectangular turf for roofing). The account was £135–9–4.

Mr Hamilton reported that further repairs were needed. The heritors then instructed Laurence Cunningham, mason, and John Lyon, wright, to report on what was required. At the inspection of the property John Aitken, mason, was also present. The survey was done "upon oath" before James Adamson, the Baillie of Corstorphine. The tradesman found that work was needed on the brewhouse and the "gavell" (gable) between "the old school" and the byre. This note on the gable links up with the 1646 statement about the schoolhouse having the manse on its east boundary and would seem to locate the manse on the southern half of the church ground. There was work for three days for the wright and two days for the two masons and their labourer.

A major inspection and renovation of the manse property was done in 1709. The survey was carried out in the presence of a deputation from the Presbytery along with the minister, George Fordyce, and tradesmen – John Cleghorn, mason, and John Lyon, wright, both Corstorphine men, and John Watson, slater, and Thomas Forrest, glazier, both burgesses from Edinburgh.

The manse had a closet and three rooms upstairs, with public rooms, a kitchen and a cellar below. The offices included brewhouse, coalhouse, byre, stable and barn. The heritors wanted to put a slate roof on the building. The report noted:

PARLOUR
Wright:
4 double trees, 48 flooring dales　　　　　　　£28–6–0

LOW DINING ROOM
Wright:
3 windows – cases, casements, shutting
board, 2 cuts knapple (clapboard, split oak),
300 flooring nails, 6 pair double jointed bands,
door lock and key　　　　　　　　　　　　£17–8–0
Mason:
14 feet hewn work, slapping (forming an
opening in wall) and putting in windows,
lime and sand　　　　　　　　　　　　　　£9–2–0

EASTER ROOM
Wright:
3 windows, knapple £4–0–0
Mason:
3 windows, 15 feet hewn, slapping,
lime and sand £9–0–0

WESTER ROOM
Wright:
windows, knapple £3–0–0
Mason:
3 windows, 10 feet work, lime and sand £7–0–0

MIDDLE CLOSET, ENTRANCE, STAIRHEAD
Wright:
windows, knapple £3–0–0
coomceiling, 40 dales £24–0–0

CLOSET
Wright:
3 windows, knapple £2–0–0
Mason:
3 windows, 12 feet work,
slapping, lime and sand £7–0–0

ROOF
200½ dales for sarking: the right to take
off the old roof and put on new dales; £135–0–0
the slater had slates, lime, nails,
and rigging (ridge) stones £300–0–0

WINDOWS
Enlarging small windows, some of
existing glass to be used for boles
(one pane windows) £48–0–0

MANSE OFFICES
Byre: wright: new door, 2 locks £4–0–0
Barn: mason: take down and
rebuild gavel, lime and sand £13–0–0
Coal house: mason: 15 threaves thatch £15–0–0

The estimate for repairing the manse and office houses, slating the roof and building the dykes about the minister's yard totalled £948–6–0 Scots.

The former manse of the Old Parish Church in Manse Road, demolished in 1959. The garden bordering St John's Road was developed for shops and rear delivery areas. The new manse was built on the south side of the garden. *(PB1041)*

Despite the repair work of 1709 the manse was visited again in 1716 by the Presbytery and the principal heritors were present. The tradesmen were David Mitchell and Daniel Wilson masons, Alexander Allan and Andrew Barclay wrights, and David White, thatcher.

The report stated that the walls and the roof of the manse were satisfactory but in the easter and wester rooms upstairs the floors needed renewing. The manse was small so that the minister was "much straitned for rooms". It was recommended that the kitchen should be changed to a bedroom and floored and plastered. This meant that the brewhouse was to become the kitchen and be repaired and thatched.

The stable, byre and barn were only fit to be taken down and rebuilt. The chimney and windows of the laigh room needed altering and heightening and the same was to he done to the walls and the "lum" of the brewhouse. The yard needed a dyke.

Mr Gavin Drummond on behalf of the laird of Ravelston objected to these proposals saying that enough, nearly £1,000 Scots, had been spent on the manse since Mr Fordyce's arrival.

Mr Fordyce pointed out that the manse, not having reached the standards required by the Presbytery, could not be declared "free and legal". He went on to remind Drummond that Ravelston had not yet paid his full share of previous repairs. The Presbytery overrode Ravelston's objections.

David Mitchell's estimate for mason work was £249–12–0 Scots; Alexander Allan and Andrew Barclay calculated timber and plaster work at £276–18–6 Scots; David White, thatcher, for eight days at £1 per day and materials charged £47–14–0.

Myrton of Gogar and Sir James Dick agreed that the estimates be accepted and that "legal diligence" (process for recovering debt) was to be taken against all parties liable for costs. In 1721 the manse was declared "free" by the Presbytery. When further glazier work to the cost of £13 was done in 1735 Charles Bruce, the Edinburgh glazier who had his country house on Corstorphine Hill and had his aisle in the church, did the work without charge.

By 1753 the manse, according to Mr Fordyce, had deteriorated. Watson of Saughton was of the opinion that all that was needed was a drain to remove damp and that Mr Fordyce was complaining in order to leave the manse and live in Edinburgh during the winter when his grandchildren could be educated in the city. Fordyce left the manse, renting a house in Corstorphine at £8 yearly. A drain was made 1754 but Fordyce then went off to Edinburgh and sent out pulpit supplies.

An attempt was made to let the manse with its garden and an offer of £5 stg was made. Fordyce objected and kept the manse keys. Despite this non-residence the manse was habitable to within three years of Fordyce's death. But since it was unoccupied it was raided, the furnishings removed, and the timber taken from the barn, the byre and the stable. No effort was made by the minister to trace the culprits.

When Fordyce died his heirs sold the manse doors to Alexander Paterson in Corstorphine and to Alexander Anderson, baxter, at Hermiston. The minister's servant, Robert Stewart, took away a cartload of partitions and made gates from the timber for the Park as well as beds for the servants at Mr Johnston's house.

In April 1768 a new manse was proposed. The heritors were willing to find alternative accommodation for the incoming minister, Mr Chiesly. A fresh site was staked out. This position is shown on the 1777 map of the village. It was at the north of the glebe where to-day Manse Road meets St. John's Road and where the shops have their delivery area. The cost for the new manse was estimated at £261 stg. The architect was George Frazer. Alexander Peacock, mason, was the builder.

James Watson of Saughton agreed to pay his share but said that the "house and office houses are too grand and the intended barn, stable, and byres are too large for any minister or his corns and are fitter for a farm". However James, as a heritor, did pay his proportion in July 1770: it was £62–4–0 and Peacock signed the receipt. Watson paid another account 1771 to John Smith, mason, for harling the manse and offices.

By January 1770 it was reported that the manse and offices had been built for £281. There was a stable for two horses as well as a byre for two cows. In February 1770 the tradesmen and the heritors met at the new manse – Mr Crocket, slater in Leith, Somers and Douglas, glaziers, Edinburgh, Deacon Punton, wright, Edinburgh, John Reid, wright, Belmont Foot, Jameson and Ramsay, masons, Edinburgh, and Francis Mitchel, mason in Corstorphine. Also present was George Frazer, Auditor of Excise, the responsible architect.

The matter under discussion was the roof. The "pairlions" (purlins, horizontal parts of timber framework) were not watertight. The tradesmen thought that this could he obviated by removing the blue slates and supplying best tiles or by raising the pitch and recovering with blue slates. The heritors chose to raise the pitch.

Water problems were destined to be Mr Chiesly's burden at the manse. He petitioned the Presbytery in April 1777 about the adverse effect of an alteration in the "water passage". It had caused his manse and glebe to be flooded by a run of water from the high ground to the north. During recent rains he had had no access to his house "without wading nearly to the bran (calf) of the leg". His crops on the glebe had suffered and the sewers that he had provided at great personal expense had sanded up and were useless till cleaned.

When Mr Oliver came 1792 the manse was not fit to occupy till repairs had been done and this prevented the observance of Communion that year. Extensions and alterations were made to accommodate the Rev. David Horne in 1835. There was also drainage work done at this time by John Lunn.

Later in the 1880's a new frontage with bow windows was built. In 1923 a strip was taken off the manse garden to allow the widening of St. John's Road. The City of Edinburgh wanted to erect a railing as the new boundary but Mr Fergusson insisted on a wall. Moreover he made it clear that his hen run was not to be disturbed.

That same year a bus owned by the Scottish Motor Traction Company damaged one of the manse gate pillars at St. John's Road. The SMT accepted no liability, declaring that the bus was proceeding "at a slow walking pace when it gave a sudden and wholly unexpected skid". The City Road Surveyor saw no reason why the City should pay if the SMT were not to compensate. In the end, however, the City did the repair as they were then building a new manse wall in return for road widening ground.

The end of the manse came in 1959 when it was demolished and part of the ground sold to provide the site for the present row of shops in St. John's Road. This allowed a modern manse to be erected on what remained of the historic glebe land – the southern portion of the old manse grounds. Some of the stone from the demolished manse was used for the new. The present boundary between the modern manse and the shopping complex roughly runs through what was once the minister's lawn and tennis court. As many trees as possible were saved.

THE SACRAMENT OF COMMUNION

Communicants in the Church of Scotland to-day generally receive the elements seated in their pews, a custom arising from the introduction of fixed pews in the 19th century. In Reformation Scotland the communicants came forward and sat at a table or tables specially set aside for the purpose. There the minister and the elders served the bread and wine. The service took place in the midst of the congregation in contrast to the way of the old church where the altar and the officiating priest were in the choir.

Bernard Hunter in April 1652 was instructed by the Session to go to Leith to buy timber for the Communion tables and for kirk forms that had been broken and burned by the "Englishes" (Cromwell's troops). Six years later new forms were got for seating at the communion tables "for this solemne worke" since what the church had "werr failed".

The Corstorphine tables in 1710 were on the north side of the nave. The Session were careful in 1729 when allowing for the erection of seats for the gentry to insist that such "seats come not out so far as the area of the kirk as to straighten the passages" to Communion. In 1738 the local wright, John Alexander, made fresh tables.

At the Thursday meeting of the Session in June 1673 the minister earnestly entreated that "all the elders should orderly atend at ye kirk doores upon Sabbath nixt ... for ye collections and at serving the tables and attending ye elements".

Communion observance was not limited to the Sunday celebration service. There was preparation before and there was thanksgiving after. The collections in August 1682 for "communion upon Thursday, Saturday, Sunday and Monday" amounted to £41–11–0 Scots.

The Thursday Fast Day service was directed to ensuring that the people understood the principles of religion and, moreover, that no ill feeling existed among members of the congregation. In Corstorphine in September 1679 Communion was delayed "till ye Spring time in respect of ye farness gone of ye year and much hatred among the people".

This reference to "hatred" is interesting for it was in August 1679 that Lord Forrester met his death at the sycamore tree. There is no mention of this violent death in the Kirk Session records but the ensuing strife among members of the Forrester and Baillie families found its way to the Privy Council. Inevitably the villagers must have taken sides and this may be the background to the minister's comment on "hatred".

A Saturday preparation sermon was approved by the General Assembly of 1645 and was observed in 17th century Corstorphine. This was the forerunner of the modern preparatory service. Sometimes the Saturday sermon gave way to a Saturday Fast as happened in 1696 when Mr Hamilton was minister. Sacramental fasts were not total, literal fasts. They could involve attending service without breakfast or having only bread and water. More generally the Fast was a day of spiritual humiliation for sin.

The Monday thanksgiving sermon was a less severe meeting. Once thanks had been given the people were free to gather socially. Monday manse dinners were times of feasting for the elders and visitors who had travelled a distance to join in the Communion services. However these dinners in time became jollifications that met with disapproval from higher church authority.

TOWARDS RESTORATION

Among the peasantry the Monday social aspect degenerated by the late 18th century into the Holy Fair type of gathering satirised by the poet Burns. Corstorphine Communions were held annually in June to fit in with the agricultural life of the community.

When George Fordyce took up his ministry in 1709 he found the church had three Communion cloths but there were no Communion cups or flagons. Mary Robertson in 1715 got four shillings for washing the Communion table-cloths. The Session in 1720 bought "twelve yards of Dornick" (linen cloth) at fourteen shillings Scots per ell (37.2 inches) for table-cloths.

TOP.
Detail of the fine silver Communion Cup dated 1719, hallmarked Edinburgh, 1717–18 *(PB2028)*

BELOW.
The 18th Century Communion Cups photographed in front of the main entrance to the Old Parish Church. The cups are still in regular use. *(PB2031)*

The heritors in June 1718 decided that one Communion cup should be gifted by the owner of the barony, Sir James Dick, and that another should be a joint gift from the owners of Gogar, Saughton, and Ravelston. By May 1719 the three lesser landowners had presented their cup. It is inscribed: "This cup is the New Testament in my blood shed for the remission of the sins of many. Drink ye all of it. Corstorphin 1719."

Dick was approached again 1721 when he excused the delay by saying the cup would come after the engraver had cut the Dick name and arms on it. This took another year. The Session records for May 1722 note: "Sir James Dick of Prestonfield had now condescended to give up to the Session the communion cup... and desired that the Session might record it in their books and the particular weight thereof".

The cup is inscribed: "May 23 1722. This silver cup is given as a free gift by Sir James Dick Baronet and Heritor and Patron of the Church of Corstorphine and that for the use and service of the said church and the weight being 30 unces 7 drop and an half". The craftsman was John Seatoune, goldsmith, burgess of Edinburgh.

The shape of the Communion cup in the reformed church derived from the popular drinking vessel of the 15th and 16th centuries – the mazer or wine bowl. Families, corporations, colleges, and other bodies owned a mazer which was handed from one to another at the table so that drinking from the same cup was associated with fellowship. Scottish Communion cups have been classified by the type of mazer they resemble. The Corstorphine cups of 1719 and 1722 are of the St. Andrews mazer type with a hemispherical bowl and mazer foot and stalk.

Possibly Sir James Dick thought that putting the silver weight on his cup would testify to the magnitude of his "free gift" and that entering it in the church books would ensure it being remembered for all time. Another age now reads the records and assesses Sir James's Christian spirit.

Two plates were got for the Communion bread in 1726 and a Communion flagon was bought in 1733 for £6–0–0. The church still possesses its 18th century pewter plates and a pewter flagon. In 1726 the price of casting one plate for the Sacrament bread was £1–7–0.

When in 1885 "simultaneous Communion" in the pews replaced coming forward to the Communion table additional silver cups were gifted by the estate owners William Traquair

Example of a flagon for holding Communion wine [GUS]

Dickson and his brother John Heatly Dickson.

Two silver plates for bread were given by John Downie. Half yearly Communion services, April and October, were introduced at this time.

Top tables, in addition to the long tables used by the people, were not unknown in 17th century Scotland. Whether Corstorphine had a top table or not does not appear in the records. However the 1905 alterations saw the installation of a massive top table, the Communion table, in the historic chancel beneath the restored east window. So time, that ever rolling stream, brought back to the medieval church building the celebration of the Last Supper at the traditional eastern end of the church.

The heritors contributed to the cost of the Communion elements. Landowners like Charles Watson of Saughton with ground in several parishes paid a share in each.

Admission to the sacrament of the Lord's Supper from the Reformation to the late 19th century was by token. Usually the token was a small disc of varying shape made of lead or of other metals or of leather. It was stamped or moulded with the initial letter(s) of the parish and K for Kirk and P for parish. Sometimes it was dated and carried the text: "This do in remembrance of me". The tokens were also referred to as tickets.

A person wishing to take communion had to give satisfactory evidence of worthiness to participate. The minister visited the people to examine them in their knowledge of the Bible and the Catechism. Tokens were not given to persons under church censure. In Corstorphine tokens were given to the elders for distribution after the Thursday service. These were returned when the communicants went forward to the table to be "served" by the minister and the assisting elders. To-day the Communion card has replaced the token.

In 1657 the Session Clerk noted "that ticcetts might be provyded since none wer had: these that wer before being lost". Thus in 1674 "the minister did distribut the tickets to ye elders to be by them disperst to the people deserving in their severall bounds. But not to give tickets to any under scandal". As late as 1882, on June 22nd, "the Fast Day ... tokens of admission were distributed."

James Warden, kirk treasurer 1711, was ordered "to cause a peutherer make new tokens ... because the old ones are lost". This work was done by Mr Heron at a cost of £4–6–8. By the first decade of the 20th century the church was paying to have the Communion cards printed.

Collections at the Sacrament services were used for poor relief. In 1777 part of the collections "at the several diets" was divided among the poor of "Corstorphine, Gogar, Saughton and Ravelston". The remainder was placed in the Box for future alleviation of the distressed.

In the 18th century country Communion services attracted people from near and far so that overflow services took place in the churchyard. A temporary moveable pulpit, known as the Tent, and constructed of wood like a sentry box was set up amid the tombstones. It had a raised floor and a board or ledge at the front "window" which the preacher could "ding" as he drove his message home. The tent did not long survive the close of the 18th century.

This additional service necessitated a second precentor. Among the local men who assisted in the mid 18th century was Harry Hews, the miller of Gogar. Perhaps his singing ability was related to his occupation and Harry was of the jolly miller breed who "worked and sang from morn till night".

Example of Communion Tokens, 1822, including the initials of the Minister, Rev David Scott. *(PB2024)*

THE TEIND YARD AND BARN: STIPENDS

Teinds in Scotland, tithes in England, were in medieval times the tax levied by the church on what the people and the soil produced. The origin of teinds was the Old Testament maintenance of the priests and Levites by the exaction of a tenth of the produce of the earth. Scottish teinds, introduced in the 12th century, still to-day, though altered, form part of the church funds for paying stipends.

In medieval Scotland "nothing was overlooked, from the tenth egg of the cottar's hen to the tenth sheaf of the farmer's grain or the tenth bird in the baron's dovecot". Sheaves were taken from the fields to the stockyard and until they were teinded the cultivator could not remove his crop. Teinds were intended to support the parish church. In practice the bulk of teinds was diverted to large ecclesiastical institutions. Corstorphine teinds in pre-Reformation times were annexed to the Abbey of Holyrood. Before and after the Reformation the revenues of the old church were subject to spoliation by the nobility.

The Crown at the Reformation took over the property of

the church and the teinds. Minimum provision for the clergy came from the allocation of a third of church revenues – "the thirds of benefices". The stipend of the reader at Corstorphine, Walter Cowper, 1570, was xxv lib. In 1587 the Presbytery of Edinburgh ordered a stipend payment to be made to the minister of Corstorphine out of the Holyrood teinds.

Having annexed the teinds James VI then granted rights of collection to his noble friends, designated Titulars. Tacks (leases) of teinds were also granted. The farmer, James Watson, 1606 got a tack of the teind sheaves of Saughton from the Commendator of the Abbey of Holyroodhouse.

Charles I in 1625 revoked all grants of church property made by the Crown since the Reformation in order to create a better scheme for maintaining ministers. He ordered that heritors responsible for stipends and church maintenance were to have their parish teinds on a nine years purchase payment to the Titulars. The Corstorphine teinds in 1630 were awarded by the Commission for the Plantation of Kirks and Valuation of Teinds to George, Lord Forrester.

In 1633 Forrester was a member of the commission for surrenders of Superiorities and Teinds set up by the King. The lesser barons wanted to buy the teinds of their own lands but feared that the wealthy Titulars would charge highly. Accordingly they asked King Charles to take over the teinds and then sell to them. The Act of 1633 ratifying the commutation of teinds encouraged agricultural improvement for now there was a definite settled payment for land. George Forrester in 1633 wrote from Clerkington to James Watson at Saughton about purchasing the Corstorphine teind yard but apparently Forrester's price was not acceptable.

Ministers were paid partly in cash and partly in produce. William Arthur in 1630 drew part of his stipend from the teinds he got from James Eleis of Stenhouse Mills. The teinds of Stenhouse were annexed to Holyrood and, in 1633, when the titulars disponed their teinds to the Crown, Charles asigned Stenhouse teinds to the newly erected Bishopric of Edinburgh.

When Stenhouse was united with Corstorphine parish the Watson of Saughton family continued to pay a proportional sum to the West Kirk of Edinburgh for stipend and Communion elements. The Watsons were also liable for teinds connected with their other properties. For Redheughs and Sacristan's Land (to-day Kirklands off Ladywell Avenue) then in Currie parish the Watsons supported the minister at Currie kirk where they had their seating in the gallery. Likewise they paid dues at Cranshaws in Berwickshire for land there. For New Saughton (Cammo) they assisted with the maintenance of the Cramond minister, the Reverend Robert Walker. Through the skill of Raeburn Mr Walker has passed into Scottish art history as the Skating Minister enjoying the winter sport at Duddingston.

When Alexander Baylie in 1689 leased ground at Claysair from Lord Forrester he was obliged to lead the teind sheaves with his own horses and "slades" (low carts or frames without wheels for carrying loads) to the Forrester barn in the teind yard in the village. In 1694 Forrester granted to Valentine Prowse of Leith a tack of a dwelling house with stable, barn and yard at the "toun head" as well as an acre and a half at the back of the house "in the Paddowholme" and another acre and a half "in the bank" on the north side of the highway. The "bank" was unploughed land left uncultivated or grassed over.

For the ground in "Paddowholme" (Paddockholm) Prowse had to pay "the teind of what shall grow" on the land and "to carrie the teind" immediately after separation from the stock "to the noble Lord's teind barn" at his own expense.

There is no obliging map to pinpoint Forrester's teind yard and teind barn. From dispositions of other properties it was certainly west of Manse Road and on the north side of the High Street. John Gordon of Buthlaw in 1765 bought property described as being at the west of the village with the Forrester lands "of old" as the eastern boundary. Gordon's ground included the Mansion House with stable and yard which was demolished in 1952 to make room for a western addition to the school. The teind yard may have been at the east boundary of the school. Bessie Ritchie in 1678 declared that her illegitimate child to Lord Forrester was "gotten at ye teinding of ye yards in September last".

The settlement made by Charles I survived with minor adjustments till 1925. Revision of stipend was done by the Commissioners for the Plantation of Kirks till 1707 when teinds became the business of the Teind Court, later part of the Court of Session. When a stipend was decided the amount was then divided proportionally among the heritors who paid their shares directly to the minister.

Apportioning the stipend was termed "localling" it. Robert Oliphant, the baker, in 1692 when the debts of the Forresters were being taken over by Wallace of Ingliston, paid £16 to

Mansion House. A fine house, now demolished, it used to stand on the north side of the old High Street on ground now to the west side of the parish school. [EW]

"Inglistoun's locality". The locality of the stipend of the parish of Corstorphine 1822–23 showed in detail what was to be paid by each heritor. The dues on pease, wheat, bear, oats and meal were given in exact detail of bolls, firlots, pecks and lippies. Then follows the decision: "The Lord Ordinary having again considered the within locality is of opinion the same should be approven and makes *avizandum* to the Lords". It was approved: the heritors were: Sir Robert Keith Dick; George Robertson; Sir Robert Dundas; Sir Alexander Keith; Mr Ramsay for Westcraigs; James Watson for Saughton.

When a minister felt he was due an increase he applied for the augmentation of the locality. In the 17th century only one augmentation was permitted. By the 18th century changes in cost of living led to men asking for a second augmentation. If the application was refused some ministers took their cases to the House of Lords.

John Chiesly at Corstorphine signed on 22nd November 1781 a receipt for what he had got for his stipend from Watson of Saughton: "...four pounds three shillings and four pence Sterling to account of augmented stipend: which, therefore, on settling the Locality now depending, shall be deducted from his Proportion of said stipend". In March 1782 Chiesly received from Watson his victual stipend in barley and meal the value of which was given as sixpence "above the highest Fiars" per boll.

Roseleaf Cottage. Now demolished, it stood to the west of the Mansion House. [EW]

Finally the Teind Act 1808 gave ministers the right to apply for an increase at intervals of not less than twenty years. This Act also provided for stipends being paid wholly in cash, the grain being converted according to fiars prices which were the average seasonal grain prices fixed by the Sheriff. The union of various Scottish Presbyterian churches in 1929 led to the modern Fund for the Maintenance of the Ministry of the Church of Scotland. The Corstorphine stipend in 1755 was £84–11–1 and in 1798 £175–16–8. In addition the minister had the manse: in farming areas parishioners were generous with gifts in kind such as butter and meat.

Two teind barns survive in Lowland Scotland. At Whitekirk in East Lothian there is a sturdy long three storey building with crowstepped gables. At Foulden in Berwickshire is another with an outside stair to the upper storey. Unfortunately the Forrester teind barn, like their castle, became the victim of neglect by absentee landlords.

Chapter 6

PARISH LIFE

CROMWELLIAN TIMES

When Civil War broke out in England between Charles I and the English Parliament, the Scots, at first, stood back from the quarrel. Royalist victories eventually made the English Parliament seek an ally in Scotland.

In the autumn of 1643 under the terms of the Solemn League and Covenant the Scots supported the Parliamentarians who agreed to set up a Presbyterian form of church government in England. In July 1644 David Leslie, who had served under Gustavus Adolphus, saved the day for Cromwell at Marston Moor. There the English infantry fled but the Scottish soldiers stood firm.

The following year the Scottish Royalists under Montrose inflicted defeat on the Covenanters at Inverary, Auldearn and Kilsyth. At Kilsyth on 15th August 1645 Lewis Paris, husband of Agnes Ronald in Corstorphine, was killed. Their daughter, Agnes, was baptised on 28th December in the village kirk where her parents may have been married.

Shortly before Kilsyth King Charles in England was defeated at Naseby. Later the Scottish army in England 1647 handed over the King to the Roundheads. There were some Scots who were concerned for the King's safety. This led to the Scottish moderates in December 1647 signing an agreement – The Engagement – to provide an army for Charles in return for a trial period of Presbyterianism in England and the suppression of the England Independents.

In reality the Engagement was a getting together of the land-owning classes against the Covenanting church. The anti-engagers felt that Charles should have been made to sign the National Covenant to ensure Presbyterianism in Scotland. Argyll opposed the Engagement and so came into conflict with Montrose. At Preston, in August 1648, the Engagers were defeated by Cromwell who, in October, came to Edinburgh in triumph. The Scottish kirk was not slow to humiliate its opponents – those who had taken part in "the sinful Engagement".

In the parish of Corstorphine the Engagers were George, Lord Forrester, Sir John Couper of Gogar, James Watson of Saughton, and several of their tenants. By December 1648 the Corstorphine Engagers were making public repentance in the kirk, before the pulpit and on their knees: John Cleghorne, George Muirhead, William Johnstoun, Thomas Dykes. For supplying money, horse and men Lord George Forrester made his repentance before the congregation but comfortably "in his own seate". The Laird of Gogar, however, repented on bended knee. James Watson of Saughton confessed to raising money from his tenants to fund the Engagers. Samuel Veitch, the baillie of Corstorphine, and James Hadden, the estate officer, were also rebuked for supporting the King's cause.

Throughout the spring of 1649 others confessed before the congregation their participation in the Engagement – Florence Greg, John Norie and Malcolm Rodger, all servants of Sir John Couper.

George Lord Forrester's son-in-law, James Baillie, took part in the Engagement. He went in 1648 to England with his father, General William Baillie, to assist the King. They were imprisoned at Newcastle for over a year by Lt. Col. William Osborne until payment for their release was made. James Baillie did not forget. When Charles II was restored Baillie sued Osborne for repayment and was awarded £118 sterling.

Charles I was executed on 30th January 1649 and on 5th February Charles II was proclaimed King in Scotland. Next year, on 22nd July 1650, Cromwell invaded Scotland. David Leslie had the Scottish army drawn up between Leith and Edinburgh to cut Cromwell off from Leith where the English fleet would give him support.

By 17th August 1650 the English army, 16,000 men, had pitched their tents on the Galachlaw, a sheltered hill slope between Mortonhall and Fairmilehead cross roads. Oliver's camp was a placename familiar to locals into the 20th century and in 1989 provided residential street names in the area. The English could get water supplies easily from the nearby stream. Here between the Braids and the Pentlands almost 300 years later "Dad's Army" – 3rd Edinburgh Home Guard 1940–44 "C" Company – exercised on the Galachlaw as it kept its "Watch on the Braids".

Cromwell, unable to take Leith, then looked towards Queensferry as a possible point of contact on the Forth between him and his ships. Leslie moved quickly to foil Cromwell. He placed a detachment with "two great guns to secure a pass towards the Queens Ferry" on the slope of Corstorphine Hill in the vicinity of Coltbridge. By the 21st August Leslie, marching by the Lang Gait, moved his forces from the ridge between Edinburgh and Leith, the area now covered by the New Town and its environs, to the rising ground between Coltbridge and Corstorphine.

Cromwell with a "forlorn" – a storming party – came within sight of some Scots at a place not named but described as having the "advantage of a passe" over the Water of Leith. Though at a distance a Scots soldier fired towards Cromwell whom he recognised for he had seen him at Marston Moor. It has been suggested that this encounter took place near Coltbridge. If so it may strengthen the tradition that Cromwell stayed a night at Roseburn House and his business may have been to estimate his chance of controlling the Water of Leith crossing there as a means of contact with Leith.

The nature of the terrain between Cromwell at the Braids and Leslie at Corstorphine was difficult. Between were the two Lochs, Gogar Loch to the west, and Corstorphine Loch stretching to Coltbridge on the east. These lochs are shown on the map of Lothian and Linlitquo in Blaeu's Atlas of 1654. Moreover the month was August, the time of Lammas floods which added surface water to the marsh lands.

Leslie made his headquarters at Corstorphine Castle with his men lying west of Corstorphine Meadow. Providing food for the troops was the responsibility of Sir John Campbell, first Earl of Loudon, Chancellor of Scotland. He sent an undated letter "in Haste" to the Lord Provost and baillies of Edinburgh:

> "My Lord Provest
> The best service you can doe your Brethren is to send out bread and chees or other meat to give them for this night and the morrow morning for they will seek noe moe until the Lord deliver us from them, or declar his pleasor in the contrary. Send out the baxters with their own bread, and hors together, accomodat them all that you can for truly they deserv it, and God hitherto is with them to our Comfort: send your Provisions in by the other syd of Corstorphin we are

drawn up from be west Corstorphin medow to the west along the Crag syd: let Mr Jhon Drumond com along with it to distribut and order it rightlie. You are desird to stand to your arms, Ply the Lord and his throne with strong prayers and supplication for us and for his Caus: It is easie with him if he will to deliver us: and ther is noe Help for us But in his name We commend you to God."

Among the Covenanting forces then quartered in Corstorphine was "Arbuthnot's troop". Sir Robert Arbuthnot, created Viscount by Charles I in 1641, supported the Argyll faction which opposed the Engagement. In 1644 Arbuthnot raised his men in the Mearns to oppose the campaign of Montrose against the extreme Covenanters. This led to the sack of Aberdeen and the laying waste of Arbuthnot's lands.

In 1650 Sir Robert was present at the General Assembly's Commission in Edinburgh which appointed "Mr William Cheyne, minister at Dyce for Lord Arbuthnot's regiment". Eighteen Corstorphine folk were made responsible for quartering Arbuthnot's men and horses. George Cochran, the kirk treasurer, had to provide for 5 men and 4 horses. This burden may have been the reason for his taking a loan in 1650 of 100 marks from the poors box. He was pressed by the Session to repay in 1653 and again in 1657 when he finally managed to clear what he had taken from "the box in the tyme of Crumwell anno 1650".

Margaret Gardner was the widow of Alexander Crawford, maltman, whose death was blamed on the alleged witch, Betie Watson. Two men and two horses were allocated to Margaret. The local smith, James Richardson, also had two men and two horses to feed and shelter: no doubt he was expected to shoe the horses gratis. When Richardson was just over 60 in 1678 he had to present for baptism the illegitimate child of his daughter Helen and James Lord Forrester.

The English left their camp at the Braids and captured Redhall, a control point near the Water of Leith at the Slate Ford. Here, too, they were within striking distance of Corstorphine. The Laird and Couper of Gogar ordered their tenants to cut their crops so that the enemy would not find fodder for their horses.

On 27th August Cromwell, with Queensferry as his objective, moved west. Leslie at once did likewise. The Scots marched to where the Gogar Burn crosses the highway (A8 near Gogarburn Hospital) and there on the right bank of the water they took up their stance.

Meantime the English were dragging their artillery across the countryside towards Gogar. They had to get their equipment across the Murray Burn and then the Gogar Burn to reach "the pitch of rising ground" near Gogar Bank. Here Cromwell found himself in the midst of marshes. The twists of the burn at Gogar Bank in the wet August of 1650 no doubt caused the stream to add flood water to the existing bogs. The English force was probably stretched out from Gogar Bank west to Norton. The Scots cannon, an invention of Colonel Wemyss the General of Artillery, appear to have been positioned in the area now covered by the estates of Gogar Burn and Hanley.

The Cromwellian troops were given the word to attack – "Rise Lord". They battered down some sheepfolds in the middle distance because some Scottish infantry, placed there within the sod walls, were firing at any English that appeared. The bog on both wings of Cromwell's calvary made it impossible for them to move forward.

The memorable action was the gun fire from the new cannon – Wemyss's "leather ordnance". The brightness of the flashes gave the battlefield its name – The Flashes – which was remembered two hundred years later in the *New Statistical Account*. As night fell the English withdrew a short distance in the hope that the Scots would advance. But next morning when the English viewed "Gawger field" they found their enemy in their first position. After some gunfire Cromwell gave up and the Scots returned to Corstorphine. Leslie then made his way by the "calsey" that linked Corstorphine to Coltbridge and so eastwards to Duddingston. Cromwell, retreating on a line near to that of the road passing Saughton towards Redhall and Colinton, returned to the hills. From there he made for Musselburgh. And no doubt the tenants and cottars at Gogar – the Barrons, the Yorstouns, the Hardies – drank their own brewing in relief and celebration.

By the end of the month Cromwell withdrew south to Dunbar. There the Scots occupied a hill position at Doon Hill. Leslie, unfortunately, decided to come down to level ground where on 3rd September Cromwell was victorious. He then occupied Edinburgh and Leith.

In 1656 James Watson of Saughton raised a legal action

against William Muir in Curriehill for the theft of a grey mare and her foal and "a two to three year old staige" which she had bred. Watson in his evidence stated that the mare was sent to Dunbar in 1650 with a servant who died there and that the animal either was seized or had wandered. He could identify the mare for it had his brand and there was another mark known secretly to him. So a man and a mare went from Saughton to Cromwell's battle at Dunbar.

On 1st January 1651 Charles II was crowned at Scone in the church Lord Stormont had built on the mote hill about 1624 to replace the ancient Abbey church wrecked by a Dundee mob in 1559. This coronation was notable in being a Presbyterian one and the last performed in Scotland. Only the north aisle of the church remains. There the visitor to Scone Palace today may see the magnificent monument in marble and alabaster of Lord Stormont in armour kneeling at prayer.

With a Scottish army Charles entered England in July 1651. Monck was left to control Scotland while Cromwell pursued Charles. On 3rd September Charles was defeated at Worcester. Meanwhile Monck had sent the public records of Scotland to London. In 1660 on their way back to Scotland the ship carrying them was wrecked and most of the records went to the bottom of the sea.

The even tenor of life in Corstorphine was disturbed over 1650 and 1651. The family at the castle supported the king. The minister was displaced by the English troops who occupied the church, destroying the communion table, the church forms, and the place of repentance (a wooden scaffolding or platform on which sinners stood before the congregation). In 1652 Bernard Hunter, the smith who had his smiddy in Barney's Slap (Manse Road), was instructed by the Session to go to Leith to buy timber to replace the destroyed church furniture. Traditionally the English soldiers were also responsible for mutilating Forrester effigies.

In 1653 Cromwell became Lord Protector. The Scottish parliament was absorbed into the English parliament. The subjugation of Scotland – something that Edward I failed to do – was formally completed in 1654 with the Ordinance of Union.

By 1654 James Baillie had become Lord Forrester and for his part in supporting the Stewart kings Monck fined him £2,500. The diarist, John Nicoll, noted that in Edinburgh on 12th June 1654 notices had been placed, under cover of dark,

These are the gates (still extant) forming the east entrance to St. Margaret's Park off Corstorphine High Street. They *may* have been the gates to Corstorphine Castle (in ruins by 1800). [GUS]

on all public places and on entrances to closes, signed by Lord Forrester and calling for assistance to be given to the King's supporters. From camp at Leny in Perthshire in August 1654 Coronet Baynes, a Roundhead officer, wrote that "Lord Foster is about 5 miles west of us with about 200". A month later Monck reported to Cromwell that Lord Forrester had agreed to bring in his forces. His estate was deep in debt as a result of his support of the Stewarts. £1,500 remained to be paid of his fine and Monck promised that if the estate could not clear the outstanding payment he would ask Cromwell to remit it.

Apparently, James Baillie, Lord Forrester, was still a prisoner in 1656 for Monck writing from Dalkeith to Cromwell advised that, since two prisoners had escaped from Edinburgh Castle, Lord Forrester should be sent elsewhere. During 1654 and 1655 creditors making claims for loans given to Forrester, on the security of the estate, included William Clersone indweller in Corstorphine; Henrie Hope, Andrew Balfoure, James Jonkins, and John Boyd, all merchant burgesses of Edinburgh; Lawrence Scott of Bavelaw; and Richard Murray in Corstorphine.

An appeal was made to the Privy Council in 1666 by Elizabeth Pittiloch widow of Captain Archibald Hereot who had been in charge of a troop of horse in Lord Forrester's regiment under the command of the Earl of Glencairn. Hereot had met the "common enemy" on Calder muir where he suffered two shots in the body. He withdrew to the hills. Not being able to get a doctor his wounds festered causing his death. His widow, on behalf of their four children, asked for help to be given her by the shire of Lanark of which Hereot was a native. The Privy Council agreed and ordered the Archbishop of Glasgow to instruct the ministers in Lanark parishes to appeal to their congregations to help the widow and children.

Cromwell's troops billeted in Corstorphine Kirk left presumably by August 1651 when the Session records resume with a note that the Rev. David Balsillie had returned. One who stayed till 1655 was James Keame. He found work with the Listons who farmed at Gogar. When he left Corstorphine he asked the kirk for a testimonial. The Session Clerk described Keame as "ane souldrome", possibly a combination of souldart (soldier) and southron (an Englishman).

Despite the upsetting experience of military occupation, life for the villagers followed its familiar ways. As Neville

Chamberlain said to the British people in the 1939 war situation – "Life must go on." Because the place of repentance had been pulled down by the English soldiers local sinners, like James Hadden, had to promise to appear at a later date to make public repentance. Marion Campbell denied the Session's charge that she had been fraternising with the soldiers. James Young was in trouble for drinking and "swaggering".

As the Cromwellian soldiers departed one wonders what they thought of Midlothian Scots. Hopefully they had formed a better opinion than that of a fellow trooper who came through Berwickshire and East Lothian a month after the fight at Gogar. He wrote home that he found the Scots to be religious hypocrites showing piety the one minute and lying and swearing the next. When the English soldiers came upon abandoned houses they found the beds "nasty and greazie, full of lops (fleas) and covenanters (lice)". Though commanded to have only one God the Scots idolised their ministers.

Murder according to the letter writer was common. Adultery was blatant. Stealing, covetousness, and false witness abounded. His opinion of the crops was more favourable than his opinion of the people. Trees were not so plentiful as across the border. Cattle and sheep were small. Fruit was sour and the weather very unpleasant. Men wore blue bonnets and the women parti-coloured plaids. The poor lived in thatched houses and the lairds lived in stone houses.

With that last observation the Corstorphine soldiers would have agreed for the castle of the Forresters was no mean building. The last of the thatched cottages in the village (Roseleaf – between the school in the High Street and Ladywell) survived till 1937 when fire brought an end to a historic type of roofing.

Ladywell, former houses close to the site of one of several wells in the old village. [EW]

DEFENCE OF THE REALM: 1660–1787

QUARTERING

The restoration of Charles II in 1660 did not bring peace to Scotland. The struggle between Episcopacy and Presbyterianism led to the wars of the Covenanters, opening with the march on Rullion Green on the slopes of the Pentland Hills in 1666 and continuing to the flight of James VII in 1688. The British Standing Army was established in 1660–61. And since wars make demands on quartering troops Corstorphine, in the second half of the 17th century, was subjected to the coming and the going of soldiers and the supplying of fodder for their horses.

In 1661 Major General Morgan complained to the Privy Council that the people in the countryside about Edinburgh were not co-operating in providing straw for the 80 animals in his garrison at Leith. The Privy Council then instructed neighbouring parishes, including Corstorphine, to furnish straw. The price of the "threive stra" (24 sheaves) was 14/– if got within four miles of Leith and 10/– if beyond. It was to be lifted and taken away by the garrison's own horses.

The decision of the Galloway men in November 1666 to march on Edinburgh created a state of rebellion that led to the Privy Council calling on fencible men to be in readiness to act and instructing heritors to come on their best horses to arranged meeting places. The commanders in West Lothian were to call local heritors to Corstorphine and Kirkliston.

Orders were given in June 1668 that the part of Chancellor Rothes's troop stationed at Dalmellington and Cumnock was to be brought nearer Edinburgh, half being quartered at Corstorphine and the other half at Dalkeith. In July the commander of the Corstorphine section received an urgent message. With a party of horsemen he was to pursue immediately William Mirrie who was travelling west by Caldermuir, having with him the wife of Sir Thomas Wallace. Mirrie was to be seized and brought back to Edinburgh. If, however, he had left the lady he was to be followed to Tarbolton where he lived. By August 1668 the Lord Chancellor's troop at Corstorphine was ordered to leave as soon as "the grass fail" and come to the Canongate.

A shift of forces in September 1669 brought H.M. Guards under the Earl of Newburgh to Corstorphine. The Earldom of Newburgh was created in 1660 for Sir James Livingston of Kinnaird: later the title went by marriage to an Italian family. The following year the Guards at Musselburgh were shifted to Corstorphine. In May 1671 the Guards at Corstorphine under the Earl of Atholl were ordered to stay and grass there till further notice. Atholl was still there in 1672 trying to get grass at reasonable rates. His men were again in the village in the summer of 1674 when the Privy Council ordered those to whom the meadows and "grassings belong" to provide the military with grass at the normal county rates.

PARISH LIFE

The Earl of Linlithgow quartered "two squads" in the parish in November 1678. The following year on 10th June the heritors and feuars were commanded to deliver 10 horses to the Major General at the Canongate Tolbooth. On 21st June Sir John Nicolson, Lt Colonel of the shire of Edinburgh militia, received an order from Rothes to provide 30 of his men to guard the carts coming from Leith to Corstorphine with provisions and munitions for the army. Those who accompanied the carts were travelling to Bothwell Bridge where on 22nd June 1679 the Duke of Monmouth, illegitimate son of Charles II and husband of Anne Scott, daughter of the Earl of Buccleuch, defeated the Covenanters under Robert Hamilton of Preston, despite the brave stand of Hackston of Rathillet.

In 1680 Foulis of Ravelston took part in discussions at Corstorphine about the "new modell of militia". Arrangements were made in December 1685 to provide army winter quarters in the village. Inevitably the quartering of soldiers had repercussions on the life of the community. Captain George Buchan and Janet Drummond in September 1667 were in trouble with the kirk Session for fornication. Janet appeared before the congregation on three successive Sundays. Captain Buchan, however, "being one of His Maties Guard and uncertainty how long he may bide in this place" asked the Session to be content with his doing one day's "sitting on the pillar". The Session agreed but increased his fine. Buchan duly underwent public rebuke. He paid £10 Scots which was used to repair the north aisle of the church and "for other charitable uses".

In 1672 Harry Antonius, kettle drummer in the King's troop, married a local girl, Margaret Harper. Alexander Moncrieff, gentleman of H.M. Guard of Horse, in 1676 married Margaret Steven of the village. When Elizabeth Weir, servant to Archibald Inglis, gardener, was pregnant in 1679 she named Gawan Muirhead of the King's Guard of Horse as the father of her child.

The coming of William of Orange, William II of Scotland, and his wife Mary, daughter of James VII, and their crowning in Scotland in May 1689 may have been glorious but it did not ensure peace and prosperity in Scotland in the last decade of the century. The Scottish parliament was faced with Presbyterian and Episcopalian tension, the treachery of Glencoe, the failure of the Darien Scheme, and within itself the rivalry of the Scottish noble families – Hamilton, Dalrymple, Queensberry. There was also involvement in William's wars in Europe.

Scottish finances suffered from mismanagement. In 1690 William had to supply money to pay troops in Scotland. Over 1689 to 1690 only two months pay and four months subsistence was given to the forces. The continuation of a standing army in what was supposed to be the peacetime placed a burden on landowners and their tenants, creating a feeling of grievance among the people. In October 1688 Thomas Baillie in Meadowfield signed for receiving from James Watson payment of £1–8–0 Scots which, with James Eastoun's payment for the same amount, completed Saughton's share of "the outraik" (fitting out) for 14 days militia pay.

Parliament in 1689 appointed James Watson a captain of militia in Edinburghshire and the following year instructed him to raise a supply for the king. An irregular baptism in 1692 in Corstorphine revealed that the father of Clara Kilpatrick's daughter was Robert Hunter in Eglinton's troop of dragoons. Later Hunter was reported to be in Newbattle's regiment. Elizabeth Duff, wife of Robert Oliphant, complained in 1692 that Janet Alexander, wife of Archibald Inglis, the kirk officer, had slandered her by saying that she knew the way to the hearts of dragoons for she fed them with baps and rolls.

When Captain Foxe's soldiers were stationed at Corstorphine in 1693 Ensign Evans was reported to the Session. His comrades threatened the informer who was forced to leave both his home and the village for some nights. Once the soldiers moved out the case went ahead against Jean Cant with Elspet Wallace as accessory. William Beg and George Coe were witnesses to what had happened in Wallace's ale house. Elizabeth Duff corroborated that the Ensign and Jean had been seen "in bed together". Jean Cant fled the parish. In 1693 John Ballantine, sergeant to Captain Archibald Dunbar, presented for baptism a child, Elizabeth, in the name of John Dunbar sometime soldier with Capt. Dunbar and then in Flanders "serving their Majesties". Service for William and Mary in the Low Countries possibly accounts for another baptism where the child's uncle, James Couts, acted for the absent father, David Couts, sergeant in Colonel Leslie's regiment.

In 1694 Helen Anderson, daughter to Jean Cockburn in Gogar, had to disclose to the Session that her child's father was a Frenchman, Patrick Shallingtoun. Where she met him is not known. However, from 1691 to 1694 the State prison on the Bass Rock was in the hands of Jacobite prisoners. They were sent provisions and two boats by the French government. These adventurers lived by seizing trading vessels and stealing sheep from the Isle of May. When the occupation ended the men were given the choice of staying in Scotland or going to France. Perhaps Shallingtoun had some link with this incident or he may simply have been a wanderer. The life of a quartermaster was not easy. As a local man, appointed and sworn in by the Commissioners of Supply and Militia, he was subject to the wrath of his neighbours when he exacted service. Instructions were drawn up for quartering soldiers in Corstorphine parish. Preferably they were to be in the "toun". If there were too many for the village the overflow was to go to Cramond, the Water of Leith, or other adjacent villages "on the road most convenient for the souldiers". In places where people kept "horses to carry coalls, straw to Edinburgh" the provision of stabling and horse corn would be more conveniently arranged.

He was not to quarter men in the country part of the parish so as "not to hinder the countrie labor and tillage of the ground". Moreover quartering and supplying corn and straw was to be borne proportionally by the places and persons concerned. Weekly accounts of expenses were made to the Quartermaster so that he could claim from the Commanding Officer. The carrot held out to the luckless individual on whom quartering duties fell was that if he did the job honestly he would not be called upon personally to provide quartering during his time of service and for two years thereafter. John Finnisone in January 1694 wrote to Sergeant Hoome to say that the Watson of Saughton tenants had paid their dues the previous December for they were on his Corstorphine account. Hoome was to refund what he had taken for St. Cuthbert's parish. The mistake possibly arose because the Watson property at Stenhouse was then in Edinburgh west parish for certain dues.

Resentment against quartering came to a head in 1692 when Captain Foxe's company was in the village. Petitions were drawn up for submission to the authorities. That to the Commissioners of Supply for the Shire of Midlothian was from Tenants and Indwellers of the parish of Corstorphine. Complaint was made that a troop of dragoons under the

Master of Forbes was quartered without "prior provision" being made. The authority of Alexander Alexander of Corstorphine, the quartermaster, was questioned.

Twenty dragoons with horses sent to Saughton forced the tenants to displace their "labouring horses" as they had not "roome for both". The soldiers threatened and abused the people when asked for payment for meat given them. If this state of affairs continued the petitioners declared that there would not be enough fodder left for the "bestiall" used by the tenants to cultivate the land. The heritors drew up the plea presented to the Privy Council. They stressed the geographic position of Corstorphine. Near Edinburgh and "upon the comone high road" meant that for Corstorphine there was "not only continual transient quartering therein but also local quarterings". Adjacent parishes which were not so burdened ought, according to the heritors, to be made to bear a proportional share of quartering. They gave an example of what was involved. Eglinton's troop consumed weekly 17½ bolls of oats and 60 stones of straw "besyde bed and coall". The loss of stabling was also a serious matter. The heritors' petition ended with a warning that if the situation was not adjusted the land would soon be waste and the people destitute.

The minister, Archibald Hamilton, expressed his feelings in a personal statement about "exorbitant quartering". He was concerned about the situation being "not precisely a case of the Revenue but a point of privat right". He would never, he assured the authorities, "dispute the payment of my proportion of supply to the Crown" but he was anxious about the parish and persons involved. What the minister asked for was a suspension of quartering. The introduction of linen bleaching at the Easter Meadow at this time may have had the attraction of countering demands for billeting. By the 1695 Act The Incorporation and Society of Linen Manufacturers got the privilege of tax free drink for employees as well as exemption from quartering demands. Despite Francis Bacon's assertion that money is not "the sinews of war" the fact remains that soldiers and their provisions have to be paid for. Quartering was a small local means of alleviating financial pressures. Parliament, however, was forced to consider various forms of taxation to meet the overall burden of King William's wars in Europe. This led to the Hearth Tax in 1690 and the Poll Tax in 1693, 1695 and 1698.

THE HEARTH TAX

The Scots Parliament authorised taxation of "fourteen shilling for each hearth in the kingdom". This tax was levied on the occupier, not necessarily the proprietor, who was described as the "possessor" of the hearth. The only exemptions from this tax were "the hearths of hospitals and of such poor as lived upon the charity of the paroch." The official responsible for collection was James Melvill of Cassingray and the money was to pay "debts due to the Country and the arrears to the army". Candlemas 1691 was the date for paying: the sub-collectors' lists vary in information noted – sometimes the names of individual householders, sometimes the estate owners, sometimes the poor. The Collector listed for "Corstorphin paroch":

Saughton's house and mylnes	20 Hearths
The Lands	41
West End of Saughton	02
Ravelston House	12
The Lands	14
Ffewars in Corstorphin toun:	
Alexr Baillies houses	10
Alexr Andersons	03
Alexr Alexanders	03
Gibsons Land	01
Tho Beg's	03
Rankin's Land	05
Jon Alexanders	03
John Johnston's	10
a part of Tho Baillie's	03
Geo Aitken's	04
Mr Herriots	09
Jon Binnies house	01
The Youngs	04
Schiels's	03
Johnston's	01
Ja Murray's	04
Corstorphin house	09
The Lands	55
Nether Gougar House	13

Corstorphin paroch

Alexr. Lindsay in My Lords Land	02
James Banneton thero	01
Wm. Forrest thero	01
Jon: Yorkston ye	02
Joan Alexander ye	02
Mrs Baylie	01
James Wilkie	03
James Broun in Sacktoun	02
Widow Tarte thero	02
Lawrance Trinent ye	01
John Whyt in Corstorphin	01
Jas: Murray Horiton ye	01
Jon: Johnston ye	01
Jon: Bog ye	01
Marion Wilson ye	01
Rot: Ker ye	01
Andrew Long ye	01
Edward Robertson ye	01
	25

The Lands	18
Meadowfield	07

In a further survey other hearths were "found out":

Alexr Lindsey in My Lords Land	02
James Banneten there	01
Wm Forrest there	01
Jon: Yorkston there	02
Jean Alexander there	02
Mrs Baylie	01
James Wilkie	03
James Broun in Sachton	02
Widow Taite there	02
Lawrance Tennent there	01
John Whyt in Corstorphin	01
Jas: Murrey Heritor there	01
Jon: Johnston there	01
Jon: Bog there	01
Marion Wilson there	01
Rot: Ker there	01
Andrew Long there	01
Edward Robertson there	01
	25

OPPOSITE. Extract from the Hearth Tax Roll for Corstorphine, 1694. The printed text is a transcript of the MS on facing page. *(Courtesy NAS, ref. E69/16/1)*

THE POLL TAX

In 1693 the Scots Parliament introduced a Poll Tax to finance the country and the armed forces. It was collected over 1694–95. Some receipts survive for poll tax payments at Saughton. For everyone who was not the head of a household the basic rate was six shillings Scots. Servants with wages of more than £6 annually were taxed at a twentieth of their wages. Children under 16 and those living on charity were exempt.

James Watson, the laird, paid for himself £24–6–0. His son being a child was not taxed. Isobel Duncan, a cottar at Stenhouse Mills, was charged twelve shillings for herself and her daughter. Her neighbour, William Brown, gardener and cottar, was assessed at eighteen shillings for himself and his wife. Six shillings were exacted from Jean Harper, a cottar. Thomas Girdwood, a hind on the estate, paid nineteen shillings. Mr James Scott, minister and tutor in the Saughton household, was charged six shillings.

List of the Tennants of the Parsonry of
Corstorphin

Robert Oliphant Baxter in Corstorphin ab:
~~Thomas~~ ... in meadow feild being excused as being sick
Robert Cunningham ab:
Alexander Laidly in Sydahill ab:
John Clerk in the hill of Corstorphin ab:
Gabriell Wilson in Corstorphin ab
James Ritchie yr ab:
p ~~...~~ ab
p ~~...~~ yr ab: present
Duncan Forrester yr ab:
p James ~~...~~ ab
Thomas ~~...~~ Wtser yr ab:
Marione Grant yr ab
George Aithine yr ab:
Agnes Williamson ab:
William Napper yr ab:
p ~~George ...~~ yr ab:
p ~~William young~~ yr ab:
James Scoir yr ab:
Alexander Alexander yr ab:
William Johnstoun yr ab:
John Gibsone yr ab
James Walker yr ab:
James Damsone yr ab:
~~Mary ...~~ yr ab pr:
John Wing yr ab:
James Waddon yr ab:
p ~~Robert ...~~ yr ab
p John ~~...~~ in the meatherst ab
p John ~~...~~ in ~~...~~ ab:
Corstorphin the 26th Jan[ry] 1692

Ilk day mr Duncan Robertsone Baillie of Corstorphin at ...
... lessons of Corstorphine signd ... all absent hopis ... asked
... day exclude the others ... in law of ... pnts to ...
Sic subscribtr ... took Instrument

MEN AND SUPPLIES

The Treaty of Ryswick 1697 closed William's wars in Europe but it did not mean an end to a standing army at home. The question was hotly debated. There were those who considered a standing army to be an infringement of public liberty. Others, keeping in mind that the neighbouring states continued to be armed, believed that security lay in armed men.

Pressing men into service was one way of getting recruits. On 25th March 1697 James Lillie, constable at Liberton, had custody of Alexander Taylor, servant to James Watson of Saughton. By 27th March Taylor was back at Saughton with a note from Sir Alexander Gilmour of Craigmillar in his capacity as a Justice of the Peace. Gilmour explained that Colonel Hamilton had refused to take Taylor because "of the want of an eye".

The attraction of the man in uniform for the local girl was as evident in 1700 as it was in 1939–45 with G.I. brides. Corporal Thomas Hamilton in Colonel James Butler's troop belonging to Lt General Echlams regiment of Dragoons married Martha Wallace: their son, William, was baptised in Corstorphine kirk on 25th February 1709.

Defence obligations continued to trouble Saughton estate into the second decade of the 18th century. John Clerk, servant to Mrs Brown, a Saughton tenant, was carried off in 1711 by a Captain Livingstone who had an order from a Justice to support his action. James Watson took steps to have Clerk released. His first move was to have the fellow concerned placed in the Tolbooth of Edinburgh to prevent his being transported elsewhere by Livingstone. Then he had a summons served on the Captain to justify his seizure of Clerk.

Next a petition was written in support of Clerk's appeal for release. When the Justices of the Peace eventually liberated John it was Watson, the laird, who paid the charges for the prisoner's maintenance in the Tolbooth of Edinburgh. He also paid the clerk who wrote the *absolvitor*, the document freeing Clerk when Livingstone failed to pursue the matter.

The Justices of the Peace in 1712 dealt with two sons of Edward Yorstoun, tenant, West Craigs of Corstorphine. On 15th March George Yorstoun took the oath to Lt Gray of Peacock's regiment. On 18th March Edward was summoned to present on 25th March his son, John, to the Justices for the shire of Edinburgh sitting then "in the laigh Councill House

OPPOSITE.
A list of the tenants of the Barony of Corstorphine, 26th January 1692. All those with 'ab' (absent) after their names were fined 40 shillings Scots for failing to appear at the baron's court. Whether they ever had to pay is a matter for conjecture. *(Courtesy NAS, ref. Ex RH11/17/1, item 1)*

of Edinburgh". Lt Hay in Douglas regiment had brought an action against Edward Yorstoun. The Yorstouns were warned that failure to comply meant a fine of £10 sterling.

The demands of the Collector of Supply in 1714 led James Watson to complain to the Lords of Council and Session. Though the Barony of Saughton was within the parish of Corstorphine part of its lands of Broomhouse lay in Currie parish. The land tax (cess) for the Currie portion was fixed at £25 Scots but Watson protested that he had paid for this under his Corstorphine assessment. When he delayed paying, having remitted his case to the Committee for Cess, the Collector of Supply warned the Broomhouse tenants that "a full party of souldiers" would be quartered on them. In the end the law supported the Collector.

In 1716 the gentry in the parish of St. Cuthberts were called on to furnish horses to draw artillery. Those who did not respond by supplying animals were to commute their obligation with a cash payment. David Lizars, tenant at Damhead near Gorgie, was responsible for collecting within St. Cuthberts parish. Watson, as owner of Stenhouse Mills, was in Lizars opinion liable for this service but Watson had already contributed to the Corstorphine parish collection. As an alternative to horses Lizars wanted a payment of £30 Scots. Watson took the dispute to the Sheriff saying that he was being asked to pay what he had already paid. He won his case and Lizars was ordered to desist.

When the Seven Years War broke out 1756 between Britain and France over colonial aspirations, the Justices of the Peace and the Commissioners of supply were called upon to enforce the Act of Parliament "for the speedy and effectual recruiting of His Majesties Land Forces and Marines".

Lord Barrington, Secretary for War, wrote to the local responsible authority. The County of Edinburgh was divided into districts and parishes. Edinburgh District included Corstorphine. The Commissioners were to raise 140 men of which Corstorphine was to find three, Colinton one, Cramond three and Currie two. Constables were given warrants to seize persons who came within the terms of the Act.

In January 1757 the case of John Weir, day labourer at Gorgie Miln, was examined. He was sober, industrious and supported a wife and numerous children "in an honest way" so did not come under the Act and was accordingly dismissed.

John Allan, labourer, born Gorgie and late servant to William Wilkie, minister, Saughtonhall, had a wife and two children but did not escape conscription. Forty shillings sterling was paid to his wife as compensation for taking her husband to join the men of Captain James Paterson of Lord George Beauclerc's regiment. Samuel McLellan, day labourer at Corstorphine and then living at Gorgie, and Robert McLellan, miller at West Mill of Colinton, born Corstorphine, were both handed over to Captain Paterson. If Robert was, as seems possible, the child baptised at Corstorphine in 1733, the record notes his mother as Agnes Lyon and his father as deceased Robert McLellan, soldier. William Hay, servant to John Crawford at Brucehill (Belmont), was not taken as he was "valetudinary". Next year the Justices and the Commissioners received a letter from Barrington praising their "zeal in the execution of the Recruiting Act", speaking of the success of "the plan of recruiting in North Britain", and conveying the "approbation" of His Royal Highness the Duke.

In 1779 Spain and France joined forces against Britain when the American colonies were rebelling. Henry Dundas, the "uncrowned king of Scotland", who watches the citizens of Edinburgh from his column in St. Andrew Square, strengthened the navy by impressing men into service. Leith, Newhaven, and Edinburgh in 1787 witnessed scenes of near riot when press gangs landed and seized about 300 men. Sailors and marines paraded the streets with drawn cutlasses. Corstorphine by the end of the century was involved in the national struggle with Napoleon.

The Smiddy, St John's Road. [EW]

Chapter 7

EDUCATION

TO 1698: SCHOOLMASTER'S LAND: THE LAMP ACRE:

Education in Corstorphine possibly began with the provision made by Dame Margaret Forrester, widow of Adam, for two chaplains and two singing boys to conduct services in the chapel of St. John the Baptist founded by her husband. Hopefully the singing boys were taught to understand the Latin they sang. The confirmation of Dame Margaret's foundation in 1429 was contemporaneous with building starting on her son's collegiate church where presumably some education was continued for the choir boys.

The Scottish Education Act of Parliament in 1496 was limited to the education of the eldest sons of gentlemen. Knox's dream of education for all, with the lad o' pairts progressing from the parish school to university, was, unfortunately, largely frustrated. The money needed to implement the scheme – the revenues of the old church – did not pass intact to the Reformed Church. The land-owning classes were greatly enriched with church property but generally showed little inclination towards generously financing education.

The kirk Session and the heritors appointed the schoolmaster, fixed school fees, provided for the education of poor bairns, kept an eye on the conduct of the teacher, and enquired into the progress of the school. Buildings were basic, sometimes a space in the kirk, sometimes a poor cottage. The curriculum covered Latin, reading mainly from the Bible, writing and arithmetic. Hours were long. Teachers were often candidates for the ministry, some of them "stickit ministers". Salaries were made up by payments from the heritors, and on occasions by what could be got from the kirk box. In addition to what the Session paid, the master, to have a modest living, had to depend on school fees and, as Session clerk, his fees for recording births, marriages and deaths.

When the Presbytery of Edinburgh visited Corstorphine in 1598 they found that there was no schoolmaster which they "desydt thame to amend". In 1646 an Act of Parliament was passed for founding parish schools and fixing the master's salary. To do this the heritors were to be taxed and if they failed to pay the Presbytery was empowered to act to see that the terms of the Act were honoured. Since the schoolmaster was usually also Session clerk it is possible that the teacher in January 1646 was Sebastian Parke who listed the poor in the Session register for 1645, a volume sadly long since lost but which is referred to in the 1646 register. In September 1646 James Chalmers, the newly appointed Corstorphine schoolmaster, was promised 100 merks (£5–11–1½) in addition to what George Lord Forrester had given to "former schoolmasters", namely a house and yards in the village. The brief reference to George Forrester's provision for the schoolmaster in his village prior to the 1646 Act indicates a care for the education of the children of his barony.

The house provided by George Forrester lay between "the minister's manse on the east, and John Aitken mason on the west". The location of the Forrester schoolhouse depends on where the manse was in 1646. It has been suggested that the minister at this time occupied the Provost's house but in 1646 Florence Gardner, titular Provost, granted sasine of the Provost's house to Margaret Forrester, daughter of George Forrester, and her husband Alexander Telfer of Reidhews. No doubt there was other residential property belonging to the church lying immediately west of the Provost's house and along the north side of the High Street – in the area presently stretching from Albyn Cottage to Augustine Cottage. If a dwelling west of the Provost's house was used at the Reformation for a manse then the schoolhouse and the bellman's house would follow westwards. Oral tradition in 1706–07 maintained that the schoolmaster's house and the bellman's house were part of the Provostry.

One of the "yards" was an acre and a half above the smithy on the east side of "the walk that goes to Cramond". This strip noted as Schoolmaster's Land on the 1777 village map ran from Belgrave Terrace to Old Kirk Road. In 1824 the heritors and Sir Robert Dick, the laird, entered into a contract of excambion. The Schoolmaster's Land at Clermiston Road and ground in the village which was part of the teacher's glebe and then occupied by John Wightman, were exchanged. The school in the High Street was built in 1819–20 on ground occupied by Sir Robert's cottars. It had a playground in front, the schoolhouse adjoined the school, and the school glebe was to the north. The glebe was a Scots acre of ground behind the master's garden. It was accessible only through the teacher's garden. The annual grazing value of the ground was estimated at £8.

The schoolmaster had another piece of land – an acre west of the "Cowesbrigge (Coltbridge) on the south side of the little house standing on the wayside commonly called the Lamp Aiker". This Lamp Acre lay on the north bank of the Water of Leith, a roughly triangular strip stretching from the entry to Riversdale Crescent eastwards to 37 Corstorphine Road.

Its position on the low lying bank of the river explains its appearance in a charter relating to the lands of Dalry in 1642 for the area of Roseburn Park was part of the haughs of Dalry. That charter states that the lamp acre was "mortified" to the Provostry of Corstorphine. How or when this medieval benefaction became attached to Corstorphine is not really explained. It lies in an area historically attached to the West Kirk of Edinburgh which, with the chapel at Corstorphine, was given by King David to his Abbey at Holyrood. Somewhere in that ecclesiastical chain of churches and gifts may be the link between a Lamp Acre at Murrayfield and the church at Corstorphine. The link with the schoolmaster is in the Reformation use of kirklands to support education. The Lamp Acre is shown on the 1797 map of the marches between the farms of Damhead and Balgreen.

The income of the Lamp Acre was part of the schoolmaster's salary till 1821. At that time Mr Robinson of Clermiston, acting for the heritors and the schoolmaster, sold the Lamp Acre to Murray of Henderland on condition that the teacher was paid the feu duty. This was calculated on the full value of 1 boll wheat, 1 boll oats, and 1 boll barley.

Between 1846 and 1855 Murray feued the ground and the new owners built the houses 37 to 45 Corstorphine Road. Ann Lawrie in 1848 had a quarter of an acre; Alexander Wightman, jeweller, Edinburgh was there by 1850 and James Penman of near Melrose invested in a rood of land.

Murray had a small piece of adjoining ground called Cripple John's Acre – approximately 55, Corstorphine Road.

Cripple John is no more than a name from the past. It may be that he was supported by the income of this acre or he may have occupied it.

When Thomas Matthew was appointed schoolmaster in 1874 his annual salary was £60 along with the Lamp Acre income and the use of the school glebe. Because the headmaster had these extras Corstorphine School Board was able to charge lower fees than in neighbouring parishes. Corstorphine charged two pence to five pence weekly, Currie three pence to seven pence and Colinton's lowest charge was three pence.

When the State began enquiring into educational endowments the Clerk to Corstorphine School Board stated that the schoolmaster had a glebe of almost an acre adjoining his garden as well as feu duty from the Lamp Acre. Then under the 1882–84 Education Endowments (Scotland) Act the Lamp Acre and the school glebe were amalgamated and vested in Corstorphine School Board on condition that the teacher then in office continued to enjoy the annual income of these perquisites till death or resignation. Part of the school glebe in 1896 was bought by the Dickson estate. It lay west of the west end of Hope Street, now Manse Street. On the death of Mr Matthew in 1902 the income from the Lamp Acre and the glebe was used to provide bursaries for children attending schools in the parish and going on to higher and technical education.

In 1938 this income was merged in the City of Edinburgh Educational Endowment Trust. Up till regionalisation the City Abstract of Accounts noted the Lamp Acre and the schoolmaster's glebe. Presently the Trust funds are mainly used for promoting interest in music, drama, and the arts.

When the schoolhouse needed repair in 1647 the Session used money got from the fines paid by sinners to buy timber and to build a wall. James Chalmers, the teacher, was a witness at the 1649 witchcraft trials.

Chalmers' successor, William Greg, when in Falkirk in 1650, acted in his other capacity as Session Clerk and made enquiries, without success, as to the whereabouts of a Corstorphine backslider. Since the master depended on fees for income he suffered when anyone else set up a school. Accordingly to protect the parish teacher the Session in 1655 prohibited Thomas Mertoune and his wife, Jean Ramsay, from keeping school.

The modern electric lamp presented to the Old Parish Church by the Corstorphine Rotary Club in 1958. (See also photo on page 39) *(PB644)*

The following year Greg was paid "out of the box" for teaching Thomas Elder, John Halden, David Lowriston, son of Margaret Hodge widow, and William Duncan, son of Isobel Mackie. All were poor scholars educated by the church.

Greg was followed by Thomas McConchy. The long vacancy in the church after the minister was deprived in 1662 for non-conformity prevented timeous official recognition of McConchy's position so in 1666 he requested the Session to grant him an Act of Admission as schoolmaster. This was to regularise the agreement made in October 1662 between himself and James Lord Forrester as patron of the kirk that he was to be the master in Corstorphine school. McConchy was then recorded in the Session records as being from October 1662 schoolmaster, precentor, and clerk to the Session. Scottish village schoolmasters generally filled these three offices in parish life: the two church positions gave additional income.

The Session in 1667 instructed the scholars to read the catechism in church each Sabbath between the second and third bells. This arrangement in March 1682 was confined to "during the long dayes". The time spent on the "questions" added to the usual church service time was no inconvenience in the summer months. In winter the members of the congregation who lived out with the village wanted home before dark as unlit, rough roads and marshy ground made travel dangerous.

McConchy in 1667 complained that a considerable part of his salary was still due him. Next year he notified the Session that he was about to resign as he had not been paid. This was the period when James, Lord Forrester, was notoriously in debt. The minister was delegated to speak to the Bishop of Edinburgh and the Town Council who had the benefit of the teinds of Gogar and Lang Saughton to see if they were willing to pay a proportion of McConchy's salary. The Session ordered local tenants and land labourers in the parish to pay McConchy two pecks victual upon the plough and a peck on each half plough or the equivalent in cash. This was additional payment to the £100 agreed by Lord Forrester.

Though the Session by 1669 paid McConchy's fees as their clerk and precentor he was still without his teaching salary. Therefore he petitioned George, Bishop of Edinburgh. He stated that he had been schoolmaster at Corstorphine for six years on an understanding with Lord Forrester that he would pay him £100 Scots yearly. McConchy was on the verge of poverty. Since the Bishop had appointed a visit to Corstorphine glebe with a view to excambion McConchy took the chance to petition to get what was due him. But the Bishop prevaricated and referred the petition to the Presbytery.

Possibly because the Presbytery were not helpful McConchy then refused to act as precentor. Mr Chisholm, the minister who had come in 1666, asked the Session what was the general opinion in the village of Mr McConchy. No one knew anything to his discredit. The complaint appears to have been settled for no more requests for payment are on record.

The Session in 1681 repaired the old schoolhouse. The Revolution of 1689 put an end to Episcopalian church government. This may have led to McConchy being displaced from his school. Whatever the reason the Session in 1689 called William Wilsone to be the master. By Act of Parliament in July 1690 schoolmasters teaching Latin had to swear an oath of allegiance to William and Mary and to subscribe to the Confession of Faith. William Wilsone conformed for Corstorphine. A document assuring him of his terms of employment was signed by Lord Forrester, Foulis of Ravelston and the elders in 1691 and then agreed to by the Presbytery.

McConchy, however, did not give up the schoolhouse and the garden. The summer of 1692 was taken up with complaints from Wilsone and with notices being sent to McConchy to appear before the Baron Court. Wilsone wanted rent from McConchy for his continued occupation of the schoolhouse. McConchy claimed that the heritors owed him money and since the place of schoolmaster had not been declared vacant he was within his right to occupy the house.

On 5th September 1692 the Baron Court of Corstorphine granted Wilsone a decreet against McConchy ordering McConchy to "flitt and remove himselfe wife bairnies family servants goods and gear furth and frae the schoolmaster's house and yeard". By December Wilsone had possession of the schoolhouse. In August 1693 McConchy confirmed that the Session had paid all that had been due to him.

The problem of others teaching "to the prejudice of the public school" forced the Session in 1693 to prohibit teaching within a mile around the village except women who taught girls what it is "not incumbent for a man to do". Wilsone inherited an extremely cold schoolhouse. The Session having some sympathy for frozen children ordered in 1694 a hanging chimney – a wide wooden canopy with one end over the open fire and the other end taken up through the roof – to be placed at the east gable. The room was also divided by a wooden partition having a door in the centre. Lord Forrester was asked for the timber. This doubtless served the double purpose of increasing warmth in a smaller teaching room and giving the master the privacy of a separate accommodation. During Wilsone's term of office the Scottish Parliament in 1696 reinforced the 1649 Act with amendments aimed at compelling heritors to meet their educational obligations.

JOHN CUNNINGHAM

Wilsone's successor, John Cunningham, had a short but colourful year in Corstorphine. The Session admitted him in January 1698 and he resigned in October. His downfall started on Saturday 12th February when he was found "lying in the highway drunk betwixt Edinburgh and Corstorphine".

In his defence Cunningham said that his intoxication was the result of "a naturall distemper" since he had gone to Edinburgh on an empty stomach, had drunk only "the share of six chopins of drinke among six men", and was affected when he came out into fresh air. The Scots measure, the chopin, is a reminder of the Franco-Scottish connection, the French chopine being a half litre mug.

The Session suspended him from holding office as precentor and Session clerk but he was left to continue his educational work until an enquiry was completed and a verdict reached. On Thursday, 24th February, before the minister, Mr Archibald Hamilton, and the kirk elders – James Murray, David Morison, John Walker, James Finny, and Alexander Anderson – there appeared John Pyrrie, shoemaker at Whitehouse in the West Kirk parish, to give evidence. Cunningham objected to Pyrrie on the grounds that he might be prejudiced against him. The two men had quarrelled over shoes that Pyrrie made for the Cunningham children. On being asked why he had taken the shoes if they were unsatisfactory Cunningham replied that the children needed footwear urgently.

Cunningham was then asked if he had tried by threats to dissuade Pyrrie from acting as a witness. To this the schoolmaster replied that all he had done on meeting Pyrrie in Parliament Close was to tell him that he did not need to appear until called to do so by a magistrate of his own parish. After further questioning about his attitude to Pyrrie the irate Cunningham "went out of the kirk in a scornful and huffing manner".

The minister informed the elders that he had heard from Mr David Williamson, one of the West Kirk ministers, popularly known as "Dainty Davie", that Pyrrie was an honest man. Accordingly the Session decided to hear the shoemaker.

Pyrrie, aged 52, declared on oath that on Saturday afternoon 12th February he was looking over the forestair of his house when he saw Cunningham coming along the road. Since he had been drinking in the Cowgate, the road Cunningham took home would follow the line of the West Port, Castle Barns (Morrison Street) and Whitehouse (beyond Haymarket). The schoolmaster was "tottering south and north on the causey. A neighbour, Isobel Young, called out to a Corstorphine woman, "Take up your Precentor".

The woman, however, left Cunningham to stumble "west of the Whitehouse till he came near the midding and there he fell". Evidently Pyrrie felt no call to help a fallen brother for he went indoors and did not look out again till half an hour later by which time the schoolmaster had disappeared. Pyrrie declared "as he shall answer at the great day" that Cunningham was guilty of the sin of drunkenness.

When the Session met again on Thursday, 3rd March, Thomas Sandars, aged 26, servant to Mrs Baillie in Corstorphine, gave evidence. In company with Margaret Wightimer, wife of the local smith James Stevenson, he was riding home from Edinburgh when he came upon Cunningham lying on the wayside. Sandars asked the woman to help him get Cunningham up on to "his horse behind him" but before she could do so James Johnstoun overtook them "at one of the big stones west of the middin". Farm middens were handy landmarks. Johnstoun dismounted and helped Cunningham up behind Sandars. Sandars said the schoolmaster put his hands over his shoulders and "nipped his ears".

On Sunday, 6th March, the enquiry continued. James Johnstoun, aged 62, gave his version of the incident. Cunningham objected saying that Johnston was "half witted" but the Session thought otherwise. To them Johnstoun was "a fewar in the town well respected". He said that he saw Cunningham stretched out on the ground and Margaret Wightimer raising him up. Three or four washerwives called to him, "Go forward and take up your precentor who hath got a sop drinke". It may be that the washerwomen indicate that the incident took place near Coltbridge where washing clothes in the Water of Leith was customary into the early 19th century.

When Johnstoun reached "one of the big stones west of the midden" he got off his horse, laid down his goods – candles and iron – and pushed Sandars and his horse near to the big stone against which Margaret had propped Cunningham. Once the intoxicated Cunningham was got up behind Sandars the trio set off for Corstorphine. Possibly the big stones were march stones. Johnstoun saw Cunningham tweak Sandars' ears for he observed "it seems he had a mind of his scholars when he nipped Thomas Sandars' lugs". John Galt recalled this habit of Scottish schoolmasters when Malachi Mailings remembered Dominie Skelp: "He nippit my twa lugs till he left the stedt (imprint) o' his fingers as plainly upon them as the mark o' Peter's finger and thumb can he seen on the haddock's back."

Though the evidence was then completed the Session did not pass judgement for Sir John Foulis of Ravelston had sent word that he did not wish sentence to be given until the heritors could be present. At the next meeting, 13th March, no heritors appeared. The Session proceeded to draw up a statement listing their dissatisfaction with Cunningham. They had five complaints. He was not fit to he kirk precentor because he knew only two tunes which he could not sing properly. He was guilty of disclosing Session business known to him as clerk of the Session. His drunkenness caused scandal. He was "light and vain in conversation and carriage" and given to "haunting ale houses" on Sundays as well as week days. Finally he did not keep satisfactory church records: "confused minutes" and neglect of the mortcloth list.

Session met again on 4th April and again no heritors appeared. Since the heritors had been written to twice and two intimations had been made from the pulpit the Session concluded that they were not interested and resolved to refer the affair to the Presbytery.

At the next Session meeting it was noted that Cunningham had been charging excessively for writing testimonials (certificates of character given when a person removed to another parish). He had taken eleven shillings when the charge was four. This led to the Session ruling that a testimonial with the name of four people was to cost a groat and for eight people of the same family six shillings Scots. Also the minister was to sign any testimonial given.

By June the Presbytery of Edinburgh had visited Corstorphine and they returned in August. The beadle, standing at the church door, called upon the heritors but none appeared. The Presbytery committee, Mr Craig of Duddingston, Mr James Hart of Ratho, Mr Hamilton of Cramond and Mr Paterson of Colinton then tested Cunningham's musical ability. His two best tunes were Elgin and French which he sang "tolerably". He knew three others – Still, London and Martyrs but was not "exact". Elgin was the tune that Burns described as "The sweetest far of Scotia's holy lays". When it is remembered that, in the days of Cunningham, the number of tunes used in church was twelve, "The Tunes o' Davit", his knowledge of five is, perhaps, not so poor a performance. His Latin was found to be very satisfactory.

When the minister and the elders were questioned about Cunningham's conduct of the school it was said that he was "frequently in the change house" and the school consequently suffered. When the Session minutes were examined they were found to contain falsehoods, omissions and nonsensical expressions. On 1st October Cunningham resigned but there were repercussions over the next six months.

In January 1699 he applied for money he considered the Session owed him. The Session demanded that he produce the registers of baptisms and marriages. They also charged him with neglecting the schoolhouse and held him responsible for repairs. Two villagers, James Weir and Robert Oliphant, notified the Session that Cunningham owed them money and requested payment out of any money the Session might be paying to the schoolmaster and this was done.

The last of Cunningham was in August 1699 when the Session agreed to give him a testimonial to be received into any Christian congregation. This was important, for to live or stay even for a short time in any Scottish parish it was necessary to produce a testimonial from the last parish of residence. It showed whether the possessor was married or single and whether free from scandal or not. A person without a testimonial could be expelled from the parish by the local magistrate.

So John Cunningham passed from the Corstorphine scene but not from history: he lives on, immortalised in the kirk records. For those who travel the road from Edinburgh to Corstorphine almost three centuries on Cunningham has left a stern warning not to indulge too freely in chopins of ale. The disciplinary power of the Session has gone but the technological age has produced its own instrument of retribution – the breathalyser.

EIGHTEENTH CENTURY MASTERS

The heritors in 1699 having accepted the minister's report that James Coupar was satisfactory in Latin and music appointed him to succeed Cunningham and then started to squabble over his salary. Hew Wallace of Ingliston who had taken over the Barony of Corstorphine from the Forrester family said that based on the valuation of his land he was liable only for a proportion of the teacher's salary. Foulis of Ravelston and Andrew Myrton of Gogar replied that they had never paid the schoolmaster as he was the responsibility of the Corstorphine estate. Ingliston argued that although in the past it had been customary for the Reader and the schoolmaster to be appointed by the patron of the parish the situation had changed. Under the recent Act of 1696 the heritors were obliged to stent themselves for the schoolhouse and the master's salary according to their valued rent.

James Coupar stayed two years. In November 1700 the Session noted that the schoolmaster without consulting them had given the children their holiday break, their "vacance". It was enacted that in future notice of the vacation had to be given either to the minister or the Session both when children were excused from classes at harvest time and when after harvest they were to return.

Laurence Waugh, schoolmaster at East Calder, started to teach in Corstorphine in December 1700. By June 1704 the ruinous condition of the schoolhouse gave the Session concern. Sir Robert Dickson of Sornberg who had bought the Corstorphine estate from Ingliston expressed his willingness to pay his share of the costs and the minister undertook to consult the other heritors. In October 1704 for giving a testimonial to John Binning of Drumcross, "a scandalous person", Waugh came under the displeasure of the Session who reported him to the Presbytery. As a result Waugh was suspended for three months from his office of Session clerk.

The reluctance of the heritors to pay their teacher culminated in 1706 when on 14th November Waugh resigned "because he wanted encouragement of an yearly salary as a schoolmaster and also wanted a schoolhouse". Waugh asked for a "testificat" for his six years of service which the Session "unanimously granted him".

No time was lost in getting a successor. William Wood was ordered to show his precenting skill in Corstorphine kirk on Sunday, 1st December 1706. The following Sunday the Session accepted him for the triple duties of precentor, Session clerk, and schoolmaster. The provision of a schoolhouse was still under debate. The year 1707 opened with the minister seeking information from his predecessor, George Henry, who said that the schoolhouse was part of the Provostry of Corstorphine and paid no rent to Lord Forrester or anyone else. An old residenter, Thomas Beg, along with James Wilkie, agreed that no rent was paid to the laird. William Stevenson and John Leishman, both old men, declared that what was called the bellman's house had originally been the schoolhouse where they, as boys, had been taught by William Greg, when David Basilly was minister. This was the truth, they declared, for there still existed a door between the two houses. James Johnstoun and James Weir testified that these houses were used by the precentor and by the bellman.

By October 1707 the schoolhouse had fallen which forced the heritors to act. The choice was to rebuild, the cost being borne by the church as in Presbyterian and Episcopalian times, or, to convert the sacristy on the north side of the church, making an entrance door from the churchyard. The heritors offered "to putt up ane lumm therein". However the sacristy was left undisturbed. It was Burn, the 1828 restorer, who desecrated the sacristy with a heating system.

Then in 1708 the Session heard that the laird, Sir Robert Dickson, had taken over the bellman's house and was about to let it. Thomas Baillie, former baillie to the estate, testified that the bellman's house was originally used by the schoolmaster and that during his 32 years as Baron Court Officer the house was never rented. Thomas Baillie signed his statement so that it could be sent to Sir Robert. That same year Mr Wood found one of his sources of income, the Lamp Acre, threatened by Nisbet of Dean. Nisbet sent his ploughmen to plough back the ground Wood had sown despite the fact that, in Nisbet's presence, the boundaries of the schoolmaster's Lamp Acre had been attested by honest men acquainted with the location.

Wood took action in the Sheriff Court of Edinburgh and the Session promised to help him with the expenses as they were anxious to preserve what belonged to the church and the school. The Sheriff came out to Coltbridge and witnesses for both parties "did perambulate" the ground in his presence. Among the Corstorphine witnesses was James Clerk in Balgreen.

Then Wood in 1709 took his complaints about salary and lack of a schoolhouse to the Commissioners of Supply. The Presbytery of Edinburgh also appeared to support Wood. Regarding his salary Wood explained that the Lamp Acre "att the Coltbridge" suffered from flooding of the Water of Leith "lying on the brink thereor", and when let did not bring him more than £18 Scots which also included his acre and a half at Corstorphine. The last straw for Mr Wood was having to collect the two pecks of oats per plough allowed him in the parish: to the dominie it was degrading. It was "unbecoming the character and station of a schoolmaster". If he did this he "would be in noe better caise than a pyper who beggs and collects in seed tyme and harvest".

The Commissioners awarded a salary of £80 Scots yearly along with the Schoolmaster's Land and the Lamp Acre. In their opinion the church "ile" proposed for a school did not belong to the heritors but to Lord Forrester and his successors in the lands of Corstorphine. Sir Robert Dickson was unwilling to hand over the sacristy for a school and the parish school was a ruin of walls and gables. The Commissioners ordered the schoolhouse to be repaired at a cost of not less than £200 Scots. Materials to he used were timber, thatch and divot.

Sir Andrew Myrton of Gogar said that his hamlet was well peopled and children could not he sent to Corstorphine school because of the distance. Accordingly Sir Andrew was allowed to keep half of his share of the Corstorphine money for use at Gogar. So in 1709 Wood got his schoolhouse but the work was not completed in 1710 for Saughton's factor was asked then by the other heritors to pay his share to allow the teacher to finish the job.

When the Rev. George Fordyce was appointed minister in 1709 the affairs of the church were reviewed including the position of the parish teacher. Wood explained that as a teacher he got a legal salary from the heritors, an arrangement which formerly had not been recognised. As Session clerk he was paid from the collections for the poor but the money gathered was small and the numbers of poor had greatly increased. In 1707 the heritors and the Session had agreed to pay Wood £24 yearly as their clerk but at Mr Fordyce's review the schoolmaster because of the state of kirk funds offered to continue the work for £16 yearly. The Session gladly accepted his offer, reserving their right to increase or decrease the payment to his successors as they thought fit.

School fees for two poor boys, William Beg and Charles Anderson, were paid by the Session in 1710. Some of the poor receiving a monthly allowance from the church did not send their children to school. Consequently the Session ruled that poor children were to be educated and that the kirk treasurer would pay the teacher by deducting the fees from the parents' monthly allowance.

A further move to regulate educational provision in the parish was made in 1714. The Session decided to issue an Act establishing the "schoolages" of the teacher and his "casualties" as Session clerk registering baptisms and marriages. Till then the system had operated on use and wont. The master was to have quarterly payments:

Latin or Arithmetic – half a crown
English and Writing – twenty pence
Reading English – fourteen pence

His Candlemas (2nd February) offering was left to parental discretion.

Candlemas was a great day in the school year. Originally the gifts made to the teacher then were expressions of parental respect. Later they were considered dues the master could claim. Sometimes the gift was a goose, or a turkey, or a book. Generally, however, it was money, sixpence and a shilling being popular sums. Pupils were cheered as they gave the dominie, seated at his desk, his Candlemas present. When half a crown was given the master called out "Vivat". When greater sums were given his exclamations were graded from "Floreat bis" and "Floreat ter" to "Gloriat". The highest giver was declared "Victor".

The giving completed the master then declared Candlemas day a holiday. The children in procession paraded the streets with their "King" or "Queen" (the highest gift giver) seated on crossed hands. The latter part of the day was used for the

OPPOSITE.
The Barony of Corstorphine, 1754. The old village can clearly be seen in the lower segments. Its basic layout has remained the same. *(Courtesy NAS, ref. RHP 1041 and Messrs Gillespie Macandrew W.S.)*

Candlemas "bleeze". Where whins were available some were lit: in Corstorphine no doubt Broomhouse provided handy material. Otherwise a bonfire was made. Sometimes at the end of the day's festivities the teacher made a bowl of punch, giving his scholars a drink to the health of the reigning monarch. Candlemas gifts survived to the early 19th century.

Another customary Scottish addition to the master's emoluments was connected with Shrove Tuesday, known as Fastern's Eve. The school was given a holiday to engage in cock-fighting. Usually the teacher provided the cocks and the schoolroom was the arena. The master claimed all the runaway cocks called "fugies". Those who brought contestant cocks paid entry money. This brutal custom lasted into the early 1800's. Cock fighting took place in Corstorphine till the turn of the 18th century.

Among the other clauses of the 1714 Session enactment was provision for paying the fees of poor children: the prohibition of private schools in opposition to the parish school was also a matter of concern.

As precentor and Session clerk the schoolmaster was to have:

> proclamation and registering of marriage – 14½ pence
> registering baptisms – 7 pence
> supplying a testimonial – a groat
> giving an extract of birth or marriage – sixpence
> fines of fornicators – 18 pence

The wages of sin were a constant source of income to the church and its officers as well as to the poor.

William Wood's service came to an end in April 1723 when he received an appointment as master at Peebles. Robert Black, student of divinity, followed straight away. Divinity students were welcome at Scottish parish schools as being suitable for their other duties as precentor and Session clerk. Black got an additional guinea yearly for assisting the kirk treasurer in keeping the accounts. In 1728 Black left to teach at Liberton.

Another divinity student who was also a local lad succeeded Black. He was James Mitchell, son of a kirk elder, John Mitchell, farmer at Broomhouse. His mother was Marion Louriston, a member of another well-known 18th century Corstorphine farming family. James had four broth-

A Plan of the Barony of Corstorphin and Clermiston one of the Seats of The Honble Sir Alexr
PRESTONFIELD Dick Bart. From a survey taken Octr 1754 by

ers and three sisters. He married Marion Broun in the West Kirk parish.

James and Marion Mitchell had six sons and three daughters. Since at the baptism of his son, Robert, the witnesses were James Broun in Gorgie with his two sons, George and John, it is probable that the Corstorphine schoolmaster had married into one of the Gorgie Broun families related to the Brouns of Gorgie Mill. Mitchell's period as schoolmaster appears to have been uneventful apart from his having to report in 1733 that a rival school had been set up by a Patrick Galbreath, an incomer.

Ralph Drummond from "Down" (Doune?) took over in 1756. School fees were a crown per quarter for Latin, half a crown for writing or Arithmetic, and two shillings sterling for English. Drummond left in 1762 to be the ordained minister at Cranshaws. He may have been directed to this Berwickshire parish through its landowner, James Watson of Saughton and Cammo.

Alexander Bannatyne who came in 1762 was a student of divinity. In 1774 a spelling book was provided for a poor scholar, Mary Whyte. The Session, however, was not too happy about the "great length" of time spent in school by poor bairns as the church had to pay fees and provide books. This led to the Session making rules about the poor. No child was to be sent to school without a warrant from the church treasurer. No child under seven years of age was to be admitted and on reaching ten years a poor child was to be dismissed. The number of children in each family qualifying for free education was to be at the kirk treasurer's discretion. Later only the Session could admit poor scholars.

Further school rules were made by the heritors and the minister. From 1st April to 1st October schooldays except Saturday were to be six hours with two intervals of an hour each: 9–11; 12–2; 3–5. From 1st October to 1st April hours were limited to four with an hour interval: 9–11; 12–2.

On Saturdays instruction was to cover three hours 9–12 without interval. The last half hour on Saturday was to be given to the principles of religion. The master was to supply copies of all letters of the alphabet either on detached slips or at the head of the paper on which the child wrote. No school was to be held on Christmas day; New Year's day; Hansel Monday (the first Monday of the New Year when gifts – hansels – were given); H.M. Birthday; four days at Sacrament time; the last two hours on Wednesday afternoon once a fortnight from 1st April to 1st October.

Perhaps the way in which Bannatyne's predecessors had used classroom time led to the Session clearly stating that the teacher was not to use the school time to read newspapers or books for his own amusement. He was to devote himself to his duties, either prescribing lessons or preparing lessons. The Session prohibited the master from granting half day holidays: only the heritors or the minister could authorise what generations of Scottish schoolchildren delighted to get and aptly referred to as "a halfie".

DANIEL RAMSAY

Alexander Bannatyne's signature last appears in the Session minutes for February 1784. No record was kept between 1784–1794. Only a few notes cover 1801–1814. Accordingly it is not certain when Daniel Ramsay took over from Bannatyne as dominie. Bannatyne was first clerk to Corstorphine Friendly Society and was active in 1804. In 1805 Ramsay became clerk. There was a James Ross designated schoolmaster living in Corstorphine in 1803 but it is not recorded where he taught. He appears to have been a bird of passage.

When Bannatyne's days as schoolmaster were coming to an end his fellow parochial masters in Midlothian were moved to protest about their salaries. In April 1799 their petition appeared before the Commissioners of Supply. The teachers argued that the 1696 Act was "for its time" but times had changed. To live comfortably in 1799 an income triple that of 1696 was needed. It was "an indesputable fact that many day labourers, common mechanics and menial servants earn a more comfortable maintenance than many parochial schoolmasters".

The 1696 Act fixed yearly salaries at a minimum of £5–11–1 and a maximum of £11–2–3. In 1803 an Act set the master's salary for the next 25 years at not under nor above £11–2–3. Then after 1828 graduated salaries related to the value of oatmeal were introduced so that the minimum became £16–13–5. The 1861 Act gave a maximum of £70 per annum.

Ramsay in 1804 was designated schoolmaster when he became clerk to the Crossroads authority. The Presbytery of Edinburgh was requested in April 1806 by Ramsay to examine him as schoolmaster in Corstorphine. The Presbytery refused to do so as there was no extract of his being elected by the heritors and the minister. In October Ramsay presented the Presbytery with a notarial copy of his appointment but the Presbytery delayed making a decision "as there were certain difficulties". However in December the Presbytery did examine Ramsay in Writing, Arithmetic, English, Latin, and Literature. He also had testimonials from St. Andrews and Aberdeen Universities. Eventually the Presbytery declared him "qualified".

On 19th July 1810 Ramsay made a declaration to the Sheriff of Edinburgh. It was the period of the Napoleonic wars when militia forces were in Edinburgh. The wives of some Aberdeenshire militia men took lodgings in Corstorphine where between 1809 and 1810 nine children were born. Ramsay collected the government allowances to militia wives at the office of the Collecter of Cess in Edinburgh and then distributed it to those concerned. Some of the women lodged with Ramsay at the rate of three pence a week or a shilling per month. His house had six rooms with fireplaces exclusive of the schoolroom. Five rooms were let to five women: there were no beds in the rooms.

In order to get payment a certificate was issued by the regiment and then the minister and the Session had to confirm the details. Finally an order was given by a Justice of the Peace authorising the allowance to be paid. Ramsay produced certificates at the Cess Office but had not got the signatures of Mr Oliver, the minister, and the elders, James Nimmo and John Menelaws. Instead Ramsay had himself written their names.

Defending his action Ramsay told how the previous winter he had met Mr Oliver at the Cowgate of Edinburgh when, in the course of conversation, Mr Oliver had complained of the trouble he was put to by militia wives coming to him individually to have their certificates completed. Later, Ramsay said, he understood that Mr Oliver was willing for him to subscribe the documents in his name. Likewise Nimmo and Menelaws were glad to be saved the trouble of signing themselves.

Apparently Ramsay retained part of the allowance he collected. The charge brought against him was forgery and fraud but it may well have been his highly individual and original method of ensuring he got payment for his rented rooms. The heritors, however, considered it "immoral conduct" and took action to get rid of him. They did not, they asserted, "seek to punish" but "to protect the infant generation". Ramsay, in their opinion, was a disqualified schoolmaster under the 1803 Act.

The Presbytery of Edinburgh served a libel on Ramsay but by July 1812 its relevancy was questioned by John Clerk and James Moncrieff, advocates, acting for the schoolmaster. They argued that Ramsay having been "served with criminal letters to stand before the High Court of Justiciary" and having "run his letters" could not be tried again for the same crime. The Presbytery, with one exception, agreed that the criminal charge was irrelevant and accordingly dismissed it.

The heritors lost the day but they made educational history for Ramsay's case was "one of the first" since the 1803 Act which made the judgement of presbyteries final in matters concerning parochial schoolmasters and "without appeal to or review by any court civil or ecclesiastical". But Daniel by then had had enough and left Corstorphine.

Ramsay was a character. He started teaching in Anstruther in the 1780's and wrote a textbook on "Mixed Schools". One of his pupils at Anstruther was Thomas Chalmers, later to become the celebrated preacher and first principal of the Free Church College, Edinburgh. His statue by John Steel controls modern traffic flow at the intersection of George Street and Castle Street.

Chalmers did not forget his teacher. Having lost his status as a schoolmaster Ramsay became impoverished and Chalmers for many years contributed to his support. Ramsay ended his life in Gillespie's Hospital erected in 1802 in what is now Gillespie Crescent as part of the charitable bequest of the Colinton snuff maker. The 14th century Wrychtishousis buildings were demolished to provide the hospital site. Later it became the Royal Blind Asylum. In turn this building in 1975 gave way for a housing development. On his deathbed at Gillespie's Hospital Ramsay spoke with deep feeling about Dr Chalmers: "No man knows the amount of kindness which I have received from my old pupil."

A delightful and characteristic story is told of Ramsay writing to the Duke of Wellington advising him in dealing with the Irish to take "the taws in the tae hand and the Testament in the tither". The tawse (belt) and the Bible must have been Ramsay's teaching equipment, tools of the trade now vanished from Scottish schools. Perhaps in the affair of the militia wives he was more sinned against than sinning, his action being imprudent rather than criminally motivated.

TO THE 1872 ACT

Alexander Simpson followed Ramsay. Mr Ritchie of the High School of Edinburgh examined Mr Simpson in 1812 and approved his academic attainments. Mr Simpson pointed out to the heritors that he would need to keep boarders to give himself an adequate income. For a time young Norwegians and Swedes belonging to trading families stayed at the schoolhouse where Mr Simpson conversed with them in their own languages. However a heavy duty was placed on Baltic timber so that the connection with Norway came to an end.

When Waterloo finished the career of Napoleon the scholars in Corstorphine were working their way through Myln's *Spelling Book* and Tyro's *Guide*. By 1818 the schoolhouse at the north of Kirk Loan was no lónger fit to be used. The new site chosen for the school and schoolhouse was north of the Cross of Corstorphine in the High Street. This, unfortunately, involved cutting down the trees that formed the Cross.

The heritors of 1820 were critical of the architect's plan for their new buildings, rejecting the "hewn work upon the front being ornamental and of no manner of use to the teacher". Work, however, went ahead and the school, a small single storey building, is still a visible part of the present buildings in the High Street.

In 1822 the heritors exchanged the Schoolmaster's Land at Clermiston Road with Sir Robert Dick for land beside the new school. At the same time Mr Simpson got a quiet rap on the knuckles for enclosing school ground without the consent of the heritors. They thought he had acted "incautiously". But they did concede that there was "rubbish left" in removing the cottar houses on the site and that there was "necessity of dispatch to enable him to improve the premises without losing a season and consequently a crop." So the Session paid the enclosure account and instructed Mr Simpson to get estimates for flooring the schoolroom with wood.

When the parish church was being renovated in 1828 the congregation for two years used the schoolroom and the schoolhouse. Mr Simpson was not slow to utilise stone disregarded by the church masons for in 1829 he removed from an arched vault in the body of the church a stone which he took to form a cover for his well: in 1833 a pump was purchased for this well.

The school roll in 1839 was from 50 to 70 children. The fees were English 2/6, Writing 3/–, Writing and Arithmetic including mensuration and Geography 3/6, Latin or French 5/–. Mr Simpson's salary was £34–4–0 with house, garden, ground in the village and the Lamp Acre. As schoolmaster Mr Simpson was known to all and involved in the life of the community. He was active in helping the sick during the cholera epidemic of 1832–33.

By 1833 space became a problem as the school roll rose towards 100 pupils. The heritors in 1846 tried to use William Watson of Saughton's £2,000 legacy to the church to build a new schoolhouse but this was not legally possible. The income from the legacy, however, could be used to buy books and paper for poor scholars.

Two years later, 1848, a larger building was provided. The old room was to be used for Classics, Arithmetic, and Mathematics taught by Mr Simpson: the new room was for an assistant teacher to teach other subjects. More playground

The entire roll of Corstorphine Public School pose for the camera before 1872. Since a long exposure was required, the children have obeyed the order to stay perfectly still. They are well-shod, well-dressed, hair neatly brushed, and make an appealing picture. *(PB560)*

space was needed for the increase in pupils so the east wall of Mr Simpson's garden was moved west. Both boys and girls were to use the larger playground.

Alexander Simpson's service as the dominie of Corstorphine ended with his death in 1848. With him closed a historic chapter in Corstorphine education for he was the last to hold the triple office of teacher, Session clerk and precentor.

George Manson, Headmaster of the Edinburgh Normal Institution (Moray House), took over at a salary of £50. Latin, Greek and French were offered at seven shillings a quarter or seven pence a week. When Mr Manson died in 1862 he was followed by William Duncan from Crail.

Music was free of charge for all but pen and ink, if provided by the school, cost a penny per month. Holidays were not to exceed six weeks. The heritors, keen as ever to avoid personal expense, decided to place the school under Government Inspection in order to get the State grant. A female assistant, Miss Margaret Sinclair, was employed. She had a Government teaching certificate of high merit for which she got a salary of £3–17–8½ for the half year with 1/10½ tax deducted. In 1867 gas lighting was installed and in 1871 a charge of one shilling was made for gas when the school was used for meetings.

With the passing of the Education (Scotland) Act 1872, education became State controlled. Each parish elected a School Board which took over the powers and obligations of the heritors and the minister. The centuries old connection between church and school was ended. The Board had authority to levy rates in order to finance education. Though the 1872 Act made elementary education compulsory it did not abolish fees. The School Board existed till the Education (Scotland) Act 1918 brought in yet another system of management – the Education Authority.

THE SCHOOL BOARD

The first meeting of Corstorphine School Board took place on 26th April 1873. The Board members were the Rev. James Morrison of the Free Church (St. Ninian's) who gained the highest number of votes, the Rev. Robert K.D. Horne of the parish church, Mr Robert Thomson, market gardener, Gibson Lodge, Mr Andrew Wight, flesher, and Mr John H. Dickson of

Saughton Mains and of Corstorphine estate. Mr Duncan, the schoolmaster, became Clerk and Treasurer. Robert Cuddie, letter carrier, was appointed Visiting Officer and instructed to carry out a census of children in the district from age five to thirteen.

The year 1873 was a busy one for the Board. An assessment of four pence per pound on the rental of the parish was agreed. The Corstorphine Friendly Society and the Corstorphine Horticultural Society were granted the use of the schoolroom for their meetings and for the Flower Show. Miss Jane McBain came to teach at £50 sterling yearly. Her duties were to teach junior classes under the direction of Mr Duncan and to conduct the Industrial Department and Singing. On a motion by the Rev. Mr. Horne it was decided to continue the teaching of the Shorter Catechism. The year closed with the Visiting Officer calling on the parents of children failing to attend.

Mr Duncan's closure of the school for three days in 1874 was approved by the Board as there was an outbreak of fever in the district. At the same time Mr Duncan gave notice of his intention to resign. The Board arranged for Mr James Matthew at Juniper Green School to become headmaster. The school at this time had a staff of three – the master, the mistress, and a pupil teacher. Coal money was levied from the children as had been done previously. Consultation went ahead with Mr Wardrop, an architect, about providing an addition to the schoolroom. There were 256 children of school age in the parish and it was noted that the village "promises to increase".

Salaries were examined in 1875. Mr Matthew was entitled to the school fees, £63 from the rates which represented the sum formerly paid by the heritors along with the value of the Lamp Acre, house, garden, and glebe. The mistress was given £35 from the rates and one third of the state grant. The pupil teacher was paid £15 yearly. The year ended with the board authorising a cart of gravel to fill up hollows in the playground: no consideration there for the skinned knees of the juvenile population.

Charles Monro became Visiting Officer in 1876 replacing the deceased Mr Cuddie. An order was given for a covered shed in the playground where there were earth closets. Later that year new desks were made by John Wight, a local joiner, and he was instructed to fit up a basin stand and towel roller in the lobby of the Infant Room. An iron scraper was got for each of the school doors. The lower panes of windows were obscured, probably to concentrate young eyes on the blackboard instead of on life in the High Street outside.

Estimates were considered for a grate for the Infant Room and for other furnishings. After some thought the Board preferred Mr Scott in the Grassmarket whose "quotations were considerably lower than those of Mr Gray" in George Street, Edinburgh. The December 1876 meeting was taken up with deciding to increase the payment to the school cleaner, Mrs Shade. She was granted 3/6 per week and was offered an extra 2/6 if she took charge of the slushing and emptying the closets. This gave her 6/– weekly. The Board hoped her efforts would keep the closets in such a state "as to give no offence to neighbouring proprietors".

A reminder that 19th century Corstorphine was a village distant from Edinburgh is in the minutes of 27th February 1877 recording that a telegram had been received from Mr Dickson stating that he had been detained in town and would be unable to attend the meeting that evening. Six cart loads of Barnton chips were ordered for the schoolhouse walks, the teacher agreeing to pay half the cost. A group of local ladies was granted use of the school for a course of twelve lessons in cookery.

An approach in 1878 from the Church of Scotland Education Committee suggesting that the Board employ the church Inspector of Religious Knowledge met with a blunt refusal. The Report from the Scotch Education Department on the work of the school was excellent. Grants from the Government depended on the attendance of the child and the standard of proficiency attained in the 3Rs. Of a total grant of 12/– one third was given for at least 200 attendances and two thirds divided equally among Reading, Writing and Arithmetic. All children over six years were examined individually. This was the Payment by Results system and explains why School Boards were so concerned with attendances and the performance of the children in basic subjects. The year 1878 ended with provision being made for a small bell and "hat pins" for the cloakroom.

Thirty seven absentees were pursued in the spring of 1879: many were "ill of scarlet fever or hooping (sic) cough". Minor panic on discovering that the infant Room had never been "sized" made the Board "unanimous in agreeing that the health of the children required that this should be attended to" and, moreover, the walls were to be tinted "a pleasant colour". Mr Monro, the School Officer, had his salary increased from £5 to £7–10–0. The year 1880 started off with a boy from Stenhouse "not yet twelve years old" being beyond the control of his widowed mother. Slate racks were fitted to the backs of the seats in the Infant Room. The fee known as Coal Money was abolished, the cost of heating the school to be borne by the Board. The Visiting Officer having resigned, Sergeant Fred Billingsley was appointed with the additional duty of giving drill to the boys for half an hour per week.

The very severe winter of 1881 affected the children with colds and "many in the Infant Room from a distance could not attend". The Fifth and Sixth Standard pupils were provided with a large map of the British Isles. A new water supply for the school premises was arranged but the fitting of a bath for the schoolhouse was "not considered necessary meantime". Miss Isabella Moffat, the junior assistant, went off to be in charge of Midlem School near Selkirk. Her successor, a local girl, Miss Elizabeth Thomson, was paid £40 yearly.

Mr Blaikie in 1882 moved that writing materials be supplied free but Mr Morrison's statement "that it is not fair to burden the public rates with charges naturally devolving upon parents" won the day. The Corstorphine Band of Hope which met in the schoolroom complained to the Board that Mrs Shade, the cleaner, had been unhelpful.

Ten years on from the establishment of the Board it was decided, largely as a result of pressure from adjoining householders, to convert the earth closets into water closets. Early in 1883 local tradesmen, William Samuel for drainage and Robert Couper for plumbing, submitted estimates for £5–10–0 and £6–13–0 respectively which were accepted. A boy, age 12, who had been at a private school was admitted but not to the Fifth standard for, on examination, he was found fit only for the Infant class.

In 1884 the widow who could not control her son agreed that the Board should arrange for his brother to go to the *Mars* Training Ship, certified by the Home Office as a means of reforming wayward boys. The *Mars* continued to help boys in need of care till 1929. Mr Stuart, the Corstorphine agent for granolithic, won the contract for paving the girls' playground.

The triennial election of the School Board in 1885 returned Charles Blaikie with the highest votes. He lost no time in

The public school in the High Street before the considerable alterations and additions of 1894. The position of the gate remains the same today. (PB135)

trying again but in vain to have writing materials provided free. He then followed up with a motion that the Board supply school books at cost price. However he was thwarted by a counter motion by Mr Morrison that there was no need for the Board to change the existing arrangement whereby books were available at a discount of two pence per shilling.

Employment of another teacher split the Board in 1886. Mr Dodds suggested a male certificated assistant at £80 p.a. but Mr Blaike proposed a female certificated teacher at £45 p.a. General Grant of Southleigh then advised a certificated male at £60 and this was accepted. Possibly what was saved on the teacher's salary helped the purchase of a cyclostyle and sewing frames. For additions and alterations to the school premises a loan of £570 was granted by the Public Works Loan Commision. Miss Boyd was given the use of the Infant Room free of charge for her Brass Work Class.

On the matter of school attendance defaulting parents were called before the Board in 1887, "suitably addressed and admonished" and dismissed "after having promised ammendment". The Inspector's report noted that the grammar of the higher standards had improved and that the children of the

Infants and First Standard were "active, honest and remarkably frank and eager". Domestic Economy was taught by the Infant Mistress with "marked intelligence": that comment must have made the teacher's day.

Certificates of merit were arranged for in 1888, bearing the heading *Corstorphine Public School*. Mr Matthew was allowed to buy wool for the knitting class in the Industrial Department at a cost not exceeding £2. Later drawing materials and instruments were granted for the use of the boys. G.U. Selway, later to write a history of Corstorphine, rented a room for a drawing class at sixpence per night to cover fuel and light.

The salary of the Headmaster disturbed some of the Board. His annual average over the previous ten years was £246–17–7½. Mr Blaikie thought it too much. Mr Morrison protested at Mr Blaikie's proposal to reduce the master's income. Mr Blaikie persisted. At the January 1889 meeting a petition signed by ratepayers against reducing salaries was submitted. At the February meeting Blaikie proposed to fix the schoolmaster's salary at £110 yearly and all the fees but the Board was to have no responsibility to collect fees. The minister, Mr Morrison, said this was a breach of faith and was

The school showing the 1894 additions, which included a second storey and extensions towards the rear of the building. (PB420)

seconded by Mr Traquair Dickson of the estate. But Blaikie and his seconder, R.C. Thomson the market gardener, got the reduction passed. It was a shabby business.

The same mean attitude appeared shortly after when Miss Agnes Henderson, the assistant teacher, got her parchment and asked for £10 increase. Blaikie and Thomson cut it to £5. By September 1889 the Board having considered the Scotch Education Department's circular on relief of school fees agreed to abolish fees. Consequently Mr Matthew had to be given £104–12–5 in lieu of fees. In 1890 a piano was bought.

When the Roman Catholic priest, Father Forsyth, applied in April 1891 for the use of the school for divine service once a month on Sunday morning the request was granted but the Free Church minister asked that his dissent be minuted. The following May when the Public Hall became available the Board hastened to advise Father Forsyth to hold his services there.

A parent's claim for his daughter's ulster and cape being taken from the school porch fell on deaf ears in 1893.

A move by the County Council to start Dairy classes created some interest. The need for more accommodation was met in 1894–95 with the building of a new school on the site where today a tablet inscribed "Rebuilt 1894" records the fact. During the rebuilding classes were held in the Public Hall. The glowing report of H.M. Inspector in 1896 must have delighted "Daddy", sometimes affectionately called "Cocky", Matthew.

The last master to preside over the young in Corstorphine as a Midlothian village came in 1902. When he died in 1924 he was buried in the old churchyard beside the kirk. George W.T. McGown published his Bible Class talks *Scottish Heroes of the Faith* and *Ten Bunyan Talks*. He was also responsible for *A Primer of Burns*. Mr McGown was the Bard of a group of Edinburgh teachers who spent happy hours fishing the Yarrow. They lodged at the Gordon Arms where in the evenings they smoked and talked of trout in the warm glow of Mrs Beattie's lamp with its red shade. This gave the group its name – Brethren of the Red Lamp.

When in 1920 Mr McGown published a book of verse it was titled – *Under The Red Lamp*. One section of this volume is poems on the 1914–18 war and two local boys are remembered: First Lieutenant Athol Robertson and John Paterson (Jacky). Another of the schoolmaster's poems was his account of the murder of James Forrester at the Sycamore Tree – *A Ballad of Corstorphine Castle*.

In 1901 the school leaving age was fixed at 14. The national Qualifying Examination began in 1903 in order to assess which pupils were fit for secondary school education. Pupils took the test at the age of 11. This was the examination known to the bairns as the "Qualy". They took it in their stride, for better or for worse, blissfully unaware of the concept of juvenile stress or pre-examination nerves. To meet the needs of others in the 12–14 age group a Supplementary Class was formed in 1905. That year Corstorphine pupils who gained bursaries went off to Edinburgh secondary schools. In 1909 there were 14 leavers who took their talents to Boroughmuir, Gillespie's, Queen Street Ladies College, and Heriot's.

Further enlargement of the school premises took place in 1912 when a central hall, a sewing room, a cookery and laundry room, a workshop, and two classrooms were provided. The Rev. James Fergusson proposed a swimming bath but it received no support. However there was no opposition to flying the school flag on St. Andrew's Day. The Headmaster was allowed two afternoons weekly free of teaching to give more time to administration. Dr Malcolmson had the use of a classroom for his ambulance lectures. A boy who stole money got "six of the best" described as "stripes". Pre-1914 physical education for boys took the shape of drill every Friday morning. Armed with wooden guns the lads marched to the playing of the pipes by the Janitor, an old pipe major of the Seaforths.

In 1913 the Scotch Education Department's recognition of the Infants as a separate department led to a confrontation between Mr McGown and the Infant Mistress, Miss Mason. When he came into her department she told him to leave and not to deal with her staff. Within a few months the lady resigned on the ground of ill health. The Board were not amused. They challenged McGown over his attitude to Miss Mason and warned him that they might have second thoughts about his position. Miss Mason was asked to reconsider her resignation but she had no wish to continue. Mrs Graham from Broughton Elementary School filled the vacancy. Typewriters for evening classes were hired at 7/6 per month per machine from Leishman and Hughes, Edinburgh.

By 1914 five of the ten teachers were graduates. The school roll was 480. The headmaster's garden was laid out as a school garden to give the pupils practical instruction. Transport was arranged for children coming from Gogar. Those from outlying districts could get soup for a penny per day. The Board stated clearly that the cost of meals was not to be charged against rates.

War coloured the school scene in 1915. One of the masters, James Blyth, joined the Motor Cycle Machine Gun section and returned, invalided, in 1918. The school hall was let to the Corstorphine Women's First Aid Corps for ambulance drill. Insurance of the premises against aircraft risks was taken but the Board did not think it necessary to insure against bombardment.

Early in 1916 the school hall was used for drilling Derby recruits: these were men who volunteered for war service under Lord Derby's scheme. Each man on enlisting was given a florin. When the war was over the school set up in its hall its own sad, impressive Roll of Honour.

The cookery room in 1916 got its first gas cooker. In 1917 when John Jordan's motor business which served the local children went out of business the SMT undertook the transport at a cost to the Board of sixpence per week per child. Though only children under ten years of age were given free transport the Board had the humanity to include a lame lad. Of the 714 school age children in the parish 452 attended Corstorphine School, 251 went to Edinburgh schools or private establishments, and the rest were apparently evading the law.

By 1919 the Board knew that their days of independence were numbered for when Corstorphine was absorbed into Edinburgh in 1920 Corstorphine School became an Edinburgh school. Over the years since then the school in the High Street has added to its reputation. The local spirit has been maintained in the varying designs of the school badge incorporating the Forrester hunting horn. The school song, words by P.A. Falconer, Headmaster 1934–44, and music by W. Craig Cairns, son of the Edinburgh choir master, William Cairns, whose charitable "Children's Choir" gave so much pleasure and financial aid in Edinburgh from 1901 to the Second World War, recalls the tradition *of The Cross of Fine Gold*. The school building was extended in 1952 when the adjoining Mansion House was taken down.

Before and after 1945 housing development and the growing population necessitated the erection of primary schools – Balgreen, Stenhouse, Murrayburn, Carrickvale, Broomhouse, Drumbrae, Clermiston, Fox Covert, Gyle.

A maypole in Corstorphine School rear (north) playground c.1918. The shed has since been demolished but the Manse Street houses are still there. *(PB46)*

Corstorphine did not have a secondary school till Forrester school was opened in 1960. Then followed St. Augustine's adjoining Forrester. Later Craigmount was built beside the old Craigs Road leading to the West.

The lack of local secondary education in Corstorphine pre 1939 led to an educational divide, some parents sending their children to the City Merchant Company schools and others taking advantage of the excellent facilities provided by the local authority at Broughton and Boroughmuir. Now at the end of the century the trend is towards an increasing use of the local secondary schools. Fortunately brain power is not the prerogative of public or private schools. A long road has been travelled since George Forrester's school was recorded in the kirk Session register of 1646.

FEMALE EDUCATION

In 1824 Dr Robert Morehead, one of the ministers of the Episcopal church, St. Paul's Chapel, York Place, Edinburgh, had a summer residence at the north east of Kirk Loan opposite Clermiston Brae. He described Corstorphine as "a quiet English-looking village with an old Gothic church and a clergy man who is a great Hebrew scholar". Until 1832 when he removed to Easington in Yorkshire, Dr Morehead read Hebrew with the minister Dr Scot. Mrs Morehead contributed to Scottish education by establishing in February 1829 a female school: "the girls of the village were rough and neglected and neither taught morals or manners nor sewing and knitting for in those days there was no female teacher in the parish schools".

A survey was made by Mr Stewart, a home missionary in the Canongate. He made frequent "walks to Corstorphine" to find out how acceptable the idea of a female school was to the villagers. A list was made of children who would attend such a school and Mr Stewart "was fortunate in the course of his pilgrimage to meet with Mrs Ferguson of the Gyle who hospitably received him in her house and gave him the warmest encouragement to proceed in his mission."

Dr Morehead, however, was worried lest Dr Scot might resent this apparent interference of Episcopalians in parish matters. But Dr Scot was "anxious to promote every plan" which would benefit his people "from whatever quarter it might originate". In fact Dr Scot had written a "recommendatory letter" to accompany the notice which was sent to the heritors and the parish householders.

At once Sir Robert Liston at Gogar donated £5. Among other gentry contributing were Mr Christie, accountant, his partner Mr Keith of Corstorphine Hill, the ladies of Mr Keith's household, Sir Alexander and Lady Keith of Ravelston, Mr Ramsay of Barnton, Lord MacKenzie and the Hon. Mrs MacKenzie of Belmont, Mr Sharpe of Hoddam, Sir Robert and Lady Keith Dick, Lady Dundas of Beechwood, the Trustees of Mr Watson of Saughton, Mrs Maitland Gibson of Gogar House, Mr Johnston, Mrs Jones of Saughton Hall, Dr Alison (author of the essay on *Taste* and fellow minister of Dr Morehead at St. Paul's), and Francis Jeffrey of Craigcrook. Village contributors included Mr Girdwood, Mr Walter Wallace, Mr Cuddie, Mrs John Simpson, Dr Scot, and Mrs Binnie of West Craigs.

In selecting a teacher the organisers looked for someone able to do more than teach sewing and reading: they wanted someone to train the girls in "good principles", "neat and orderly habits", "respectable and civil carriage", "courtesy and decorum of manners", "habits of delicacy and cleanliness which used to be thought too much disregarded in this part of the Island but with which our Southern neighbours find now that every day they have less occasion to reproach us".

The lady who met all these requirements to bring civilisation to Corstorphine was Mrs Bonner from Berwick. The site of this school may have been the old parish school at the north east of Kirk Loan near Dr Morehead's house. Furnishing a room and kitchen house for Mrs Bonner meant providing a tent bedstead, a feather bed, bolster and pillows, English and Scots blankets, a quilt, a chest of drawers, a mahogany table, a washstand with blue crockery, a dressing glass, curtains, two rush chairs, kitchen towels, quantities of check gingham, sheeting, bed lace, and pack sheet. Among the items supplied by the ironmongers were brass candlesticks, table knives, a Britannia metal teapot, a tea boiler, a tea caddy, a coffee pot, and a corkscrew. Other items bought were ashets, wine glasses, a small "batchelor's" oven, a carpet, and eight mahogany chairs.

Fitting up the schoolroom involved the local wright, Andrew Henderson, in providing benches, tables, desks, cloak pins, gravel and a little outhouse. Other supplies were a square box with 80 divisions and 200 balls, knitting needles, pencil cases, and linen for pinafores for 70 children. Text books were the First and Second Instruction Book, Johnson's Dictionary, and a ready reckoner.

In 1830 Mrs Bonner's yearly salary was £30. Fees were 1/6 a quarter. The cost of running the school for the first year was £116–2–10 which included £45 for furniture for the lady and her expenses in coming to Edinburgh.

The venture was quickly seen to be successful for in a few weeks "a very marked change was observed in the demeanour of the children. The little girls became neater in their dress and more courteous in their salutations ... Even the boys ... caught a good deal of the contagion and in the bye lanes and corners where they were not likely to he objects of ridicule ... might be seen touching their caps and making their bows."

In addition to the Scriptures the pupils were taught arithmetic and writing. Lady Dundas of Beechwood gave a spinning wheel and Mrs Ferguson of Gyle "in true Scottish spirit" showed the girls how to spin. The village schoolmaster, Mr Simpson, sent two of his daughters to be trained "in the finer arts of needlework".

In June 1830 there was an exhibition of work done by the girls and Morehead reported to his patrons. He began by speaking of the pleasure he and his wife had experienced since living in Corstorphine – "the great improvements in the external aspects of the village", "the neat houses and gardens which were coming, in the room of the decayed and inconvenient cottages and, at last, the old ruinous church assuming an enlarged and embellished form".

The raising of the quarterly fee to 2/6 caused Dr Morehead to express the opinion that "Education is not a Boon of that kind which ought to be thrown before those who might make some exertion to pay for it but would rather spend their money on less useful or worthy objects and it is apt to be despised by those who are not required to give reasonable remuneration for so precious a prize".

Dr Morehead wished to include in the management of the school local people with knowledge of the local situation – the minister, the Session, some of the ladies – and they would be able to report who would like to send their children to school but had not the means to do so. He also wanted to ensure that the education given was suited to the needs of the parish and the "training of that most important and interesting class of inhabitants – its future wives and mothers". For the boys there was the parochial school which Dr Morehead described as "that old and excellent institution engrafted upon the Church of Scotland".

A feature of the school that was particularly noted was the library, a great part of which had once formed the collection of "an individual of this parish, of humble rank." This library had passed to the Edinburgh Gratis Sabbath School Society who, in turn, entrusted it to Dr Morehead for the use of the school. Mr Jeffrey of Craigcrook presented some volumes to the collection. Among the visitors to the school was Mr Wilderspin, an educationalist interested in infant teaching, who had devised teaching methods to attract the very young by using balls and pictures. A set of these teaching aids was presented by Mrs L'Amy living at Gogar so that "Mrs Bonner could immediately apply these pieces of ingenious mechanism to the instruction of the youngest child."

While out walking in the village on summer evenings Mrs Morehead saw that the boys seemed to have nothing to do to occupy their leisure. She decided to have them taught to knit stockings. The help of a local woman, Mrs Smith, was enlisted and soon the Corstorphine boys, "even some of Mr Simpson's crack scholars" thought it "no disgrace to take the wires into their hands."

When the knitting lessons were going on in Mrs Smith's house parables from the gospels, hymns and psalms were read to the students. Sometimes Scott's *Tales of a Grandfather* were read, an activity which Dr Morehead believed would have delighted Sir Walter – "recalling to the boys of Corstorphine the contrast of the old stirring and bloody times of their country while they are sitting quietly knitting". Of this youthful industry Dr Morehead wrote: "I suppose I shall wear nothing else but Corstorphine hose for the remaining of my life."

Even after leaving Scotland to live in Yorkshire, Dr and Mrs Morehead maintained their interest in Corstorphine. In April 1837 when Dr Morehead was staying with his relations, the Jeffreys of Craigcrook, he found himself invited to the examination day at Corstorphine Female School. He described the scene in a letter to his wife: "The children, about forty eight very nice-looking clean tidy girls ... Mr Horne (parish minister) and a Mr Wilkie, a clergyman from Edinburgh, occupying chairs in front of the children and behind them, on a bench, the elite of Corstorphine and neighbourhood – the Misses Dunsmures, Miss Crawford, the Flemings, Mrs Horne, Mrs Chapman (Broomhouse Farm) ... the children did uncommonly well ... the ministers were much pleased ... Mr Horne said he must announce to the children that this was Dr Morehead under whose auspices the school had been formed ... I said ... Mrs Morehead had with great zeal and perseverance had it established ... of all the sights which I had seen since my return to my native country, the spectacle of this day had been the most interesting ... the whole ended with a distribution of prizes, consisting of elegant silk work-bags, pin cushions and other works of the kind from the ladies. In short, my dear Margaret, your school is in prodigious favour ... I saw too sons of our old neighbours such as David Cuddie who is now swelled out to a great fat man ... Agnes whom you tried to make a good cook has now got a most smart-looking house, quite an elegant hotel ... I drive up in a dashing curricle...to old Mrs Keith's who is in great preservation at the age of eighty four."

When Mrs Bonner became too old to teach, the heritors superannuated her by paying her salary and house rent. She died in 1877. The introduction of a female assistant for the Industrial Department of the village school ended the need for Mrs Bonner's type of school.

Dr Morehead was an interesting character in the Edinburgh of Sir Walter Scott and Christopher North. He was Episcopal Dean of Edinburgh, 1818–32, and cousin of Francis Jeffrey of Craigcrook. One of his sons, Robert, had a successful business career. He began with a Glasgow insurance broker, progressed to being a cotton manufacturer of shawl and zebra cloth in Glasgow, and then in 1840 he was appointed manager of the Scottish Australia Company. In July 1841 he arrived in Sydney.

The Moreheads, father and son, were active in a period (1820–1846) noted for Scottish emigration to Australia. Dr Morehead, as editor of the *Scots Magazine* in the 1820's published articles strongly supporting emigration to Australia. The emigration of Corstorphine folk to Australia in 1841 may have been another Morehead influence on the life of the village.

Dr Morehead had some poetic leanings and Scott used to quote to his visitors at Abbotsford a couplet by Morehead and then ask the authorship:

"Calm slept the clouds on cloven Eildon laid
And distant Melrose peeped from leafy shade."

A Morehead scheme which was abortive arose from an idea he had when walking between Corstorphine and Edinburgh in 1825. It was to produce a cheap journal to instruct the lower orders. He approached Constable who, however, was too deeply involved otherwise to take up the proposal.

Dr and Mrs Morehead were in the tradition of school patrons depicted in Scottish art by Thomas Faed. His painting *The Patron and the Patroness' Visit To the Village School* (Dundee Museums and Art Galleries) is alive with detail. The dominie, not young, with spectacles on nose, is calling the patron's attention to the barefooted bairns standing in front of him displaying their reading skills. At one end of the room a boy's attention is taken up with something he sees outside: at the other end the dunce stands cap on head while a friend seizes the chance to chalk on the blackboard. Others are enjoying private ploys. The black boy behind the lady is probably her personal attendant. Thomas Faed came to Edinburgh in 1843 and stayed till 1852 when he left for London. One of his Edinburgh pleasures was walking over Corstorphine Hill.

Mrs Bonner's type of school was painted by the Victorian artist Alfred Rankley in *The Dames School* (Christopher Wood Gallery, London: Bridgeman Art Library). Here all is neatness and order while the mistress, a motherly figure in frilled cap, teaches the alphabet with a child at her knee.

OTHER SCHOOLS

Mr Simpson, the schoolmaster, about 1840 noted that there were three private schools in the village. The non-parochial schools were private ventures with various designations and varying standards – the sewing school, the dame school, the adventure school, the private school. Some were exclusively for girls; some were mixed establishments. Needlework, knitting, cookery and some or all of the 3Rs were taught depending on the education of the teacher which might he almost non-existent or more or less satisfactory.

In the 1760's Mary Liston at Larbour (Calder Road / Wester Hailes Road) was teaching poor scholars. About 1770 the sewing mistress, Janet Stewart, later convicted for infanticide, had a schoolroom at the north end of Kirk Loan where she also lived. A Mrs Smith had a dame school which ended about 1829 when Mrs Bonner came to Mrs Morehead's school.

When Mrs Smith taught is not recorded but there was a small, tiled schoolroom on the north side of St. John's Road opposite Manse Road. At the Disruption in 1843 the Free Church used this schoolroom for services. Dr Guthrie from Edinburgh frequently preached there. It became known as the Free Church School. In time James Lind, the baker, had it as a flour store. When shops east of St. Ninian's were built the schoolroom was taken down.

The adventure school which became a thorn in the flesh to the School Board was run by Miss Jane Maitland, also associated with the Female Industrial Home. She set up her school in Manse Road on ground a little north of the south west

Pupils of the Misses Gun's School at 18 St John's Road c.1923. Kenneth McKenzie, after whom the McKenzie Room in the Corstorphine Heritage Centre was named following his generous bequest to the Trust in 1997, is 4th from the left in the second back row. *(PB1030)*

corner. The school ran from 1864 to 1889. Miss Maitland lived at various Corstorphine addresses as well as Manse Road. For a while she boarded with the Thomson family at Gibson Lodge.

Miss Maitland's schoolroom had an area of 294 square feet. The roll was 45 of which the average attendance was 32. In 1877 the School Board requested Miss Maitland to close down. When she refused the Board wrote to her again expressing the hope that she would not accept any child over the age of six. Two years later the Board asked for a list of those attending her school and a monthly return of absentees.

Then in 1885 the Board arranged with Professor Laurie to

examine Miss Maitland's school under the terms of the 1872 Act. He reported that the school was not satisfactory, "a mere refuge for those who find the fees, discipline and rules of the Public School disagreeable to them". The lady had 17 pupils, 13 girls and 4 boys, of ages from 6 to 13. Eventually the Board got Miss Maitland's school closed about 1889 when she was aged 75.

A private school in Gladstone Place run by the Misses Eliza and Nicholas Dow with a roll of 12 gave up in 1875. Miss Johnston's school was examined and found satisfactory in 1885. The Watson family in 1891 at Bellevue, Forrester Road, taught a variety of subjects. Miss Jean specialised in English and Music and called her school a "seminary". Her father taught Writing and Arithmetic. Her sister, Mary, offered Language and Drawing. When Corstorphine joined Edinburgh in 1920 the Misses Gun were active with small children in their private school at Virginia Bank.

PLAYGROUND AND STREET NAMES

Playing games has always been an essential part of a child's life and the school playground has had an educational function of considerable importance. In the playground of the school in the High Street around 1914 *Cuddie Weichts* was a popular activity for which strong back and an ability to jump were needed. The cuddies had to bend down and take the weight of those who jumped over their backs. *Spinning a Peerie* (top from the French poire indicating the shape of the toy) demanded dexterity of the wrist. Boys' pockets were usually filled with marbles, always referred to by their Scots name *bools*. The game of bools had its own terminology – Glessies were highly prized glass striped balls. The Knuckler was used for playing the marble off the thumb knuckle and Plunkie involved using a semi-circular hole at the foot of a wall. Backie meant standing three feet from the playground wall, bending down and playing by looking between the legs. Another popular game was *Sookers*. This needed a small piece of leather with a centre hole through which went a length of string knotted to prevent it slipping through. The leather was wetted in some handy dub and then trampled on the road or on anything that could lift, such as a water toby. The fun was in applying the suction power of the leather.

In the evening, especially a long summer evening, the village street was the place for *Kick the Can*. A boy or a girl termed "het" (i.e. hot) shut eyes and counted to 100 while the others dispersed to hiding places. When the "het" person opened his eyes he had to find one of his chums. Once a boy was spotted the "het" called out his name, ran to the old can that had been placed on the road, kicked it down the street and rejoined his friends. The test of ability was to prevent the boy who had been seen getting to the can and kicking it before "het" could do so. It was a noisy game, not popular with older folks in nearby houses.

A *girr* or gird was a large, slim, iron hoop made by the blacksmith for a few pennies. To use it a cleek was needed. The cleek was a short straight piece of iron shaped at one end to guide and propel the girr along the road. The user had to maintain an even balanced speed for otherwise the girr wobbled and fell to the ground.

The girls enjoyed a monopoly in the arts of *Skipping Ropes* and *Peevers*. Whenever winter passed peever beds appeared chalked on the streets and pavements. The skill was to hop from one square to another without standing on the chalk lines and to move the peever forward at the same time. The peever could be a simple round disused tin of shoe blacking or a grand circle of marble or granite. When Dr John Oliver of Moray House College in 1954 chanced one evening to pass a peever bed chalked out in the solemn precincts of Parliament Square, Edinburgh, he was inspired to write a humorous poem in which he saw the great legal dignitaries, the Lord President and the Lord Justice Clerk, competing at peevers. The Lord Justice Clerk won, taunting his opponent with "Ye're no worth a dawm at the Peevers".

If a Corstorphine Brueghel had drawn his village children at their games he would have caught their excitement and pleasure as did the 16th century Flemish painter in his *Young Folk at Play*. Time and place may vary but children's games are largely universal. Corstorphine bairns, like Brueghel's Flemings, knew the fun of Leap Frog, spinning tops, marbles against a wall, and trundling a hoop. The joy of playing games is something the school cannot really teach: it is an experience that bairns in all generations find for themselves in the playground and now to a lesser degree in the street because of modern traffic hazards.

Chapter 8

LAW AND ORDER

JUSTICE AYRES

After the death of James V in 1542 Justice Ayres (circuit courts) largely fell into abeyance but under the Regency of Morton between 1573 and 1577 there was a revival mainly in the Lothians and the Borders. They served the useful purpose of bringing in, through fines, sums of money for the Treasury. The offenders, appearing in Edinburgh, were generally tenants and cotters involved in such activities as supplying provisions to the rebel forces of Kirkcaldy of Grange holding out in Edinburgh Castle for Mary Queen of Scots.

A group of Corstorphine folk in 1576 were fined from £10 to forty shillings for dealing with the rebels and breaching the regulations for the sale of malt. The offenders were James and William Cleghorne, Andrew Ranken, Alexander Ramsay with his servant Thomas Gibson, James Scott in Clermiston, William Henderson, Christian Thomson, wife of Patrick Easton, and Alexander Murray. Thomas Baillie in Meadowfield and Andrew Greg in Corstorphine Hill were guilty of "intercommuning" with the rebels. James Cleghorne in the West Craigs was fined £10–6–8 for opposing the supporters of King James at the Battle of Langside in 1568 where Mary Queen of Scots was defeated.

BARON COURTS: SAUGHTON AND CORSTORPHINE

At baron courts tenants could seek justice in civil disputes with neighbours: criminal offences were subject to fines, imprisonment or death. The Saughton area in the 16th century came under the jurisdiction of the Court of the Regality and Barony of Broughton which met at the Canongate Tolbooth. The court book recorded in 1569 that David Michelsoun charged with theft "within the toun of Sauchtoun" agreed "of his awin frie motive will to be baneist" and never to return till he satisfied the indwellers there.

The same year Gelis Lokhart of Leith was in trouble for owing money to William Henderson in Corstorphine who had supplied her with "ane mask of grund malt". Then in 1570 when John Aikman in Corstorphine lent Elizabeth Sclater £48 the baillies meeting in the Canongate Tolbooth accepted William Kintraa burgess as her cautioner.

In 1598 Margaret Smith of Gogar had a busy, criminal weekend. On Saturday she was banished from Edinburgh for the theft of clothes and the next day she broke into the home of George Melville in Canongate where she was disturbed before she could take anything away. Then on Monday she stole clothes from the house of Francis Brundie, a Frenchman. Her career came to an end on Wednesday when she was given the death sentence.

George Wilkie in Saughtonhall was murdered in 1592. William Barker, whose father Andrew lived at the Water of Leith (Dean Village) was charged and acquitted.

In October 1596 at Hallow E'en cattle thieves Weir and Thomson, acting on orders from Thomas Lowrie, weaver, went by night to the Craigs of Corstorphine, stole two oxen, one black, the other brown, belonging to Archibald Greiff, and drove them by the Lang Gaitt (Princes Street / George Street) to the sheepfold at Craigengalt (Calton). There John Aitken, a weaver in the Pleasance, kept the beasts till Lowrie slaughtered them. For this Lowrie was given the death sentence. The others were whipped through the Canongate and their goods were forfeited.

The 17th century court was usually held in the forenoon at the Parkhead of Saughton. In 1691 when Adam Erskine, mealmaker, complained that Robert Alison, wright, had not dealt fairly over a firlot of meal the baron baillie found Alison guilty. On 28th May 1694 the baillie's work was to list the people liable to pay the government poll tax. The December meeting was concerned with payment for "muck upon a plough of land".

James Watson, the laird, in October 1696, complained that his tenants were not paying their kain dues. John Clerk, writer, who was acting as judge ordered the outstanding kain to he paid in a money equivalent. In addition he decreed that overdue rents were to be paid at once and repairs were to be done by the tenants to their houses as required in the terms of lease.

The rotation of the crops was not to be altered.

At the same time James Easton, tenant, was summoned to appear at the "manor place of Saughton" to explain what he had done with the crops that his deceased father owed Watson. Easton admitted having 4 bolls of oats ground at Stenhouse Mills but of that a quantity had been given to the estate herd. Some oat and pease straw he had taken to the Edinburgh market. The rest of the crop was still in the laird's barnyard.

The dispute dragged on to the next year when Easton's servant, Thomas Allan, was charged with raiding Watson's stacks in the barnyard. At the sitting of the baron court a warrant was produced signed by Lord Forrester for Allan to be brought before the Justices of the Peace. Accordingly he was taken to the prison at Corstorphine to await trial. In a few days, however, he escaped.

Andrew Dewar, the constable, was given a warrant in May 1697 to arrest Allan along with David Easton, brother to James, and another servant, Christina Greig, as all were implicated in the grain theft. Another warrant was issued for another accomplice, Thomas Craw in Outhouse, Kaimes (Liberton).

The laird was not happy about Allan's escape. He interrogated Dewar. Watson wanted to know if Dewar had been pressurised to free Allan or if he had given the key to anyone. He also asked who had spoken from the kirkyard to the prisoner shut up in the kirk tower. Allan's wife was also questioned about the stolen corn and about her husband resetting what David Easton had taken. She was asked who had helped Thomas Craw, employed by David Easton, to lay the crop on the horse and carry it away "in the night time".

The Eastons appear to have been the culprits. By the end of 1697 Thomas Allan who was then living at Swanston paid Alexander Alexander what he owed for bread and drink which Alexander had provided while Allan was imprisoned at Corstorphine. The baron officer in 1733 was John Currie who was paid in meal. His successor was John Mitchell, tenant, Broomhouse.

After the Forty Five the government, as a move to curbing the influence of landowners over their tenants, passed an Act in 1747 for abolishing heritable jurisdictions. From then the administration of justice was to be done by Crown officials, sheriffs and their deputes. Landowners presented claims for compensation to the Court of Session for their loss of power.

James Watson, "Baillie of the regality over the lands of Saughton, part of the regality of Broughton", claimed £600. The claim does not appear to have been sustained.

In the 18th century baron courts fell into desuetude as their functions were taken over by other courts. For historical pageants or ceremonial purposes the office of Baron Bailie, without power, has been on occasion revived in the past century. The present holder of the superiority of Corstorphine which was sold in 1988 may, if he wishes, continue to hold a baron court. The Baron court of Corstorphine met at the collegiate church with the baron or his bailie presiding. There were usually three Head Courts held at Yule, Easter and Whitsun with intermediate sittings as required. Lists were made of the vassals (people holding land not as out-and-out owner but conditionally on annual payment of a feu duty) who were bound to attend the court to assist in the business. Absentees were fined. Petty debt, theft, drunkenness, slaughter, and disputes over cattle and land were routine business.

At Corstorphine the kirk tower served as the local prison. Persons convicted of breach of peace were imprisoned till they paid 4/– Scots for their release. Anyone kept more than one night had to pay an additional payment for every twenty four hours of detention. In 1604 Thomas Johnstoun complained to the Privy Council that he was held in prison in the kirk of Corstorphine but he had committed no crime. Harry Aikman in Broomhouse, the baron bailie, and Matthew Hadden, the court officer, had imprisoned Johnstoun. The Privy Council ordered Aikman to appear before them but he failed to do so and, presumably, Johnstoun was freed.

On occasion the Session called on the baron court to support their enactments. When Janet Alexander in 1683 did not repay the money she was due to the church the baron bailie was "required to give ye Session justice against Janet". Local concerns involving local personalities evidently provided the women of the village with a popular meeting point for John Benny, the court officer in 1691, had to get power from the Laird to exact a fine of six shillings and eight pence on any woman disturbing the court proceedings. William Wilson, the schoolmaster, brought claims against Thomas Menzies, the litster, and Thomas McConchie his predecessor in the school. Regulations about drinking beer in the town of Corstorphine were issued to retailers of ale. David Morisone got into trouble over payment for "Gibisones Aiker" which was possibly the land designated on the 1777 village map as "Gibies Yard" (close to the north west corner of Saughton Road North).

Failure to produce receipts for payment of feu duty led to Thomas Baillie being fined. James Alexander, however, could show the court that he had paid his meadow rent. An acre of George Girdwood's land had been assigned by Lord Forrester to Major Murray and Girdwood had to agree that he had paid no rent "to rent ye Major as yett". The business of payment for the house possessed by Elizabeth Muire was referred to Lord Forrester. Some of the debts were outstanding payments in meal and bear. For his house James Walker paid a boll of meal and kain hens as well as £8 Scots. In January 1692 Robert Oliphant, the baxter, admitted he owed rent on his bakehouse in the Huntingtoun of Corstorphine. Apparently he took exception to pressure from the Baron Court for by the end of the year he was again before the court charged with deforcement – assaulting an officer when doing his duty.

Among those who acted as Baron Bailie in Corstorphine in times past were: John Stanhop 1491 / William Cleghorne 1500 / Harry Aikman 1604 / James Haldan 1638 / Samuel Veitche 1648 / John Livingston c.1650 / John Swinton pre 1665 / Cuthbert Nilson 1668 / David Heriot 1679, 1703 / William Cathcart 1681 / Thomas Baillie 1665,1667,1682 / Thomas Forrester 1684 / Duncan Robertson 1691, 1692 / James Murray 1696 / James Adamson c.1699 / David Howison and Andrew Deuchar 1709 / James Hamilton 1730 / Andrew Garvie 1741.

BURLAW COURTS

In addition to the Baron Court there was the Burlaw Court the members being chosen from the feuars. The Burlawmen or Birleymen were concerned with regulating agricultural matters.

Villagers had the right of common pasturage and quarrels often arose over the number of animals using the pasture. Cattle and sheep were numbered in proportion to the soumes. One soume could be one cow or six big sheep while a horse could be two soumes.

The Outfield was the land occupied by the tenants in common as pasture. Each tenant was entitled to "soume" or pasture in summer on the Outfield in proportion to the number and kinds of cattle he was able to "roum" or fodder in winter on his share of the Infield which was the best land.

In Corstorphine in 1692 the Birliemen were James Johnstone, John Girdwood elder, James Patersone younger, and John Leishman younger who swore to be true "betwixt master and tennent and between tennent and tennent". A roll was made of feuars and their soumes for pasture within the "meikle myre, Hermiston myre and moore, and Cramond Moore". Their obligations were also set down. They had "to keep up sufficient bridges about the place of pasturage and to cleanse and keep fenceable the stanks or ponds surrounding the same".

The Girdwood property in 1824 – the west half of Templelands – carried the right of pasturage "of half a horse and half a cow". Dr Johnstone's property (Corstorphine House area) in 1815 had "the pasturage of two soumes of cattle".

JUSTICES OF THE PEACE

Keeping the law was also dealt with by the Justices of the Peace set up in the opening years of the 17th century. To carry out their orders they had a constable. In Corstorphine in 1684 he was John Kilpatrick. That year the Justices banished Florence Lauriston "ane flagicious contumatious person".

James Easton, farmer, Saughton, complained in January 1687 that John Wood, a lodger, had gone off "betymes in the morning" with blankets, a "cod" (pillow), and a covering as well as two shirts and a cloak. In August Wood came before the Justices at Corstorphine and admitted the theft of the bedding but not the other items.

When arrested Wood had some money and a horse laden with cheese and butter. The horse belonged to Wood but the butter and the cheese were the property of Robert Wyseman. The Justices ordered the horse to be sold and confiscated the cash before liberating Wood.

Another case concerned a horse stolen from James Watson. Eleis of Stenhouse Mills, one of the Justices, on 7th August questioned David Crawford of Gogar Mill about his dealings in horses. Crawford admitted that he was at Innerleithen Fair on 1st August where he sold a grey mare that was not his. When asked where he got the animal he replied "in the south upon lee ground in the night time".

Robert Wallace, formerly employed by Watson to look after the horses, described one in detail – dark grey, a little whiter in the face "which some call a star", and "well legged". Other witnesses told of the strange behaviour of the minister of Corstorphine's servant, Andrew Rodger alias Wallace. He was seen in the month of July acting suspiciously at Saughton.

John Tait saw him, whip and stick in hand, after sunset loitering between his barn and the stone dyke. When challenged Wallace said he was on his way to visit the herd who had married the minister's nurse. Thomas Clark, the herd, confirmed that Wallace had called between 8 and 9, adding that when he left he could hear Wallace "beating the road with his stick".

But the minister's man had not returned to Corstorphine. Next morning after Adam Erskine, the mealmaker, had gone off to the mill between 4 and 5, his wife Helen Leishman was disturbed by Wallace coming to the door wanting ale which she refused to give. Agnes Girdwood saw him at 6 o'clock sleeping beside a whin bush. Later he gave her a halfpenny for a chopin of milk.

There is no evidence to connect Robert Wallace and Rodger alias Wallace but someone had the intention to steal the laird's horse and did so. A generation later an Andrew Crawford at Gogar had a servant Robert Wallace who married a Gogar girl, Catherine Lyon. There seems to have been some link between the Gogar Crawfords and the Corstorphine Wallaces.

Notes of a thieving incident, possibly about 1697, concerned an unmarried woman. When living with James Lees in Muttonhole she stole the key of a chest belonging to the lass who sold ale there and took money from the chest. She also helped herself to shirts belonging to her landlady. Then she robbed her grandfather at Currie of about £16. She fled from Currie towards Corstorphine but on the way was caught by James Lees and some others who took the shirts and some money. Thomas Murray, servant to Widow Baylie, witnessed this rough justice. When the thief got to Corstorphine she spent some of the money but grandfather followed and claimed what remained.

The kirk Session, on occasions, had their power reinforced by the Justices. In 1712 the Session heard that John Yorston, son to Edward Yorston in West Craigs, had been drinking in time of divine service in George Pinkerton's house. Accordingly they called him to appear before them. However the

Justices of the Peace saved the Session bother by having the constable arrest Yorston for drunkenness and other "irregularities". Recalcitrants who refused to meet the Session after repeated warnings were liable to be referred to the magistrate who had power to imprison.

CRIMINAL MATTERS

Andro Rewll, weaver in Corstorphine, was charged in July 1597 with the death of his son. The twelve year old boy was struck by the lead part of a sword pommel somewhere between Corstorphine and Edinburgh. The blow was under "the vayne organ" (the jugular vein). The father was sentenced to be taken to the Castlehill of Edinburgh and there his head to be struck from his body. His goods became the property of the crown.

Thomas Hodge who lived at the Mill of Houston in West Lothian was molested several times in 1604 by Robert Ross. Again in March 1605 Ross attacked Hodge between Edinburgh and the Water of Leith. A week later on Monday 25th March, the principal weekly market day in Edinburgh, Ross with some friends overtook Hodge and his companions beyond the toun of Corstorphine at the East Craigs. There Ross and his party, well armed and on horseback, attacked Hodge's company with drawn swords, whingers and batons. They were knocked off their horses and Thomas got six or seven bloody wounds on his head as well as a broken right arm "put the same furth of joyntour". After taking the swords and whingers belonging to Hodge and his friends Ross's party also took from Hodge a purse with £20. Despite the facts the Privy Council allowed Ross to go free because Hodge and his witnesses failed to prove the charge.

In a case before the Justiciary in 1618 John Johnstoun in Corstorphine and his wife, Agnes Cleghorne, were accused of battering Bessie Home, wife of John Wattirston in Corstorphine, with a baton to the extent that she died within a few days. What the outcome of this assault was does not seem to be recorded.

Bessie Weir, servant to James Lourieson of Overgogar, confessed in January 1619 to murdering her newly born child about midnight in her master's yard. The father of the child was James Threipland in Biggar. Bessie was sentenced to death on the Castlehill of Edinburgh.

On 4th December 1629 James Crawford in Corstorphine was brought from confinement in the Tolbooth of Edinburgh to answer the charge of killing John Fairlie, younger, servant to the Marquis of Hamilton. The case was brought by Fairlie's father who lived at Fortisset in the parish of Shotts, and by his widow Janet Murehead and her only child Gawin.

Crawford, however, on the advice of his "freindis", presented a statement that he was willing to be "banisched furth of His Majesteis dominiones". He admitted the killing and promised to leave by "the first day of Merche nixtocum". This was accepted and Crawford was set free to prepare for his departure.

Fairlie's master, the Marquis of Hamilton, called by Montrose "Captain Luckless", later became the 1st Duke of Hamilton: his daughter Anne was married in Corstorphine kirk.

When the kirk Session in 1654 felt that they could not deal with the strife between Thomas Landall and William Clarkson they referred the matter "to a higher justiciary". This was because it involved "blood and bloodwyte" (riot with bloodshed).

3 Mile House now demolished, on the north side of St John's Road. This property used to incorporate a milestone indicating 3 miles to Edinburgh. [EW]

BLACK MARKET POULTRY

Black market trading was a problem for the City Fathers in the Edinburgh of August 1658 when they were presented with a petition asking for action to he taken against people who "lyes in waitt" at several places outwith the city including Corstorphine "and buyes up all the foulles and pultrie comeing to the cittie and sellis the samen" at "exorbitant prices". The Council issued regulations to allow the country people to trade freely within the town. To control unscrupulous poultrymen a price list for the poultry market had to be strictly observed.

CAPTAIN JOHN SWINTON

In 1659 Lord Forrester disponed to Captain John Swinton, merchant, burgess of Edinburgh, the dwelling house or smiddy, stable and barn with the yard lying to the south at the Loanhead of Corstorphine (Kirk Loan area Kirk Care housing). Swinton was to plant trees about the yard. James

Forrester was to have the services of the smith in making and repairing plough graith and other "necessaries for labouring" as well as having his horses shoed.

Swinton and his servant were obliged to work eight days yearly at the "winning" of the hay in the meadows of Corstorphine. Forrester made Swinton the bailie for the barony. The following year Swinton gave his wife, Margaret Cuninghame, her liferent of the property.

Four years later, 21st April 1664, Swinton stood trial for the murder of his wife. During his occupation of the Kirk Loan property Swinton set up a change house and inn which doubtless was a profitable business situated as it was close to the highway between Edinburgh and the West.

However Swinton became unfaithful to his wife, keeping company with "women of bad fame" and beating Margaret when she complained. He discontinued marital relations and ate his meals outwith his own home, keeping company with Jonet Brown, a widow in Corstorphine. Margaret appealed to the Justice of the Peace who ordered Swinton to stop visiting Jonet but the association did not stop. The women witnesses at the trial, servants to Jonet, reported what they had seen. Agnes Johnston saw them "in the Act". Helen Miller and Mary Scott who saw them in bed added a significant detail: they "heard a noise".

Swinton, influenced by Jonet Brown, decided to get rid of his wife. When he, his wife, and his lady friend were together in the house at the Loanhead he sent the servants off on false errands. Then Swinton and Brown got to work. Margaret was given "divers mortall wounds". The blood-covered body was hidden in the cellar. One of the servants, returning to the house, found the doors shut. It was sometime before Swinton came to open the door, protesting that he had been wakened from sleep. Several witnesses testified to Swinton beating his wife.

Jonet Brown was "cleanged" of the murder but Swinton was found guilty. The nature of the wounds was such that they could not have been self inflicted. The matter of adultery was referred to the Justices as there was a question of whether it was "nottour" or "simple". "Nottour" was flagrant bedding or the procreation of children.

Swinton was beheaded at the Mercat Cross of Edinburgh on 1st May 1664 and interred in Greyfriars burial ground. Lamont in his *Diary* noted the execution and commented that

Swinton had said his wife "was a scolding woman with whom he could have no peace and Satan suggesting this tentation to him, he gave place ... he wearied also of his life."

Jonet Brown was a widow. She may have been the Jean Brown who on 1st August 1661 was charged with child murder along with her midwife, Margaret Wylie. Brown at that time was designated as relict of the late George Cochran in Corstorphine, ale seller, whose house had accommodation for servants. The two women were found not guilty. They were not strangers to prison for a month earlier, 5th July 1661, they appealed to be set free, on caution of 5,000 merks, from the Tolbooth prison where they had been put on an alleged witchcraft charge.

Jonet Brown went back to Corstorphine after the Swinton trial. In the week following her lover's execution three of her servants, including Helen Miller of the trial with the sharp ears, were before the Session for unruly behaviour on the Sabbath evening. Jonet appeared before the Session in July and confessed her sin with Swinton. The Session suspended punishment until they had consulted with the Presbytery of Edinburgh. The Presbytery remitted the disciplinary action to the church who then ordered her to sit, before the congregation, dressed in sackcloth, for 25 Sabbaths. In 1669 Jonet was again before the Session for strife with Christian Lowristonne in which the offending word passed between the two women was "whoredom". Another summons to the Session later in 1669 indicates that Jonet kept an alehouse for she was "sharply rebuked" for selling drink to Lord Forrester's servants on a Sunday night when respectable folk would be abed.

Jonet was incorrigible. Again in 1673 she came to the Session but this time she was the complainer. She objected to some of the villagers saying that she kept "a baudie house". From her previous record it is more than likely that her neighbours spoke the truth.

A CONCEALED PREGNANCY

Readers of *The Heart of Midlothian* will recall that concealment of pregnancy followed by the death or disappearance of the child placed the mother in 18th century Scotland on a charge of child murder. Corstorphine had its Effie Deans. She

JANET, alias JANNY STEWART, late sewing mistress in Corstorphine, now prisoner in the Tolbooth of Edinburgh, You are indicted and accused, at the instance of JAMES MONTGOMERY, Esq; his Majesty's advocate, for his Majesty s interest: THAT, WHEREAS, by the laws of God and nature and the laws of this and all well governed realms, the crime of Parricide, or of murdering innocent children, is a crime of a high nature, and severely punishable: More particularly, by an act of the second session of the first parliament of King William and Queen Mary, entitled, ' Act anent
' murdering of children, it is enacted, ' That if any woman
' shall conceal her being with child during the whole space, and
' shall not call for, and make use of help and assistance in the birth,
' the child being found dead, or a-missing, the mother shall be
' holden and reputed the murderer of her own child; and ordains
' all criminal judges to sustain such process: And the libel being
' remitted to the knowledge of an inquest, it shall be sufficient
' ground for them to return their verdict, finding the libel proven,
' and the mother guilty of murder, though there be no appearance
' of a wound or bruise upon the body of the child.' YET TRUE IT IS AND OF VERITY, That you the said Janet, alias Janny Stewart, are guilty actor, art and part of all, or one or other of the foresaid crimes; IN SO FAR AS, upon the 14th day of the month of August last 1770, or upon one or other of the days or nights of the said month of August, or of the months of July preceding or September following, You did bring forth a living child in your own house, or lodging, in the village of Corstorphine, within the parish of Corstorphine, and county of Edinburgh, without calling for any assistance in the birth, and which child, by keeping it under your bed-cloaths, you smothered, or by some other inhuman means bereaved of its life; and thereafter you buried, or concealed your said child in a hole dug in the earth under the floor of your room, having previously lifted one of the deals or boards thereof for that purpose; and a suspicion being taken by persons in

Janny Stewart

was Janet, alias Janny, Stewart, the Corstorphine sewing teacher. As a prisoner in the Tolbooth of Edinburgh she made a full statement on 22nd August 1770 before the Sheriff-Depute.

She admitted giving birth to a child on a Tuesday morning at daybreak when she was in bed in her room below the property of Mr Moubray. Martin Moubray was one of the clerks in the General Post Office, Edinburgh. His wife who was a witness in the case was Jean Johnston, daughter of William Johnston, brewer in Corstorphine. She and her sister, Ann, wife of Mungo Ponton, farmer, Balgreen, were given by their half-brother David, brewer and portioner, ground, houses, and yards at the Loanhead (north east end Kirk Loan).

Janet thought the child was born alive but she did not take it out from under the bedclothes and so probably smothered it. One of her pupils, Janet Hay, daughter of John Hay, labourer Broomhouse, came, as usual, between 7 and 8 to light the schoolroom fire. Questioned about the father Janet replied that he was a chance acquaintance whom she met on the shore between Cramond and Leith. The child's body was found hidden below the floor boards of her room.

She said that she had disclosed her pregnancy to Elisabeth Dickson, daughter of Andrew Dickson, gardener,Dalry, near the toll on the road west out of Edinburgh for she hoped to get a room from the Dicksons when the birth was due. Her statement is signed clearly and legibly "Janny Stewart".

Neighbours, suspicious of her condition, brought the matter to light. When she was arrested Mr Chiesly, the minister, sent some women to be with her. One was Isobel Cramond, relict of Archibald Lowrieston, a local innkeeper. Her case was considered by the Court of Justiciary on 22nd February 1771 when she petitioned to be banished rather than tried and this was granted.

The magistrates of Edinburgh and the keeper of the Tolbooth were instructed to hand her over to a merchant or a ship master trading to the American plantations. From Edinburgh Janny was taken to Glasgow Tolbooth. There, in March, Patrick Colquhoun, merchant, became caution for James McLean, master of the ship *Crawford*, to transport Janet to one of the plantations in America. McLean was instructed to send a certificate to the Court of Justiciary of having landed and having handed Janet over to the American authorities within the space of a year.

OPPOSITE.
Indictment and signature of Janet Stewart, sewing mistress, Corstorphine, for child murder, 1770. *(Courtesy NAS, ref. JC26/193/2)*

Speculation is raised by Janny's statement that the child's father was someone she did not know, by her admission that she had met him a second time though, as she averred, accidentally, and for her request for banishment rather than trial. In a trial detailed evidence would be forthcoming. Was she sparing her parents social disgrace or was she deliberately shielding the father?

Whatever the truth the sewing teacher paid a stiff price for a situation about which the poet Burns some later years wrote:

"Then gently scan your brother man,
Still gentler sister woman:
Tho' they may gang a kennin wrang,
To step aside is human."

It is to be hoped that even handed Justice caught up with the other party jointly responsible for the sad affair and that Janet found a new, happier life in America.

THE MURRAYFIELD MURDER

In the month of May 1813 James Black, Borthwick's Close, in the old town of Edinburgh, was aged 17 and an unemployed slater. His friend, John McDonald, a 17 years old unemployed painter, lived with his mother in Gosford's Close.

Black who was lame in one leg wore a long, blue coat, grey breeches and a black vest. McDonald had a yellow and brown cotton neckcloth. Without work the youths were penniless, a state which McDonald proposed to remedy. He suggested to his friend that highway robbery would enable them "to live like gentlemen".

On Monday 10th May they set about buying pistols. The prices at McLaughlan in College Street and Edmonstone in the Grassmarket were too high. In the High Street, at the Royal Exchange, James Kyle, assistant to Mr Muir, hardware merchant, sold them two pistols costing twenty shillings for a down payment of nine shillings and sixpence. They also paid sixpence for a powder horn. As well as powder they bought swan or slug shot.

On Wednesday 12th May they decided to try their luck on the road to Corstorphine for Wednesday being market day there was the chance of travellers with money. Their route from the old town was by the narrow road beside the West Church poorhouse, Tobago Street where they loaded the pistols, and then by Whitehouse toll (Donaldson's Hospital) to the west.

At Coltbridge they stopped at the public house on the east side of the bridge. It was then between six and seven o'clock. Helen Binny, daughter of the landlady, showed them in to the wester room upstairs and served them with a bottle of porter and a gill of whisky. Later when they left she noticed Black putting something into the left breast of his coat. They paid eleven pence for their drink.

They lounged about outside till it was almost nine, watching a man fishing in the Water of Leith. As they walked westwards from Coltbridge McDonald told Black that there was a road nearby which they could use to get to the Queensferry Road – the road to Ravelston (Murrayfield Road). They went into a field close to the Ravelston road and while they were sitting there the Glasgow mail coach passed on its way west. At this point McDonald said it was time to move so they got over the wall on to the highway.

A little west of the Ravelston road they saw an old man approaching. McDonald said, "We'll do for him." When they came face to face McDonald asked the time. Taking his watch out the old man said, "Look for yourself. You can see better than me." But when the youth made to grasp the watch the old man drew it back. This led to a tussle in which the watch chain broke. McDonald then threatened to blow the man's brains out.

At this the man laughed, "You'll surely not do that", and pushed McDonald aside. Immediately the youths fired and their victim fell against the dyke, gradually sinking to the footpath. Quickly the ruffians rifled the body, seizing the watch, and then making off uphill by the road to Ravelston.

It was a clear, bright moonlit night. Just before they came to Ravelston House the youths stopped to wash the blood from their hands in a burn. Near Blackhall on the Ravelston quarry road where there was a crooked tree and a wheat field they hid the pistols in one of the earth ridges. They returned to the old town by way of Stockbridge and the New Town.

On Thursday McDonald was in his mother's house when the police arrested him. Black spent Thursday and Friday in the West Port, and on Saturday he was lying in the Meadows when he, too, was taken into custody. There was no honour among thieves in their declarations, each making out the other to be the instigator and the murderer. What is clear is that they were plausible rascals and jointly responsible.

Black, in describing his whereabouts on the fatal Wednesday night, was sure he was in the Grassmarket before nine o'clock because he recollected looking at the clock on Heriot's Hospital. As for McDonald he heard the eight o'clock bell ringing as they were passing Whitehouse Toll on their return to town after drinking at Coltbridge.

The trial was held on 7th June 1813. William Muirhead, blacksmith in Calton, son of the deceased William, explained that on the night of the murder his father, expressing his intention of taking a walk in the country, left the house between six and seven. When he did not return by midnight his son went out to look for him.

James Brown, son-in-law to the murdered man, told how he was at a meeting of the Incorporation of Calton that night. Shortly after midnight Captain Brown of the police called him out of the meeting room. When in Leith Wynd they met his brother-in-law, William Muirhead, and told him his father had been murdered.

Muirhead and Brown then proceeded to the City Guard House where the body was lying. Having identified the corpse Muirhead returned home to get a tablecloth to cover the body of his seventy years old parent. Brown described how he and Muirhead watched the body all next day in the Guard House "to prevent improper visitors being admitted to inspect it."

William Inglis, butcher in Corstorphine, testified that when he was making his way home from town on the Wednesday in question he saw the lads about eight or nine near Ravelston entry.

Another Corstorphine man, Alexander Muirhead, said that he left Edinburgh about half past eight and met the two lads a little on the Edinburgh side of Ravelston road. They jostled him as he passed but he kept on walking and, then, a little below Belmont he met William Muirhead travelling towards Edinburgh. Muirhead was known to him as an old smith in Calton. He had a staff in his hand and was quite sober. The Corstorphine man stopped to speak, asking the traveller if he was not afraid to be out so late. To this the old fellow replied that it was a fine night and he had no fear of travelling alone.

Robert Young, writer, told of finding the body. He left

Glasgow at four o'clock in the *Telegraph* coach. About half a mile west of Coltbridge he spotted a man lying on his face on the footpath. He called to the Guard, James Sword, to stop. Then he got out, examined the body, found a wound on the left breast big enough to put three fingers into, and saw a great deal of blood on the ground. It was then about ten o'clock and moonlight. Young went to Coltbridge to raise the alarm.

The Coltbridge witnesses, John Binny, a journeyman skinner, and his sister, Helen, told how their mother kept an ale house and how they were suspicious of the accused. Helen heard the report of two pistol shots sometime between nine and ten: John who had spent the evening fishing in the Water of Leith close by had heard shots about nine thirty. Binny was sent to Edinburgh to inform Captain Brown of the police.

Adam McCaul, servant to Mr Lindsay at Coltbridge, described being sent by his master to get out a cart to take the body to the West Port police office but Captain Brown instructed him to take it to the City Guard House. Margaret Smith who had directed the accused to the ale house identified both and said they had left about nine o'clock.

Andrew Inglis, sergeant major in the police, told how captain Brown, as soon as the murder was reported, sent him to the scene of the crime. He found part of a steel chain, a key, a seal, and a button. He knew that a description of a lad with a lame leg, thick lips, and black hair, fitted the prisoner Black. He had seen him frequently at the police station. On Thursday he went back to examine the wall but found no bullet marks.

George Dechmont, sheriff officer, next described taking McDonald in a coach to Blackhall and turning upwards to Ravelston Quarry. McDonald directed him to a wheatfield beside a crooked tree and to a ridge where he unearthed the pistols.

William Lockhart, watchmaker, recognised the watch, chain, and seal, because he had cleaned the watch for Mr Muirhead on 26th December 1812.

Then came the medical evidence in a certificate given by Dr Farquharson and Dr Inglis. They had examined the body on Thursday in the City Guard House and found a triangular wound, about 4 x 3½ x 2½ inches, in the left breast. The ribs and breastbone were very much shattered and, on laying open the thorax, the wound was seen to extend to the bottom of the heart. On Saturday they had again examined the body in the victim's house and had extracted three bullets which were before the Court in a sealed parcel. It was swan or slug shot.

The jury were unanimous in their verdict of guilty and the sentence of death was passed. The judges were Lord David Boyle (Lord Justice Clerk), Allan Maconochie (Lord Meadowbank), Lord Adam Gillies, and David Monypenny (Lord Pitmilly). The Lord Justice Clerk spoke of "youthful depravity" and ordered the youths to be hanged by their necks by the common executioner upon a gibbet at the place where they had robbed and murdered. He went on to say that "it was from no lenity to the pannels, nor regard to the feelings of their friends, but respect for the inhabitants of the neighbourhood", that he would not "appoint their bones to wither in the winds of Heaven."

Throughout the trial Black had been silent but McDonald frequently interrupted witnesses and heard the death sentence with indifference. When the Lord Justice Clerk wished God to have mercy on his soul McDonald shouted, "He will have none upon yours."

So the prisoners were returned to the Tolbooth jail and fed on bread and water till Wednesday 14th July. About eleven thirty that morning they were brought to the hall of the prison where the chaplain of the jail and a Roman Catholic clergyman for McDonald prayed with them for fully an hour. At one o'clock the procession left the Tolbooth.

Heading the cavalcade were the High Constables followed by the City Officers with halberts, the magistrates in robes with staves of office, the clergymen, the open cart with the two condemned men and the executioner, and another body of High Constables. They were escorted by the 7th Dragoons of the Norfolk and Northampton Militia and a party of police.

Their way was by Bank Street and the Mound to the West End of Princes Street. The streets were crowded with spectators and every window was filled from which a sight of the prisoners could be got. The heat of the day and the pressure of the crowd were almost intolerable. Black appeared unconcerned and McDonald kept looking at a book in his hand. At the end of Princes Street the officials handed the lads to Sheriff Rae representing Midlothian where the crime had been committed.

The procession started off again led by the Sheriff on horseback carrying the white rod and accompanied by sheriff officers on horses. Following in carriages were the sheriff substitutes, the clergy, and the superintendent of police. The escort was a detachment of the Royal Midlothian Yeomanry Cavalry.

At two o'clock the place of execution was reached. A psalm was sung on the scaffold and after a prayer the youths mounted the drop. Black in a firm voice then asked McDonald "if he was ready" and had to ask three times before McDonald gave a barely audible affirmative reply. Black took McDonald by the hand, saying, "Lord Jesus Christ have mercy on our souls."

The hangman did his job. Almost immediately heavy rain descended on the bodies swinging from the gibbet "so constructed that the feet of the culprits hung over the spot where they had committed their atrocious crime."

When life was extinct the bodies were cut down and "with the view of impressing the spectators with more awe" were conveyed without covering to the university where the two famous doctors, Alexander Monro, senior and junior, were publicly to dissect and anatomise them.

If fancy is indulged to speculate on the idea that history repeats itself and that evil may have geographical location, could the 1813 murder have its parallel in the 1938 murder of a woman by the gardener in the villa *Ormelie* then occupied by Sir William Thomson? The house, with wall along the main road, is a little west of Murrayfield Road and possibly is the site of the mugging of the old blacksmith from the Calton.

TRANSPORTATION: THE FEMALE INDUSTRIAL HOME

Getting rid of persons considered undesirable was done till the mid 19th century as in previous centuries by banishment either from the county or from the country.

On a Tuesday morning in April 1812 a woman on the old Glasgow road just east of the entry to Saughton House was stopped and found to be carrying poultry and eggs. She was taken to Slateford where a servant from Saughton identified the goods as stolen. The woman was sent to Edinburgh where the Sheriff sentenced her to twelve months imprisonment and thereafter banishment from the county.

Transportation was still a punishment in 1851 when Elizabeth Douglas, born in Corstorphine but living in Edinburgh at Carrubbers Close, was on trial for assault and theft.

Peter Cowe, joiner, age 28, came to Edinburgh from Glasgow on 7th February 1851, and was making his way to the North British Railway Station to get a ticket to Berwick where his father was a fish curer.

He stopped at a shop in Leith Wynd, the infamous Victorian "Happy Land", and asked for a light for his pipe. Susan Willis, standing at the tenement close by, offered a light from her fire upstairs. Cowe followed her, and having lit his pipe was about to leave when Elizabeth Douglas and another woman, Mary Adams, the wife of a groom living in Leith Wynd, came in and closed the door.

The three women then attacked him. He was seized by the throat. A man came in and assisted the women. Cowe was stripped of his silver watch, twenty shillings and sixpence in silver money, two sovereigns and a purse. He was left on the floor and when he recovered he went for the police.

The women denied the charge but each was sentenced to 10 years transportation. The Corstorphine girl, Elizabeth Douglas, sailed on the *Anna Maria* which took 200 female convicts on 4th October 1851 to Van Diemen's Land. Transportation to Tasmania ceased in 1852.

In 1856 a Female Industrial Home was set up in Corstorphine in Kirk Style House, once the house of the Provosts of the old church. The ladies who launched the scheme hoped to reform young women who had got into trouble by placing them in the environment "of a well regulated Christian family". Inmates were free to stay or leave as they chose.

Despite the management claim of being concerned with "Higher Class Females" the local heritors said in no uncertain terms that Corstorphine was not the place for what the Victorians called "fallen women". If the heritors had taken a look at their Session records they might not have been so smug. On their own doorstep between 1821 and 1853 there were 52 cases of fornication and 52 illegitimate children.

During its existence from 1856 to 1885 the Home's annual admissions varied between 20 and 37. It was funded by donations from charitably disposed persons and by the sale of goods, mainly woollen work done by the girls who also undertook needlework and washing to order. On Sunday evenings visiting speakers came to address the women. Among the lecturers around 1866/7 was Robert Shinnie of the Aberdeen carriage building firm described in its time as the largest in Britain. Mr Shinnie spoke on religion and temperance.

Miss Jane Heriot Maitland was in overall charge of the Home assisted by a matron or superintendent. The matrons who served included Mrs Hay 1858, Elizabeth Ross 1861, Alexandrina Dalziel 1871, Elizabeth Boyd and Ann Forbes 1881.

A disappointing inmate for Miss Maitland in 1858 was Christina Goldie, an unmarried Irish girl of 19. She had been friendly with a young shoemaker, John Corbet, living at Shakespeare Square, Edinburgh, (north east corner of North Bridge / Waterloo Place). When she suggested to Corbet that they should live together he had replied that if she went to the Home at Corstorphine for 6 months he would leave the town and come to live with her at Corstorphine. She fulfilled her part of the agreement.

Then one night in December 1858 she came to town to his lodgings where she stabbed him with his shoemaker's knife. Dr Littlejohn, York Place, in his evidence reported that Corbet, despite a large loss of blood and a wound close to the main artery, had recovered. The matron of the Home said that the prisoner during her three months stay sat in the school-room most of the time. She was quiet and inoffensive but ignorant and badly brought up.

In her defence Christina said that Corbet had promised to marry her but she had heard that he was about to marry. Corbet denied any promise of marriage but admitted having slept with her several times. He thought that the attack was because of his forthcoming marriage. Christina was sentenced to 18 months imprisonment.

Gogar Church when it was ruinous. It was refurbished and re-opened in 1894. [GUS]

THE KIRK SESSION

While great political events were taking place in the life of the nation the parishioners of Corstorphine pursued the even, and sometimes the not so even, tenor of their way under the ever vigilant eye of the kirk session. For two centuries from the opening of the earliest extant Session record on 7th January 1646 the church was the power in the parish to which laird and labourer were answerable.

The kirk session was made up of the minister and the elders representing the strata of local society. Corstorphine elders in 1646 were; Sir John Couper of Gogar; George Broune in Gogar; John Yorstoune in West Craigs; Adam Leishman, Richard Murray, Florence Gairner, Mr James Binning all in

Corstorphine; Mr James Watson, portioner of Saughton; George Foulis of Ravelston.

At this time there were also deacons who looked after church finances and provision for the poor. They were Florence Listoun in Gogar; Thomas Baillie in Meadowfield; James Steinsone, Robert Graham yr, James Wilkie yr, all in Corstorphine; John Hodge in Sighthill; Thomas Lauriston in Broomhouse.

Each elder was responsible for the conduct of the people within the area allotted to him. These areas or "bounds" indicate the extent of the parish. In 1709 Alexander Anderson had the north side of the High Street starting at the west end of the town all eastward to Bernard's Slap (Manse Road); Francis Glog had the south side of the High Street from the west end to Mistress Heriot's house (opposite) Manse Road. James Warden was given both sides of the High Street from Manse Road eastwards to the easter Kirk Style including the Mansion House of Corstorphine (the castle) and Parkhouse (approximately Roull Road).

John Cunningham's section was from the easter Kirk Style to the east end of the town including Meadowhouse and Greg's Hill; Thomas Tod was given Huntingtoun (north side St. John's Road west of Clermiston Road / south side St. John's Road east of Kirk Loan) and Whitehouse. John Mitchell had Broomhouse and the Lairdship (south of Broomhouse); Thomas Ferguson was responsible for Sighthill, Larbour, Bankhead, Peelshire: Robert Duncan's portion was Saughton House, Parkhead and the Easter and Wester park dykes of Saughton. William Hill supervised Lonend and Stenhopmilns (Stenhouse); Thomas Allan covered Gogar House, Gogar toun, Mains of Gogar, Marchhall, Golfhall and Carse Hall. Robert Cunninghame had Meadowfield, Wester and Easter Craigs, and the Goyl (Gyle); the final section was Ravelston whose elder had just died.

Being an elder was a responsible position. When Thomas Hardie, farmer in Gogar Mains, was ordained to eldership on 4th March 1714 it was a solemn occasion. Mr Fordyce preached from 1st Timothy 5:17: "Let the elders that rule well be counted worthy of double honour." The sermon was followed by seven questions being put to Thomas on his belief in the Scriptures, salvation by faith and the Westminster Confession, his renunciation of doctrines contrary to the Confession of Faith, his acceptance of Presbyterianism, his promise to support Presbyterian church government, and his acceptance of the responsibilities of eldership.

Mr Fordyce met his elders on the first Monday of every month in the church at nine in the morning so that they could "spend some time in prayer and conferences about the state of the paroch" and "he would endeavour to explain to them a part of the Confession of Faith". An elder twice absent from any Session meeting without valid reason had to pay sixpence to the poors fund. The elders who were so busy judging others had an annual inspection of themselves called "privy censures". The 1707 inspection must have been gratifying for "they all reported well of one another".

Session meetings were also controlled by the agricultural life of the parish. In November 1703 the Session clerk noted that there had been "no Session since August because of the harvest."

At these Session meetings, in reality church courts, parishioners were called to account for behaviour and if guilty were fined and / or made to undergo public repentance in the kirk before the people on successive Sundays. Public repentance in 1692 was done by the sinner standing at the kirk door in sackcloth from the ringing of the second bell till the third bell and then appearing on the place of repentance inside the church. The sinner had to "sit upon the pillar" until the minister pronounced the Blessing.

In 1680 Grissel Weir defied the order to repent wearing white sheets by saying that if the minister gave her white sheets she would make them "goe back worse than they came". Another refinement of punishment was given to James Dyks in 1683 when he had to stand barefooted at the church door.

Public repentance as the Session noted in 1655 was for "edification to the congregation". In the Reformed kirk all were to participate, even in the humiliation of their neighbours.

A.J.P. Taylor, the historian, once made the generalisation that "before the French Revolution what we call history is the story of what is happening to a few people at the top". Though that is true of medieval Corstorphine history it is far from true of the Post-Reformation period. In the records of the kirk Session the people at the bottom come alive across the centuries. Though much is naturally of local interest there are occasions when the folks in the pews appear against the broader canvas of national affairs.

JAMES WARDEN

James Warden had a varied career from 1705 to 1725 as farmer, kirk elder, and kirk treasurer. He acted as depute bailie for Corstorphine estate then owned by Sir Robert Dickson of Inveresk and managed by his factor, John Dickson. Because of his position on the estate the Session in 1708 chose Warden who was already an elder to be the "magistrate" to ensure that their decisions were obeyed.

In 1710, acting as "proctor" (procurator) for Sir Robert, he protested at a Session meeting about other heritors allocating kirk seats without consulting his master. Next year when kirk treasurer he was given one of the keys of the kirk box and was commissioned to get new communion tokens. In 1713 he entered into a marriage contract with Jean Blakater or Blackadder.

Two years later Warden and his wife were involved in a quarrel with Janet Heriot, servant to George Pinkerton. The Session heard the evidence. Janet according to witnesses had called Mrs Warden, her father, and her children "bastards". Pinkerton declared that he had heard it said that James Warden "sang at the back of Mary Johnston's fire for the sowen pot." Sowen was a flummery made from oats. He also alleged that Warden had been "put out of Greenock". The Session, however, supported their elder and rebuked Janet Heriot.

When Warden died in 1725 he left a large number of debts and a large number of children. The Session in 1726 lent Mrs Warden £3 sterling. Then in 1728 the Session heard that she was in debt, was suffering from ague and had four children ill. One child was at the point of death. She was given £12 Scots to buy "druggs and necessaries."

In 1739 in seeking to he "exonered" (discharged of liability) she recorded the "goods and gear" belonging to James when he died. The inventory included:

a stack of bear about 8 bolls	£43–04–0
a stack of oats about 8 bolls	£41–06–0
3 stacks of peese about 12 bolls	£54–00–0
a brown mare	£37–00–0
a white horse	£9–00–0
a brown horse	£22–00–0
a blew colored little mare	£18–00–0
a cow (being one of two the other having "broke her legg" and died shortly after Warden's death)	£15–00–0

2 oxen both at	£36–00–0
11 sheep	£11–00–0
an old cart	£10–00–0
a pleugh and graith	£6–00–0
3 harrows	£0–16–0
other small labouring utensils and whole household furniture	£70–00–0
All of above in Scots money	£373–06–0

Rent for land Warden cultivated at Cramond belonging to Sir John Inglis was calculated at;	
12 bolls meall	£76–16–0
12 bolls bear	£70–16–0

There was £100 in money and there were funeral expenses.

The inventory designates Warden as "tenant in Corstorphen". About 1720 he was farming at Corstorphine Ridge and in 1723 he was cultivating Southfield in Cramond parish an area near Corstorphine Rig. He may have been a brother to John Warden (1629–1713) the miller at Mauslie on the Cammo estate.

Jean Blakater appears to have been a second wife. Despite a marriage contract she was left with little financial support. She survived her husband fully thirty years, her name appearing in the Session records as a person given financial assistance from time to time in the 1750's. Finally she became "an enrolled pensioner" at 2/6 per month.

FORNICATION

Hearing cases of fornication and adultery kept successive Sessions busy and their clerks active in writing records of discipline. When Edinburgh was plague stricken in 1646 John Veitch merchant came out to Saughton with his servant Margaret Lowrie and there she met Robert Haldane also an Edinburgh dweller and brother to James Haldane portioner of Saughton. As they were both Edinburgh citizens their association was reported to the Presbytery of Edinburgh who ordered them to do their repentance in Corstorphine, the place of their "fault".

The plague was also the cause of James Cunningham having to account to the Session for his wife having a child born "a long time before the due time according to the date of their marriage." James denied responsibility. His wife, Janet Gray, had to admit that when George Garner, burgess of Edinburgh, came to live in Corstorphine at the time of the plague she had an affair with James Whitehead, servant of the worthy burgess.

In 1681 Janet McCandlish, servant to John Yorstoun, farmer in "gray Crook" (Craigcrook), chanced to meet John Scott at a point on Corstorphine Hill called "ye Scots whinnes". There he annoyed her. His defence was that he was drunk, that he meant no harm, and that his advances were "but in merriment". The Session concluded that rape was not proven and took into consideration "the credite of his parents" and his family as he was married. On his knees he begged the Session's pardon for being drunk and for any evil towards the girl. After a sharp rebuke from the minister he was absolved.

When Margaret Moneylaws, servant to the Laird of Saughton, was reported in 1694 to the Session as being pregnant she denied it. The Session then called in the village midwives to examine her and they found the report was true; there was little chance of hoodwinking a vigilant Session. That same year one of the midwives, Agnes Baily, was cited to the Session and censured for not asking who was the father of a child she had recently delivered because to question the mother about paternity was the "usual custom" of the midwife.

There were, of course, bolder spirits like Florance Murray who "bid the minister and the reider both to go and hang themselves", and like Elspet Wallace who in 1693 declared she did not "give a fart" for the Session. Others were driven to desperate measures like Thomas Meinzies, litster, and Mary Beg who found themselves in the position of adultery. Thomas pleaded with Mary to name someone else as the father or to "make up such herbs as might cause her to part with child". Mary did neither. When he had to admit responsibility Thomas said she tempted him by "kitling" (tickling) him. That was in March 1693.

In April it appears that Thomas got more than he expected from his wife, Elizabeth Wallace, for the Session had to listen to Thomas's tale of how his wife beat him, tore his shirt over his head, and set a dog on him which bit him in five places. The Session had the last word. Thomas was ordered to buy a new sack gown and to appear in it at the kirk door and to stand there from the ringing of the second bell to the third bell when he was to proceed to the place of repentance near the pulpit.

Margaret Thomson, servant to Andrew Crombie gardener Ravelston, admitted fornication in November 1730 and named a fellow servant John Whyte who had removed to Carlowrie in Kirkliston parish. Margaret went off to Edinburgh where she had her child. The following year, after a period in the Correction House of Edinburgh, Margaret was transported to Virginia.

In 1796 Christian Greig, living with her widowed mother, gave birth to a child the father of whom she confessed was Alexander Chieslie living at Bunkers Hill as it was popularly known, otherwise 3 North St. James's Street. The Session at once wrote to Chieslie to avoid having to keep the mother and child on the poor fund. He replied, promising to support the child. No further proceedings were taken against him or the girl, possibly because Chieslie was the son of the former minister. The child was baptised William, the name of his maternal grandfather. Cases of discipline for fornication continued to be rebuked into the mid 19th century but by then the rebuke was done privately by the minister.

The 17th and 18th century place of repentance was near the pulpit which was then at the north west corner of the present north transept. David Allan's picture *The Black Stool* 1784 has given posterity a lively, detailed portrayal of repentance and the place of public rebuke in Scottish parish churches.

Sometimes cautioners had to be found to guarantee that accused persons would appear when cited to the Session. In 1692 Laurence Cunningham, mason in Corstorphine, who agreed to be a cautioner was noted as "presently working in Fife".

Alexander Petrie and Helen Walker, both servants to John Yorston in the Hill, denied scandalous behaviour in May 1704 despite witnesses testifying to their being together in the byre. Helen went off to Currie parish and the Session arrested wages due to Petrie till he paid his fine. When Helen failed to re-appear before the Session her brother, George Walker, was called upon for the £30 Scots he had promised to pay as cautioner. The Session threatened to have him imprisoned till he paid.

The power of the Kirk Session in the 18th century undoubtedly concentrated the mind of many a man on the subject of marriage. John Galt summed up the situation: "It's a sore thing for a man to be frightened into his first marriage by the bow-wow o' a kirk session."

SELLING ALE

Selling ale during the time of the church service and drunkenness were serious offences. Ale was the drink of the common people. Tea was not to displace it till Victorian times when Mr Gladstone repealed the tea tax. Wines were for the upper classes. Spirits were for special occasions like funerals.

Brewing in 17th and 18th century Corstorphine was as much a domestic as a commercial activity. Barley for making malt grew in the surrounding fertile Midlothian soil and wells of fine fresh water were to hand. In 1644 when the Covenanting army needed money consideration was giving to raising funds by means of Excise duty. Accordingly an Act of Parliament was passed imposing Excise duties on ale, whisky, imported wine, tobacco and textiles. Fourpence was charged on every pint of ale or small beer. The next step in 1647 was to farm out the Excise. At the Union of 1707 the Excise brought £50,000 yearly to the public revenue.

Records for the malt brewed in Corstorphine parish were kept in 1644, the first year of Excise duty, and continued to 1648. The first list of brewers notes the amount of grain for each person: Florie Liston 10 firlots; Thomas Liston 3 bolls, Thomas Walker half a boll; Wil Greive half a boll; John Young 2 bolls; Margaret Garner 3 bolls; Tam Jonston 6 firlots; George Cocheran 4 bolls; Florie Garner 6 firlots; James Wilkie 2 bolls; Thomas Bailzie 6 bolls; Mr James Watson 4 bolls. The Collector of taxes for Corstorphine parish in 1648 was James Watson of Saughtonhall. The firlot as a corn measure varied: it could be a quarter of a boll. The boll did not exceed 6 bushels. At this time there were three women brewers – Margaret Garner, Jean Cunningham, Barbara Thomsone.

William Johnston was the leading brewer by the second decade of the 18th century. His business, carried on by his son David, continued till the early 19th century. Writing to Watson of Cammo in 1783 David Johnston was able to say that if Lady Margaret wanted strong ale he had "some from new malt and new hops". He also recommended his table beer. In 1792 he supplied the family at Cammo with four gallons of strong ale for 15/–. No doubt he also supplied the people licensed to sell liquor in Corstorphine parish 1795 – Mrs Brownlie at Golfhall; George Burn at Saughton (Stenhouse Mills); and in the village – John Fyfe, Joseph Davie, Mrs Torbett, and Peter Shanks.

The Johnston brewery complex with barn, kiln, coble, and well was sited at the north east end of Kirk Loan. The barn housed the basic raw material, barley, which was converted into malt by steeping in the coble, a wooden cistern stone or lead lined. Water from the well may have been hill water. While the barley was soaking it was repeatedly gauged by the Excise Officer. After the water was drained the barley went through the process of germination and finally was dried on the kiln floor. There after the brewer converted the malt to ale and the gauger was ever present to ensure the law was observed.

Part of the site is now covered by the shops and flats at St. John's Road opposite Clermiston Road. The Johnston family in 1832 built Corstorphine House on the southern part of the site.

Parishioners were constantly in trouble with the Session for excessive drinking. Repeated church enactments were made against selling ale in time of divine service. George Cochran in 1656 was called to the Session to explain why absentees from the kirk service were drinking in his house. Robert Cunningham went on his knees before the minister and the elders in 1698 for imbibing too freely.

On occasions the Session showed some sympathetic understanding of a situation as when John Frizzal in 1693 was reported for having a celebration party in his home on a Sabbath evening. When he explained that only a quart of ale had been drunk and it was the day that his wife had been "kirked" (first appearance at church service after the birth of a child) he was saved from public repentance. Instead the minister rebuked him privately and the Session re-enacted the laws against selling liquor in time of divine service. For a first offence the penalty was £5 Scots and for a second £10 along with a public rebuke before the congregation.

James Weir and his wife, Agnes Landall, were in trouble in 1695 for allowing some gentlemen of Their Majesties' Guard to drink at their house in sermon time. Thomas Edward also found himself in 1695 explaining the statement he had made in the village that the elders had a drink themselves on the Sabbath when they were supposed to he looking for missing churchgoers.

James Finny, a kirk elder, created a scandal on Wednesday 14th March 1705 when being the worse of drinking brandy he met, on the highroad between Corstorphine and the Goyle, an old woman mounted on one horse and leading another westwards. Cursing and swearing he seized the horse on which the woman was seated, saying it was his. He finally pulled the woman off her mount, drove both horses away and took home the horse's branks (bridle).

When questioned Finny remembered nothing of the incident but admitted he had been drinking. A witness to the events, James Somervel, went to the woman's assistance. When a bystander warned Finny that he would be reported to the minister, Finny "answered indecently, not fitt to be mentioned". He was publicly rebuked and in October the Presbytery suspended him from the eldership.

In April 1706 Janet Waddel, wife of William Lithgow, was charged with providing drink in church time. She said that Colonel Hamilton in H.M. Foot Guards, Mr John Murray advocate in Corstorphine, and Rueben McCrabbie periwig maker in Edinburgh, were in her house but she refused to serve them. They then ordered McCrabbie's man servant, William Hamilton, to give them ale.

At the Union of 1707 the Scottish Excise Department became an independent department of the Civil Service and continued so till 1823 when it was incorporated into the Excise Department of Great Britain and Ireland. In its early years many of the officials were Englishmen. Excise was collected by officers known to the people as gaugers. Those associated with Corstorphine in the 18th century and up to 1816 were:

St. Ninian's Church on St. John's Road as it looks today (former Corstorphine Free Church). [RG]

William Wilson 1710 / Thomas Pearcieval 1712 / Thomas Drummond 1714 / John Trotter 1724 / John Malcolm 1728 / James Balvaird 1730 / John Touson 1731 / Alexander Brodie 1732 / George Mitchel 1735 / Ninian Trotter 1741 / George Robertson 1747 / Alexander Watson 1751 / Alexander Gardner 1752 / Alexander Bean 1770 / James Fraser 1790 / William Renton 1802 / John Jardine 1814 / William Fulton 1816 / Anthony McMillan 1816.

Of these Percivell was one of the English excise staff sent to Scotland in 1707 at the Union. Thomas Drummond, the gauger, appeared before the Session in 1714 guilty of fornication with Bessie Hill, servant of Robert Lithgow, brewer. Drummond asked to do his public repentance by sitting twice on one day instead of two Sundays "because of the uncertainty of his residence...not knowing when he may be commanded elsewhere by his masters the Commissioners".

Collecting excise was generally resented by the Scottish people. It was the attack at Pittenweem on James Stark, Collector of Excise, 1736, that led to the Porteous riots in Edinburgh. Scott in *The Heart of Midlothian* attributes the Pittenweem affair to a *customs raid* but in this instance our literary Homer nodded.

Modern Corstorphine continues the practice of providing a choice of hostelries weekdays and Sundays for the traveller and the resident.

PROFANING THE SABBATH

Doing household jobs and engaging in normal business affairs on the Sabbath were equally abhorrent to the Session. Margaret Hunter was rebuked for carrying a barrel on a Sunday evening in 1657. Robert Braid, gardener, in September 1693 shook a dozen plums off his tree and had to appear before the elders.

When Margaret Charity, servant to William Walker in East Craigs, was charged with carrying a sieve on Sunday 20th August 1699 she explained that she had waited till the sun set before she lifted it. For her the Sabbath ended at sunset. It was a nicety of timing, the kind of situation Sir Walter Scott created so vividly in *Old Mortality*. There the Covenanters watched the hands of the clock advancing towards midnight when the Sabbath would be ended and they would be free to kill Henry Morton.

Margaret was on her way with the sieve to Matthew Comb's mill at Cramond. Meal was needed to feed the shearers who would be busy from early light on the Monday morning. The informant to the Session was James Dundas of Southfield over the hill from East Craigs.

Thomas Edward's wife, Jean Weir, was accused of having clothes out drying on Fast Day 1699. She pleaded that she was from home and two of the children had committed the offence. When Richard Beg appeared before the Session accused of building his yard dyke on the Sabbath he explained

This replica hour glass stands next to the pulpit. Its predecessors would be turned once (or more!) by the Minister to determine the length of his sermon. (PB2022)

that some cows had got into his yard and were eating his kail. After he drove the beasts out he picked up a stone that had been knocked off the head of the dyke and replaced it. In an age of dry stone dykes this was possibly a true statement but the Session did not accept it and Beg was rebuked.

Hugh Jackson's wife scandalised the elders by sending Anna Pollok to Edinburgh on the Lord's day to buy "three dozen of baps".

The Laird of Gogar's servant, George Scot, met Margaret Fairy on a Wednesday in May 1701 as she was leaving Edinburgh to return to Corstorphine. She had some cloth with her and Scot arranged to buy a coat length at thirty two shillings Scots the ell (the plaiden ell 38.416 inches). The following Sunday George went to Margaret's house, paid for the cloth and took it home to Gogar. The Session appealed to the Laird of Gogar to punish his servant but the laird refused, saying that George was an idiot. It was generally accepted that an idiot could not be "an object of discipline". Daft or not, George Scot the next year decided that Corstorphine was not for him and crossed over to Cramond parish.

Patrick Bell, accused of shoeing a horse on the Sabbath in 1703, protested that he had nothing to do with the incident. He told the Session that a passing soldier on his way to "Carrin" (Carron) had taken the key of the smithy and shoed his horse himself. In 1708 it was reported that several people were profaning the Lord's day by bringing water into their homes so the elders were exhorted to be on the lookout for such offenders.

Cutting "pot herbs" and walking "idly in the fields" were "gross prophanation" of the Sabbath in 1710. The elders in 1718 were instructed to admonish those who went "in companies through the fields". In 1712 when a search was made of the village for church absentees George Pinkerton's maid was cutting kail and beets. When questioned Pinkerton declared that some men had come to his inn with a French prisoner who could eat only pot herbs. Accordingly he sent the girl to cut some.

Games were another form of Sabbath profanity. Alexander Greg and James Irvine found themselves in trouble for playing during sermon time 1657 at "casting of the bullots". This ball throwing game used balls made of lead or iron. Two elders were chosen in 1665 to make sure on Sundays that children were not indulging in games. Two years later Robert Girdwood, Thomas Clerk, George Cowane, James Girdwood, and George Walker were reported to the Session as "mikle boyes that playes after sermon". Boys were again in trouble in 1674 when James and Alexander Greg, encouraged by the promise of a groat from James and John Cleghorn in Currie, went on a Sunday to get a cow from Marion Law and tormented Marion Weir. The Session ordered them to learn and to repeat the Ten Commandments within two weeks because they were "young ignorant boyes".

When the elders searched the village in 1708 they found people playing at pennystone (a flat stone used for playing quoits) in the yard of William Lithgow, gardener, who was serving them with drink. Lithgow's story to the Session was that the young men came in uninvited and forced him and his wife to provide drink "contrary to their inclination". He declared he knew none of his unwanted visitors but the Session, not wholly convinced of his innocence, rebuked him in their presence instead of before the congregation.

THEFT AND HOUSEBREAKING

Elspeth Cranstounne apparently raided the Laird of Gogar's fruit garden during church time. Her version was that the herd lads who happened to be there kindly gave her some fruit. In 1697 when Margaret Rinde, employed as a shearer, was away from home at harvest time her house was broken into in the night time and her possessions stolen. The Session ordered a collection to be taken throughout the parish to compensate her.

John Crawford on a Saturday night in 1701 burst open Marion Laurie's house door. She was not at home so he lay on her bed all night. The Session decided that the minister should speak to the baron bailie to punish Crawford for housebreaking and entry while they would deal with the offender for the scandal caused.

SLANDER AND STRIFE

Village life was not all idyllic sweetness and light. In 1647 the Session had to deal with cases of women "flyting". Men were equally as quarrelsome. Thomas Walker took a "claught of John Wemys his hair" and Wemys in turn scratched Walker's face when they were both visiting William Seves in 1677. Alexander Greg indulged in wife beating in 1681.

Agnes Paterson in 1697 angered Robert Duncan who reported her to the Session for saying that "all mealmakers were going to hell upon their own feet". She seems to have taken the traditional view, perhaps from personal experience, that millers worked to their own advantage not that of their customers.

In 1701 Alexander Alexander, on a Sabbath morning, so savagely beat Christian Graham's cow that it died. He defended his action by saying the cow had been destroying his crop. The Session took the view that driving a cow out of corn was not Sabbath breaking but what the Catechism termed "a work of necessity". He was rebuked but the death of the cow they felt was a civil matter to be settled by "the magistrate".

Mary Hamilton, servant to William Thorn, had her past life exposed to the village and her reputation further damaged. The culprits were Marjory Smith and her daughter, Anna Wilson. Apparently Hamilton had been scourged through Edinburgh, the usual punishment for prostitutes. The marks of the hangman's whip were still visible on her back. Marjory's inference was that Hamilton was kept as a whore to Thom's brother and brother in-law. The Session rebuked Anna Wilson for slander and ordered her to pay a fine of £3 Scots for the poors fund.

Thomas Tod, an elder, fell from grace in 1712. When drunk in the house of John Stephenson, the smith, Tod had been seen "kissing and clapping" Agnes Tait, wife of William Walker in East Craigs. Agnes was "under the scandal of adultery" and had not made her public repentance. Moreover it was alleged that Tod had taken Agnes to his home, beaten his wife, "put her out in the night time in her shirt" and bolted the door to prevent her returning.

Tod denied the charge. He said that Walker's wife had taken "a colick" and came to his door for help. His wife put Agnes to the back of their bed while she lay in the middle and he lay at the front. He admitted that he and his wife had differences but refuted the alleged ill treatment.

The Session decided to hold an enquiry. One witness had seen Tod and Agnes in the stable at East Craigs in oat seed time. Other witnesses testified to Tod and his wife being constantly the worse of drink. The Tod affair was so great a scandal that the Session reported it to the Presbytery of Edinburgh who passed it to their committee for difficult cases. The Presbytery advised removing Tod from the eldership and rebuking him and Agnes for scandalous behaviour. In addition the minister was to make the facts known from the pulpit.

NATIONAL COLLECTIONS

Fortunately the time of the Session, though largely, was not exclusively concerned with sinners. Nor was their concern narrowly parochial. When appealed to, the Session arranged for money to be collected for special purposes. In 1657 Corstorphine kirk responded to the appeal for the harbour at

North Berwick. £4 Scots was given in 1695 for Lanark bridge. A contribution in 1700 was made to repair Kinghorn harbour.

Money was gathered in 1712 for the work of the Society in Scotland for Propagating Christian Knowledge. This body, set up in 1709, provided schools in the Highlands till the 1872 Act ended that aspect of their work. The SSPCK still exists, directing its aid today to the third world.

Contributions in 1722 went to help the erection of a church at Durness in Strathnaver. As a result of this appeal £1,500 sterling was raised throughout Scotland, allowing this widely scattered North West parish to be divided into three parishes, each with its own minister – Durness, Tongue, and Eddrachillis. The harbour of St. Andrews needed help in 1729.

Two guineas were given in 1822 to the fund for erecting the National Monument of Scotland. This appeal had the support of Scott, Lord Cockburn and Lord Elgin. The monument was for those who fell in the Napoleonic wars. It is the unfinished replica of the Parthenon, in Craigleith stone, which graces the top of Calton Hill, Edinburgh.

HELPING OTHERS

John Scot had a physically handicapped son whose legs were so weak that he could only walk with the aid of a stilt. His father suggested to the Session that if the boy were taught a trade he would be able to support himself instead of being a burden on kirk funds. Accordingly the father was given money in 1692 to help apprentice the lad.

A cripple who arrived in Corstorphine in 1683 was transported to the next parish, for which the kirk paid three shillings to a person with a horse. Over the hill at Cramond kirk on 10th April 1690 the minister reported that the collection for Sunday 30th March had been given to "Mistress Brisband in Corstorphin" to help her pay a "chirurgeon for cutting her sone of the stone gravell". This was done because Corstorphine had written to Cramond – "at the paroch of Corstorphins earnest desire by their letter for help from this paroch".

A soldier wounded at Sheriffmuir got five shillings in 1716. Alexander Somervel was assisted in 1737 to buy a horse. The overturning of a cart brought sudden death in 1758 to the husband of Widow Cleland in Loanend so to help her over a difficult time the Session gave financial support. A poor man on his way home from Edinburgh Infirmary 1782 travelled by way of Corstorphine where he was given money to assist him.

In 1794 John Stuart, a young man mentally deranged, was maintained in the Edinburgh Bedlam at a cost of £10 yearly. By 1799 the members of the Session who visited Stuart noticed that he seemed calmer but they were disturbed by the condition of his cell. His legs were cramped with cold and contracted because of the posture in which he kept himself. The Session thought that he would improve if brought back to Corstorphine. They consulted the Bedlam physician, Mr Wood, surgeon, who agreed that return to ordinary life was the best course for Stuart, advising also that friction and warm baths would help the limbs.

In 1796 the Session gave financial support to the Edinburgh Public Dispensary from which several people in the parish had received medical treatment. A widow with three children travelling towards Greenock in 1804 was given two shillings. The Session was responsible in 1834 for placing John Samuel in the Blind Asylum, Edinburgh.

Blackhall was part of the parish. In 1825 the church paid £9–7–10 on behalf of James Ross, a mentally inflicted Blackhall villager, who was taken to an asylum in Musselburgh. The return journey included tolls £1–0–6. Two men were paid for confining Ross a day and a night at Blackhall and going with him "in the night time" to Musselburgh £1–2–4.

CARING FOR THE POOR

Whatever the judgement passed by sociologists on the moral and punitive aspects of Kirk Session control over the lives of men and women there can be no denigration of the church's care for the poor. From the 16th century to 1845 Scottish poor relief was organised on the principles that responsibility for the poor person was the business of the parish of his birth, that the able bodied were not to be helped for they could help themselves, that families should support their members, and that parishes could impose an assessment to get funds.

The linking of person to parish brought about the testificat or testimonial of character. Robert Stewart, servant to William Morisone, weaver, about to leave Corstorphine, asked the Session for a tetificat to cover the period of his living in the village which was Whitsunday 1690 to Whitsunday 1692. He produced the testificat he had brought from the Session of Dunblane mentioning his "honest behaviour and Christian carriage" from his infancy to 1690. The Session finding nothing against Stewart's character ordered the clerk to give him a testificat.

During Mr Fordyce's ministry, 1709–1767, the Session were empowered to remove at once anyone who came into the parish without a testificat. These certificates were not mere formalities. The one issued in 1716 to Peter Cramond, litster, and his wife Susanna Corstorphine when they were leaving the village was endorsed with a note on Peter's "unnatural and unchristian behaviour towards his spouse".

In 1717 the Session, worried about the strain on the poor fund created by people "lately come to the parish", imposed a minimum residence of seven years for applicants wanting to be added to the poor roll.

Since the able-bodied were not to be assisted beggars were not tolerated. Help was refused to anyone receiving support elsewhere. Consequently William Johnston in 1696 was not placed on the Corstorphine poor roll because he was a King's bedesman, a licensed beggar given a blue gown and a badge and entitled to beg throughout Scotland, not like other beggars who were confined to their own parishes. The Blue Gown was immortalised by Scott in his character Edie Ochiltree whose lively personality delights readers of *The Antiquary* and whose prototype Andrew Gemmels lives on in the sculptured figure on his tombstone in Roxburgh kirkyard.

The poor had their obligations to church and state. In 1698 "a famine of victuall" made the Session grant extra payment to the poor but at the same time the Session announced that those who did not attend church would have their pensions reduced. Anyone who spoke against the Government would be "deprived instantly". Furthermore the poor were to sit by themselves in the church porch so that minister and elders could see absentees.

When, at times, the poor fund could not meet demands the heritors assessed themselves proportionately to the valuation of their lands. In 1707 the fund was 1200 merks. The minister was empowered to lend out the money to get the best possible return of interest which was then used to provide relief. Usually a bond was arranged with the gentry. This was

LAW AND ORDER

done in 1745 with Cockburn of Ormiston and in 1749 with the Duke of Hamilton.

The poor money in 1768, deposited with the bankers Mansfield and Co., amounted to £579–8–4 sterling. The interest of four per cent was not satisfactory. Henry Dundas, "Mr Solicitor Dundas", was asked his opinion on investing with the Trustees of the Turnpike Roads for the District of Corstorphine. His reply was that a group entrusted with the management of money for the poor should invest to have security and high interest and he considered the District Turnpike Roads satisfactory.

In February 1780 the Session formally regulated what had long been done by use and wont. Whenever a pauper died an inventory was to be made of his / her effects so that they could be rouped (auctioned) and the proceeds added to the fund. Three months later the Session rouped the goods of Anna Water for which £3 were got. This was used to pay her debts and funeral charges.

When Sir David Dundas of Beechwood died in 1819 the church got a legacy of £40 for the poor. The following year two seats near the east door were let to bring more money to the fund. Captain Charles Hope Watson's legacy in 1841 added £100 and in 1844 under the will of William Ramsay Watson of Saughton the poor got £2,000. These legacies form the basis of the Corstorphine Bequest still in existence.

The first extant volume of the Session records, January 1646, opens with the statement that two elders had "in ye time of the trouble" (plague) given financial assistance to the distressed. For two centuries till the State woke up to its obligations the kirk records continue the story of a caring church.

Janet Potter, widow of James Sklate in Gogar, with three small children was granted £3–8–0 Scots, the price of half a boll of meal, in 1714. James Wilson and his wife had their allowance reduced by sixpence to half a crown monthly in 1715 because the Session thought they could "make some small shift for their living". That same year when two houses were destroyed by fire the kirk did its utmost to raise money within and without the parish for those who had lost all. William Stevenson, tailor, was given cash and John Lyon got beds and household furniture and timber to restart his wright's business.

Isabel Paterson, wife of William Swan, weaver at Stenhopsmiln gave birth to triplets in 1737. The family was so poor that scarcely one child could be supported and the mother was ill to the point of dying. In desperation they applied to the Session who put two of the children out to be nursed and paid the nurses' fees.

A severely cold season at the beginning of 1740 caused so great a dearth of meal that the Session took £10 sterling from the poors box for the elders to distribute among distressed households. Later the Session felt it better to give supplies of meal rather than money. In January 1741 meal was bought from Sir Robert Myrton of Gogar and from Watson of Saughton at a shilling per peck.

When Christian McKenlay in the Goyl had a long illness during which she used all her means she was left in 1744 unable to pay the account to Mr Kirkland, surgeon. The Session agreed to pay the doctor and ordered the Treasurer to make sure that he got a receipt. The great dearth of 1757 made the Session realise some of their capital that was out on loan to give assistance. They realised £77–10–0 sterling. Meal was fifteen and a half pence the peck but William Torbet, a local mealmaker, agreed to supply it at fifteen and a quarter pence. A farthing was a consideration in 1757. The meal was sold to the poor at eleven pence a peck and where a family had several children the price was eleven pence the one week and no charge made the next.

Again in 1773 high prices led to distress. From January to July 1783 David Johnston, on behalf of the kirk, bought 110 bolls of pease "for the use of the poor". At that time the heritors were assessed £50 for meal for the poor, the cost being shared proportionally. The winter of 1795 was exceptionally severe, preventing labourers from working and so making heavy demands on the poor fund. The Session appealed for donations throughout the parish which raised £35 sterling. This was used to buy coals and meal and to give small sums of money. The Session "were thus enabled to afford a seasonable relief" to near seventy families who were "impressed with a just sense of gratitude due to the benevolence of their benefactors". Alexander Keith of Ravelston sent two bolls of oatmeal to be handed out as needed.

By 1798 the demands occasioned by adverse weather so depleted the funds that the heritors agreed to be assessed and accepted a rating of eight shillings for each ploughgate of land possessed. 1799 was a year of rising meal prices. Excessive rains had damaged crops. Relief was given by making meal available at a subsidised price. The following year oatmeal was extremely expensive. The heritors accepted a plan put forward by the minister to provide a cheaper mixture of wheat and barley for making bread. About 50 families were supported at this time whereas in less trying times around 24 families needed assistance.

Miller and Company, merchants at Leith, were in 1800 tenants at Saughton Mills then within the parish. They generously ground the grain for poor relief free of charge. In June 1814 the kirk received for the benefit of the poor two guineas handed over by George Robinson owner of Clermiston House. It was the fine paid by J. Baillie for destroying young trees in Clermiston wood. Destruction of certain types of tree was punishable in Scotland and is remembered in the verse:

Oak, ash and elm tree,
The laird may hang for a' the three;
But for saugh and bitter weed
The laird may flyte, but mak naething be't.

In 1817 there was a distribution of 342 cwts of coal to 45 families, most of which was conveyed free by neighbouring farmers. Thomas Hodge needed 11 weeks attention before his death in 1825 but was without the means to pay for help. Accordingly Mrs Watson was paid by the church for attending Hodge and washing the bed clothes. A cart of coals was sent to keep his cottage comfortable. When death came the church paid the arrears of his house rent and arranged his funeral when bread, spirits and candles were used.

The years 1830 to 1836 were years of "great agricultural distress" aggravated by the cholera outbreak in 1832. When cholera attacked poor folk the Session and the heritors paid for medical attention. The coffin and the funeral of a woman shearer who died of cholera in 1832 at Saughton Mains farm were provided by the church. The church also paid the schoolmaster Mr Simpson for superintending the distribution of soup in the kitchen set up by William Keith of Corstorphine Hill and for arranging the burials of cholera victims. Dr Henderson 1834 attended the poor and supplied medicines.

Expenditure in 1838 in cash monthly payments, supplying meal and coals and paying rents as well as wages to those managing the relief work, amounted to £260–11–4. A statement in 1839 showed £450–0–0 capital in the poors fund with an annual income averaging £213. The Poor Roll was revised. No one with a son, whether he lived or not with his parents, was to be admitted to the poors list.

Charles Watson's legacy was used in 1841 to buy "a perpetual right" of sending two patients to the new lunatic asylum at Morningside. The Session was human in its gifts to dependants for in 1841 William Morrice at Four Mile Hill got 4 ounces of snuff.

John Thomas of Gogarburn in February 1845 raised the question of assessing for the poors fund to include tenants as well as proprietors. However his fellow heritors decided to do nothing as there was a "prospect" of legislation about poor law. The "prospect" became a reality in September 1845 under the Poor Law Amendment Act when administration of poor relief passed to a Board of Supervision with an Inspector of Poor.

WITCHCRAFT

Much of the work of the kirk Session was concerned with cases of scandal reported by the elders or by neighbours. Sometimes these libels were made out of religious zeal: sometimes out of personal spite. In 1692 to safeguard themselves against unfounded accusations being brought to them the Session enacted that when a libel was given a half crown had to be paid to the Treasurer. If a charge turned out to be true the money was refunded but, if false, the church used it to benefit the poor.

In 1649 Corstorphine Session was presented with accusations made by neighbour about neighbour: witchcraft was the charge. By a statute of 1563 witchcraft became a civil offence punishable by death. An order in Council in 1597 gave the Privy Council a large measure of power to authorise commissions to try alleged witches. From 1640 to 1649 the General Assembly of the Church of Scotland passed a series of acts against witchcraft which appear to have stirred up prosecuting activities.

Witches were generally middle-aged or old women. The old were often living alone and verging on senility: the younger were often involved in malicious quarrels with neighbours. In an age when women were mostly seen but not heard there may have been some ladies who found, in having a reputation of a witch, a psychological, compensating feeling of power.

When an accusation of witchcraft against a person was made to the church the Session set up an investigation. Evidence was heard from neighbours. Any confession made provided the material for prosecution before a higher authority. Searches were made on the stripped body of the accused for a witch mark. This was done by a man known as the witch pricker who pushed long brass pins into the flesh. If the victim felt no pain and no blood appeared the test was judged positive.

Though women were the main victims of persecution there were, on occasions, men involved. On 31st July 1603 James Reid in Corstorphine was convicted of sorcery. He admitted meeting the Devil in the likeness of a horse on Corstorphine muir. The Devil showed him how to use south running water as a healing charm. For this Reid was burned. The burning of a witch was a public entertainment. Usually the witch was strangled first and the dead or almost dead body was burned in a tar barrel. Some, however, were burned alive. In Edinburgh burnings took place on the Castlehill where today a tablet marks the spot where the last alleged witch was burned in 1722.

On 13th May 1649 Beatrix or Betie Watsone, wife of Alexander Scot, weaver in Corstorphine, gave a bill of complaint to the Session against James Chalmers, the schoolmaster, challenging him for calling her a witch. Proceedings began with the reading of the complaint whereupon the schoolmaster denied calling Betie a witch but said he had heard others declare "she was not cannie".

Allegations by others then followed. Marion Weir, servant to George Cochran, related that on Friday 4th May Betie came to her master's house and said to her that if her mistress did not pay the money due for webs that had been spun for her the unpaid silver would become black silver. Marion followed Betie into the house where a quarrel ensued between Betie and Cochran's wife, Jean Broun. On being asked how she could make silver black Betie gave no answer.

Marion continued by telling how the following morning her mistress turned ill, being hot and cold in turns. By Tuesday Jean was unable to speak and "quhen any did lift up hir handis they fell down incontinent". On Wednesday

Alexander Scott and his wife came to Jean's bedside. Scott could not feel her pulse but Betie grabbed the sick woman's arm and "pitter pattered some wordis". Then she said three times, "God send thee thy haill Jeane Broune and thy tongue". At this Jean "rackseld out hir two armes" which before had been lifeless and there was a great cracking sound.

Marion the servant was sharing her mistress's bed being at the back. She declared that there came out between her and Jean a large black thing "furth under the cloathes lyk a great rotton" (rat). The bed shook. After this Jean Broun fell into a deep sleep and when she eventually awoke her powers of speech had returned and her health thereafter improved daily. A witness to these events was Agnes Fairlie.

Doubtless modern medicine could find an explanation for Jean's temporary incapacity and, keeping in mind living and housing conditions in 1649, a rat might well have got itself into the bedding.

The second person to give evidence was Margaret Gardner who said that her late husband, Alexander Crawford, before he died blamed Betie for his dying condition. Whenever he went to or from Edinburgh he would be sure to meet her on the way and she even troubled him in his sleep. One wonders what Freud would have made of the latter statement.

Third to speak was Widow Christian Williamsone who also blamed Betie for her husband's death. When Betie visited him on his deathbed he said, "Take away that tinker", and the nature of his "sickness was not ordinary".

John Ramsay told the tale of how his cow wandered into Betie's yard and she uttered threats against it if it returned. Consequently when it paid a second visit Betie sent it away in such a frenzied state that it chased the stirk everywhere and only with difficulty was it brought home. It "rowted all night" forcing Ramsay to rise and what he saw was a sow lying across the threshold of his door. This happened on four or five nights. The strange thing was the appearance of the sow for no swine were kept in the village.

David Wilkie and James Patison jointly said that when going to get coals one day they met Betie who wanted to go to town on one of their horses. They refused. Then at the coalhill one horse ran about so badly that it lost all its "graiths". On the way back home the horses shed their loads, four of them failing to the ground.

John Yorkstoun and John Cleghorn followed with their

evidence. When ploughing the minister's glebe at the back of the kirk Cleghorn saw Betie coming through the kirkyard and exclaimed, "God save the cattle." The minister who was beside Cleghorn asked him why he said that. Cleghorn replied that Betie was not "canny" for she had the evil eye. The words were scarcely out of his mouth when the oxen bolted with the ploughs.

Others present spoke of how she had foretold her death to her husband and how, before being apprehended, she had gone to Jean Cunningham "in the Greenbanks within St. Cuthbert's parish" to "take hir leave of hir" for it would be their last meeting.

The minister, David Balsillie, consulted with Mr James Robertson, one of the Justices, about the action the Session should take. Robertson advised the Session to consult Lord Forrester and to request the baron bailie to keep the prisoner "fast till farther tryal". Betie was placed in the church steeple and watched till 23rd May when being alone she hanged herself. James Hadden, the baron officer, was, "put out of his place for his carelessness". Whether Hadden's "carelessness" was deliberate, perhaps to give Betie a chance of escape, or just plain dereliction of duty, will never be known. Betie, at least, cheated the system and her enemies of the spectacle of her burning to death.

Former cottages at Ladywell, now the site of Featherhall Avenue. [EW]

On 3rd June the Session convened to hear William Kniblo's complaint that his wife Margaret or Magie Bell had been called a witch. Margaret Aikman reported that her son, John Hunter, having been engaged by Bell to look after her cows changed his mind. This led to Magie saying that Margaret Aikman would get little good from the lad and shortly after he turned ill with a fever condition. He only recovered when Magie at his mother's request came to see him and said repeatedly, "God help him."

Among others giving evidence was Bessie Scott, daughter of Betie Watson, who, after refusing to give Bell some thread, turned ill. Her mother told her to go to Magie Bell's house and ask for her health to be restored. When she did this she was also to "pouke hir taile" (pull or pluck). This she did and when she got home she fell asleep. On awakening something like a rough worm came out of her mouth and at once she recovered.

An alleged accomplice of Magie was Kett (Catherine) Gibb in Gogar. Kett admitted to having met the Devil when she was a young woman and to having renounced her baptism in order to be baptised by Satan. She also admitted to meetings with the Devil and other witches. One such coven took place on Clermiston Hill in the Spring. A plough was being drawn by swine. The Devil promised that if the plough went to the head of the hill they would get the corn that year. Kett named several local people as dealing in witchcraft. However age saved Kett from retribution from the unco guid for she was 80 years old and before the law could take her she died "upon Lambes Even in Gogar" (Lammas night 1st August).

Eventually Magie made a confession. She said that eighteen years previously when living at Merchiston she met the Devil behind "the place of Merchiston" (Merchiston Tower) and was baptised by him. When she lived at the West Port of Edinburgh she met the Devil at the back of the town wall "at the quarrell hollis". The witches who met there had all died in the time of the 1646 Plague. When she came to living in the Park of Corstorphine she often met the Devil "in the Broome". Magie took her time with her confession but had to face the death sentence. She died denying she was a witch.

In August Bessie Scott confessed to going to the Park in the gloaming with her mother, Betie Watson. There they met Magie Bell and William Scott who was Bessie's uncle. When the Devil baptised her he nipped her severely.

William Scott, warlock and weaver, described his baptism by the Devil who nipped him "through the sark" and it was "the sorest nip that ever he felt". John Kincaid, the notorious witch pricker, found the Devil's mark on both Scotts. They were burned on 28th August 1649.

A further trial took place on 9th September. Marion Inglis was apprehended on statements made by Magie Bell and Kett Gibb. George, Lord Forrester, called in Kincaid who found two marks of the Devil on Marion. The Presbytery however were not satisfied and instructed the minister, David Balsillie, to bring Kincaid back for a second investigation. This time the finding was different for Marion cried pitifully and blood appeared where the pins had been pushed into the flesh.

Witnesses from Cramond accused Marion of being an envious, scolding woman and said she had caused the death of a cow at Cammo. David Broun, a young boy whose father was the miller at Gorgie, was on Corstorphine Hill at harvest time. Marion Inglis asked him what he was doing. When he replied that he was hunting she said to him to wait and she would give him a cunning (rabbit). Soon Marion's cat came in with a rabbit in its mouth but the young Broun was afraid to take it. And so a very natural harvest time incident – a cat catching a rabbit among the crop – became evidence of witchcraft.

Thomas Rutherford, servant to John Watson in Damhead, was gathering whins on the hill in winter when Marion and her daughter objected and said his fingers would be full of whins. Within a fortnight he suffered a very sore hand. Whatever caused Rutherford's sore hand Marion's objection seems a reasonable re-action to the situation for she lived on the hill and, probably, needed all the natural fuel she could get to counter the winter winds as they swept the hillside.

But another year, laird and people had more than witch-craft to worry about. English soldiers were in the Lothians. Cromwell's regime did not harass so-called witches for they found that in many cases there was more malice than proof. But the minister and the Session in 1657, when considering who should be admitted to Communion debarred, by the advice of the Presbytery, those that were "under the old scandal of witchcraft".

A last echo appears in the records for December 1681 when an incomer to Corstorphine, David Cook, was required to furnish a testimonial for himself and his wife. They came from Bo'ness where Mrs Cook had been "booked for a witch". Forty five years later, in 1736, the laws against witchcraft were repealed in Scotland.

FOUNDLINGS

The elders in 1656 were instructed by the minister to find out if any children had been brought into the parish for fostering and to ascertain the parentage. The church considered that allowing children to be fostered without checking that there were valid reasons for so doing would be condoning immoral-ity. Moreover boarded out children might in time become a burden on the parish poor fund until able to support them-selves.

When foundlings were discovered efforts were at once made to trace the mother but seldom succeeded. An abandoned child was baptised as quickly as possible and given a name. Sometimes the Christian name was that of the person who found the child or the kirk officer or the elder holding up the bairn to be baptised. Often the surname was the name of the parish or the place where abandoned.

"A found child" presented by John Snodgrass in July 1667 in the name of the Session was named Janet. A boy left "beneath the hill of Corstorphine" in 1688 was brought to baptism by the bellman John Knight and recorded as John.

The Session, worried that the "wickedness of parents is concealed" by the system of fostering, enacted in 1693 that no one was to bring a child to Corstorphine without a "testimony" to prove that there was no scandal. The foster mother was to inform the minister or the elder without delay. This problem also concerned the West Kirk of Edinburgh when in 1697 the Session questioned Margaret Borthwick about a child sent to Corstorphine where it died.

Cramond Muir, east and west of modern Drum Brae, was owned by estates partly in Cramond parish and partly in Corstorphine. When a child was left there in 1695 Cramond parish passed the bairn to Corstorphine Session who promptly returned it. Next year Cramond appealed to the Justice court and got a sheriff's order compelling Corstorphine to aliment and remove the child. It cost Cramond £44–16–8 to get rid of this foundling.

William Ferguson, wright, was called to the Session in 1703 about the child in his house. He said the child was named William Armstrong and his father was a sergeant serving in Flanders. Ferguson assured the Session that the minister would be consulted about the child by William Turnbull, litster, and John Wilson, both in Edinburgh. In due course the litster produced a satisfactory testificat for the child.

Jannet Bonner came to Corstorphine in 1705 with a child that she was fostering for Reuben McRabbie, an Edinburgh periwig maker. He refused to appear before the Session but the West Kirk pursued Jannet. Apparently there were charges of fornication with two other men who had "gone abroad". Finally in 1706 the West Kirk set her "in the joggs with a shaven head".

Five foundlings occupied Session deliberations in 1706. Agnes Thomson got Elizabeth Paterson, mother of the fostered child to hand over a testificat but it was so "blotted" that the Session had to apply to the Session Clerk of Edinburgh to have it confirmed. This was duly done, the girl having satisfied the Old Kirk Session in Edinburgh. Again the Session was content when Margaret Aikman showed a testificat from Canongate Church to the effect that the child's mother had done her repentance.

The third foundling was with Jean Cassie in the Lairdship who also had a testificat for her foster child. The mother was Margaret Seaton, daughter to the Laird of St. Germans who had committed fornication in Corstorphine in 1704 with Colonel Stewart of Sorbie. Later the Session, being informed that Margaret had married at Glasgow and was living there, decided to write to the church authorities at Glasgow to ensure she satisfied church discipline.

James Somervel had a boy staying with him whose parentage had not been disclosed. Accordingly the Session clerk was instructed to ask the church authorities in Edinburgh if a certain Janet Alison had satisfied the church for her fornication with Colonel George Somervel. When questioned about his foster child, the 5th foundling, all that Augustine Sklate in Gogar could say was that the child was named Alexander Cairns.

A woman beggar who lodged with James Girdwood went off in the night in 1724 leaving behind a three year old girl. The minister and the Session having been told that the woman addressed the child as Jean decided she had already been baptised. Jean was put to board with Margaret Hutchison who two years later took in another foundling. This time the six months old girl was left at the door of John Mathie, gardener. The child was baptised Margaret, perhaps after her foster mother.

The kirk officer in 1728 took in a year old girl left at the east end of the village. She was named Isobel and like all foundlings she was fed and clothed by the poor fund. In 1732 two women put up for the night in the barn of Alexander Read in East Craigs and departed leaving a three weeks old boy. Next year a three months old girl left on the doorstep of the gauger's house was baptised Mary. The male child abandoned at the door of Charles Turnbull in 1739 was called Charles. The mother who laid her little girl down at East Craigs in 1749 was traced and made to take her child back.

A month old boy was left at the Lonend in 1752 with a note attached requesting that he be baptised Andrew. An advertisement to trace his mother was placed in the Edinburgh newspapers but without result and the child was boarded out in Corstorphine. The schoolmaster, Alexander Bannatyne, gave his name to a foundling baptised in 1773. Employment for Corstorphine foundlings in 1815 was found in the cotton mills at Slateford. The minister, Dr David Scot, in 1821 named a 12 days old child left at West Craigs – Thomas David Corstorphine. Another child put down at the gate of Gogar Camp 1828 was baptised Alexander Osborne Scott, the proprietor of the property being Alexander Osborne and the minister being Dr Scot.

One of the abandoned children who carried through life the name of Corstorphine had an eventful history. About two months old she was left at the school door on 25th February 1734 and was boarded with the wife of the smith, Andrew Nielson. The Rev. George Fordyce baptised her Marion. Her schooldays over, she went to work as a servant in the house of Henry Trotter of Mortonhall. This was the old house, the present one being built in 1769.

In July 1753 Trotter assaulted her "most barbarously and cruelly", tying her hands and feet and beating her with sticks and horse whips so that she lost a great deal of blood. Then he "put her into a dark cellar stripped naked and kept her there all night". She saw no one till ten the next morning.

As soon as she was able she made her way to the manse of Corstorphine where Mr Fordyce gave her shelter. But he did more than that. He took steps to have Trotter brought before the Lords of Justiciary. Trotter, however, bought his way out of public exposure. He paid over £100 sterling of which £50 went to Marion, £25 to the poor of Corstorphine, £10 to the poor of Liberton where the crime was committed, and £15 to the Edinburgh Infirmary. He also had to pay Marion £10 sterling yearly till she married when he had to provide a lump sum of £100 sterling.

The next year, 1754, Marion married William Turnbull, the minister's servant, but strangely they were not married by Mr Fordyce but by one Patrick Douglas who conducted what the church termed "irregular" marriages. On 16th August 1755 they had a daughter named Fordyce, doubtless recognition of the kindness of the minister who had befriended Marion throughout her orphan life. But Marion's web of time was to be cut short by early death. Perhaps the vicious attack by Henry Trotter impaired her health for on 23rd February 1757 she was carried to the kirkyard beside the old church, her coffin draped with the large new velvet mortcloth. She was baptised Marion but the Session clerk in reporting the Trotter affair also left on record the name by which her contemporaries knew her, the old Scots Mysie. Marion's daughter Fordyce married Robert Shedden and they had two children, a daughter Margaret, 1773, and a son William, 1775.

BAPTISMS

The Reformed church firmly believed that baptism be done in public before the congregation: "where the people may most convenient see and hear." The Act of the General Assembly at Perth in 1618 stating that "baptism may be administered at home, when the infant could not conveniently be brought to church" was short lived. Some relaxation of the principle of public baptisms did develop in the 18th century.

An Act of Parliament in 1617 instructed parish kirks to have two types of baptismal vessel, the laver and the basin. Just how exactly these were used is not clear but possibly the basin was placed under the baby's head and the water taken from the laver. The medieval stone fonts being relics of the old religion were not acceptable to the reformed church. In 1705 the Corstorphine Session decided to speak to the heritors about the lack of a basin for baptisms. Apparently the request was shelved for in 1709 though the church had three baptismal cloths it had no laver and no basins. Presumably a basin was in use by 1717 when it was decided to cut old communion cloths to make both baptismal and basin cloths. The basins referred to on this occasion included those used for church collection money.

When the Laird of Gogar died in 1720 he left money to be used as thought best for the church. The Myrton family accordingly presented a beautifully embossed silver laver depicting the Israelite spies returning from the Promised Land with the grapes of Eschol. It is inscribed: "This baptismal laver was gifted by Sir Andrew Myrton of Gogar to the Session of Corstorphine 1722". This is still used along with the ancient Gogar stone font. When a baptism takes place in the old collegiate, now parish, church the font and the laver are fine artistic symbols of a long line of Christian practice in Corstorphine.

The Reformed church also believed that Christian privileges entailed Christian duties: the person who wanted the child baptised had to accept sponsorial responsibility for bringing the child up in the faith. The Session in 1656,

The beautiful baptismal laver presented by Sir Andrew Myrton of Gogar in 1722, refurbished in 1829, and still in use today. (PB2027)

concerned that parents might be guilty of ante-nuptial fornication, formulated a rule that recently married persons with a child to be baptised were to notify the Session of the name chosen and the Session had to be sure that the parents were "free of scandalous conversation before marriage". This was revised in 1707 to the effect that the parents had to come to the minister with their elder when asking baptism for a child.

Parents were obliged to have a child baptized as quickly as possible, not "anye longer than the nixt Lord's Day eftir the chyld be borne". However parents under church censure or very ignorant had to delay baptism to get sponsors to act for them.

In December 1701 Andrew Purdie, servant to James Nimmo in Sighthill, was accused by Mary Lamb, five months married to Charles Marshall, of being her child's father. Purdie strenuously denied her statement that he had been with her in the Easter Meadow house. Finally in May 1702 he took a solemn oath of purgation before the congregation that he was not guilty.

Then in November 1703 Mary Lamb asked for baptism for the child then two years old. The Session ordered her "to take on the engagements for the child" and Andrew Dewar, kirk officer, was instructed to present the child. Mary appeared twice in the place of public repentance and on a third appearance Marshall had to appear with her before the pulpit to be rebuked. He had admitted relations with her before marriage. Marshall who was fined £5 Scots remained under censure till 1708 when he paid £2, the outstanding £3 being got by arresting his wages.

Janet Muir in Golfhall was reported to the Session as pregnant in 1710. She confessed that the father was Thomas Allan, a gardener living at Abbeyhill in the parish of South Leith, but said there was a promise of marriage between them. Allan went to the minister and confirmed Janet's statement. Each was fined £10 Scots and ordered to make public repentance, which Janet did at once.

Allan who had to leave the district for a while "on necessary business" promised to give public satisfaction later. Possibly his business was employment at the Binns for in his daughter's baptismal registration entry he is described as "gardener at Binns". One of the witnesses at the baptism of Mary Allan was James Stevenson, gardener at Abbeyhill.

The religious struggles of the late 17th century are reflected in the complaint made by the Rev. George Henry that one of his parishioners, Alexander Lowrie, in Marchhall, Gogar, had his child baptised by an "unconformed" minister. Lowrie was pressurised by the Laird to disclose who had performed the baptism. Finally in 1677 he signed a statement that he would attend the established church. He was fined 6 rex dollars. Florence Greg and his wife Marion Walker in 1666 became the parents of triplets – Clara, Janet, and Agnes.

For registering a birth in 1714 the charge was seven pence to be given to the Session clerk and a groat to the beadle. Baptisms done out of church meant a loss of the customary payments and so in 1726 it was enacted that the parent of any child not baptised in church must pay twelve shillings Scots to the poor. When James Watson of Saughton was baptised in 1737 the ceremony took place "at 5 o'clock at night".

The 18th century like the 17th had its religious struggles. Dissatisfaction with the Established Church led to the formation of the Secession Church under Ebenezer Erskine in 1733. One of the leading seceders, Adam Gib, in 1745 objected to the oath sworn by burghers in certain towns as it "involved approval of the Established Church". Those who agreed with Gib then formed the Anti-Burgher party in the Secession

Church. Gib was minister at Bristo Street Church, Edinburgh. Gibb's entry at 78 Nicolson Street is a reminder of where Adam's manse stood.

Between 1744 and 1751 Adam Gib baptised the children of George Anderson, tenant, Saughton Mains. Hugh Nimmo at Sighthill also had a daughter baptised by Gib. These baptisms were noted in the Corstorphine records.

During his ministry of 58 years in the parish 1709–1767 George Fordyce baptised 33 sets of twins. David Black and Anne Lawson were twice parents of twins. Generally the girls at this time were named Anne, Catherine, Elizabeth, Helen, Isobel, Jean, Margaret, but some young ladies were destined to go through life with more arresting Christian names. They were Crawford, Dalrymple, Lucretia, Katherine Thankfull, Carolina Wilhelmina, Fordyce, Strachan. Dalrymple was the daughter of Janet Lyon and Hugh Smelie, professional cook in 1717 to the Laird of Dornock in Annandale, in 1720 to Sir David Murray of Stenhop in Tweeddale, and in 1722 to Sir James Campbell of Auchinbreck. He was, however, at home in 1726 for Dalrymple's baptism.

Boys were George, James, John, Thomas, and William but there were a few departures from customary usage. In 1740 there was Christopher, in 1754 Normand, and in 1758 Stewart. The Sclates of Gogar faithfully named their boys Augustine from 1683 to 1747 when Augustine Sclate, weaver at West Craigs, carried on the tradition for his boy.

Naming a child after the father's master accounts for Mungo Shanks, 1733, whose father was a servant to Mungo Ponton, farmer at Balgreen. The gardener to the Keith family in Ravelston had a child baptised in 1737 named Keith Ramsay. When John Gordon in 1755 was a tenant farming on Corstorphine Hill which belonged to the Dickie family, his son was named Dickie.

Between 1793 and 1810 irregular baptisms were listed separately. Against some entries between 1810 and 1819 a note "in church" has been added. The 19th century opened with the country caught up in the Napoleonic wars. Some soldiers' wives accompanied their men throughout their campaigns as did Betty Duncan of Old Machar, Aberdeen, wife of Joseph Rose in the parish of Spynie. Their daughter, Rosanna, was baptised in Corstorphine in 1800 with an explanatory note beside her name – "brought forth on the road".

In July 1807 at a family gathering at the mansion on the hill

Elizabeth, daughter of George Robinson of Clermiston and wife of Alexander Gordon 95th Regt of Foot, had her son George baptised. Present were his Robinson grandfather and his grand uncle Lt Col. James Innes of the Honourable East India Company. The child's father was absent with his regiment "on the expedition which brought the Danish fleet in triumph to British ports". To this detailed entry the Session clerk added "the parent who introduced him to the Christian church was his mother".

Between 1809 and 1810 nine children were baptised whose fathers were in Edinburgh with the Aberdeen Militia: the mothers were lodging in the village. Alexander Keith of Ravelston and Corstorphine Hill and his wife Georgina Lamont had a son William Campbell who was born in North Knapdale in December 1815 and registered there but was baptised by the Corstorphine minister in February 1816. In 1839 Isabella Brisbane, daughter of Archibald Weir, mason, was recorded in the register of baptisms as having been baptised by the minister of the Relief Church (a Secession group) in Bread Street, Edinburgh.

Two abandoned children, a boy left at Beechwood Mains in 1850, and a girl discovered at the West Meadows in 1851, were boarded with William Samuel mason. In 1855 they were both baptised in the name of their foster father Samuel. On 17th August 1854 John George Graham, son of Rear Admiral Graham, was baptised at Fixby, 199 St John's Road. Some of the Free Church bairns were baptised by their own minister, Dr Burns, but appear in the closing pages of the register: Peter, son of Peter Keddie, mason, Mary, daughter of Thomas Garlick, smith, and George Mackay, son of George Sutherland, railway station master.

Former office and house of the manager of the horse buses, now demolished. It stood adjacent to the former Horse Bus terminus on the south side of St John's Road. [EW]

Compulsory civil registration of births came into force on 1st January 1855. The last two children baptised and registered under the old church system were Ann Gray daughter of Thomas Gray, farm servant North Gyle, and Jane Mason whose father Andrew lived at Braefoot. Both girls were baptised on 24th December 1854. The last child born in the village in 1854 was Robert Horne Mollison on 31st December. His father James was a quarryman. As the 19th century advanced home baptism became popular. "*The Scottish Christening*" by John Philip (1817–67) depicts in detail a cottage baptism which could have been a scene in 19th century Corstorphine.

MARRIAGES

The Reformed Church was concerned that the common people should participate in all its services. Marriage like baptism became a public act before the congregation. The First Book of Discipline, 1560–61, stated that marriage should take place "in open face and public audience of the kirk" and this was repeated at the General Assembly of 1571: "all marriages be made solemnly in the face of the congregation".

Those seeking to be married had to give their names to the minister or to the Session clerk and thereafter their intention to marry was announced to the congregation on three successive Sundays. This notice of marriage was the banns, a Latin ecclesiastical term meaning proclamation. The phrase "proclamation of banns" is church tautology: ordinary folk spoke of "crying the banns".

A sum of money, the marriage "pawn", was deposited with the Session clerk as a token of serious intention to solemnise the marriage without scandal. The kirk Session of Corstorphine in 1654 decided to charge "two rix [rex] dollars" for banns. The charge in 1701 was a half crown to be used for the poor. In 1714 for the proclamation and registration of marriage the Session clerk got fourteen and a half pence. Anyone coming from Edinburgh to be married in Corstorphine kirk in 1705 had to pay 14/– Scots to the poor box.

The authors of the First Book of Discipline possibly thought Sunday was the most expedient day for marriage since the congregation being at church to hear the sermon would be present at the nuptial ceremony without any upset to their working lives. However the Westminster Assembly of 1643 was against Sunday so thereafter marriages took place generally on the weekly sermon day. Corstorphine Kirk Session in 1695 enacted that if anyone married on any other day than Thursday a fine of 14/– Scots was to be paid to the poor.

When George Fordyce became minister in 1709 there was a tightening up of church administration in Corstorphine. In 1710 the former practice of the kirk officer having the collections at marriages for his own use was changed. In future an elder was to take charge of marriage gifts of money so that they could be used for the poor. Mr Fordyce found that marriages had been taking place on Fridays but in 1711 reverted to Thursdays and the people were instructed to behave "circumspectly". He was against Friday marriages because they were followed by Saturday festivities where drinking was carried on "to profane the Sabbath".

High spirited wedding celebrations in Corstorphine were no new problem. In 1646 the kirk Session was not happy with what went on at "penie brydles", the marriage feasts to which neighbours contributed one shilling Scots the equivalent of one penny sterling. The penny bridal was the 17th century version of the modern "bring your own bottle and eats" party. The kirk hired out its forms at a fee of 14/– Scots to seat the guests. In Scottish art David Allan's theme of the Penny Wedding led the way to an even greater portrayal of such an occasion by David Wilkie.

In 1648 Charles Hamilton and Anna Clark were married on a Sunday. By evening the celebrations got out of hand when Florance Lowristoune and James Ballantyne started pitching stones at the kirk windows. They soon found themselves in trouble with the Session. Alexander Taylor and George McCala in 1699 caused a disturbance "in time of divine service" at the marriage of John Jack and were fined and made to stand before the congregation. John Alexander and Agnes Cunningham in 1726 were granted the "privilege" of being married on a Friday. It cost them £1–10–0.

Though the Reformed Church ordered marriages to be in public there were private house weddings in the 17th century. This upset the Session in 1697 because of "the great inconveniency" and the loss sustained by the Session clerk and the kirk officer who were deprived of the dues got at church weddings. A house wedding was permitted in 1740 when Andrew Wilson married Anne Lindsay but a charge of £1–10–0 was made.

Church weddings, however, declined in the latter part of the 18th century so that by the early 19th century the church wedding was the exception not the rule. Mrs Story in her *Early Reminiscences* describes her marriage in 1863 to the Rev. R.H. Story, later to be Principal of Glasgow University: "The ceremony took place in our own drawing room, owing to the strong objection of Mr Story's mother to a wedding in church. She was of the old school and nourished strong objections to all modern innovations."

The First Book of Discipline did not recognise a marriage intention without the consent of parents unless no reasonable ground for refusal was proven. An instance of parental objection came before the Session of Corstorphine in 1708. David Fyfe in West Kirk parish in Edinburgh and Isobel Oliphant gave notice of their wish to marry. The Session, however, being told that Isobel's father did not approve called him to explain his objection. Oliphant said that his consent had not been asked and as for the proposed marriage "his heart could not give him to it." The Session took the view that there was no legal impediment so they allowed it to go ahead.

An objection to marriage between Marion Listoun and Abraham Stevenson was made in 1652 by John Cleghorn. He asked that the banns "be stayed" because Marion had promised to marry him. The Session said that if he was willing to take civil action they would delay the banns. When Cleghorn failed to do anything further the Session concluded that he had acted "maliciously" and allowed the banns to be called.

The church would on no account admit the marriage of persons within the forbidden degrees of relationship. Any defiance ended in excommunication. In 1695 John Thomson, widower, in the Lairdship gave up his name to be married to Jean Lauriston. The Session stopped the proclamation and ordered John to appear. He declared he was ignorant of any blood relation between Jean and his deceased wife Marion Lauriston. The Session then ordered both parties to a further meeting when each had to swear that there had been no "carnal dealing" with each other. Having satisfied themselves that there was no incest the Session proceeded to fine John two dollars and finally they "did assoill him".

Possession of a marriage certificate was important for incomers especially if baptism was needed for a child. Isobel Tait came to Corstorphine in 1716. She had no testificat from her last place of residence so the Session questioned her about her personal affairs. She said she came from Kelso and that her first husband was Daniel Cameron, a soldier in Captain Biggar's company, Bretaign's regiment. Daniel's brother had informed her that her husband had died more than a year ago "at Innerlochy". Isobel then married Alexander Connel, servant to Captain Stuart in Disney's regiment. She was able to produce a certificate of marriage to Connel performed by Mr John Wood, episcopal minister at Thurso, dated 29th March 1715. Wood was deprived of his church at Thurso in 1690.

The Session were not sure about the death of Cameron and

about the witnesses on the second marriage certificate so they reported the matter to the Presbytery of Edinburgh. The Presbytery advised baptism for the child which was done and the Session were relieved of any further enquiry about Isobel for she moved to the town.

The most common cause of conflict between the Session and the people in marriage matters arose over what were termed "irregular" and "clandestine" marriages. "Regular" marriage was marriage in accordance with the practice of the established church. Celebrating a marriage outwith the church was "irregular". This took different forms and was subject to public rebuke and fines.

After 1690 when Presbyterianism displaced Episcopacy marriages performed by Episcopalian ministers were irregular in the eyes of the established church. Between 1716 and 1719 Gilbert Ramsay, formerly minister at Cummertrees, officiated at the marriages in Edinburgh of Alexander Learmont in Golfhall and Margaret Brown; of Thomas Anderson and Agnes Muirhead in Gogar; of John Yorstoun in West Craigs and Jean Haldan. Mr James Graham, an Episcopal minister, married Robert Cleghorn, mason, and Janet Shepherd.

There were several irregular marriages from 1730 to 1760. The services which took place in Edinburgh were conducted by some genuine clerics and also by some doubtful characters. The most notorious of these "ministers" was David Strange who gave a certificate to James Girdwood, gardener, and Helen Baxter both servants in 1738 to Charles Bruce at Bruce Hill (Belmont). A George Blackie in 1750 married James Porteous and Rachael Cockburn who later became the mistress of James Watson of Saughton. Sooner or later the partners in irregular marriages got a summons to appear before the Session to be rebuked.

No indication is given in the Corstorphine records of why some people chose to have an irregular marriage. There may have been parental disapproval. There may have been breach of promise on the part of one of the persons concerned. Perhaps there was a legal impediment. More likely there was reluctance to face the minister and the Session whose inquisitorial methods could have drawn admission of ante-nuptial fornication. Whatever the kirk might do or say the irregular marriage was a fait accompli and there was a certificate to prove it had taken place. In Scotland where a valid marriage could be effected through simple acknowledgement by the parties involved that they were man and wife and had lived together, it is interesting that the irregular marriage was preferable. Possibly the security of a marriage certificate influenced the girl.

The married state certainly earned money for the kirk coffers. Apart from the marriage fees, fornication fines and hiring charges for the use of kirk forms at the wedding feast, there were donations from families when the gentry married. In 1679 "the twentie two pound" collected at the marriage of the Laird of Gogar's daughter was "put in ye box". The income from marriages in 1733 was £33 and in 1767 it was £21.

In an agricultural community the demands of the land largely dictated the times of marriage. In 1710 marriage dates ran from 29th April to 29th July, one in August, and then 9th September to 20th October. Marriages in 1750 took place from 30th March to 25th May and then in September. Between 1710 and 1766 an August wedding was rare and few took place between November and February.

Of the last two marriages registered in the kirk books before 1st January 1855 one was of William Potts, huntsman to the Linlithgow and Stirlingshire Foxhounds, and Jane Rattray Scott, Golfhall, daughter of Charles Scott, postmaster, Rose Street, Edinburgh. The other was John Kerr, smith in Corstorphine, and Janet Cowan, daughter of Hugh Cowan, implement maker. They were married at Corstorphine by the Rev. Mr David Horne, the parish minister. On January 6th 1857 Mr Horne went down to Corstorphine railway station house at Saughton and married David Smith, railway clerk, of Durham to Isabella Dryden.

FUNERALS

The ceremony and the ritual of the medieval church at death were abhorrent to the Reformers. The Book of Common Order, 1560, stated that at burials "the minister, if he be present and required, goeth to the church ... and maketh some comfortable exhortation to the people, touching death and resurrection". The Westminster Assembly of 1643 directed interment "without any ceremony". It forbade "praying, reading, and singing both in going to and at the grave" as such behaviour was "no way beneficial to the dead". Funerals were not considered part of a minister's duties.

Boswell, the biographer of Dr Johnson, in writing of his wife's funeral noted that "it is not customary in Scotland for a husband to attend a wife's funeral. I privately read the funeral service over her coffin in presence of my sons." Funerals, however, were family occasions. Before interment mourners were given refreshments and on return from the churchyard a funeral meal was provided on as lavish a scale as means permitted.

When James Warden, kirk elder Corstorphine, died in 1725 his funeral expenses included the cost of providing bread, cheese, pipes, tobacco, brandy and two gallon trees of ale for the mourners. A tree of ale was a barrel. The coffin cost £12 and kirk dues £10 and the total expenses were £44–4–0. Drink was considered a funeral necessity: "respect was shown to the dead by the intoxication of the living."

Coffins for the poor were supplied by the church. Robert Adamson, a Corstorphine wright, was paid for a "dead chist" for William Clatchie in 1680. In 1704 the Session must have been dissatisfied with the quality of pauper coffins and turned the tables on suppliers whose goods were "not sufficiently made" by paying only half the usual price. John Lyon in 1714 was paid 4/– sterling which the Session agreed would be the regular cost of a coffin.

The General Assembly in 1563 ordered corpses to be buried "six feet under the earth" and in 1576 the Assembly "thought meet that in every parish there be persons to make sepulchres". Digging graves became the job of the kirk officer or beadle as he was later known.

The parish of Corstorphine had two burial grounds, the churchyard in Kirk Loan, and the ground at Gogar beside the medieval chapel of St. Mary. In 1677 Florence Bartholomew got into trouble for digging graves at Gogar as this was the exclusive right of the bellman, James Alexander. When a pauper's grave was dug the church paid the bellman.

Despite church disapproval of ritual a funeral party as it walked to the churchyard was proceeded by the kirk officer ringing the mort bell. Corstorphine had the choice of a small hand bell, the mort bell, and the tolling of the great bell of the kirk. To have the great bell tolled in 1670 cost 30/–. By 1699 some of the feuars were objecting to paying for the great bell, declaring that it was something to which they had free right according to their land charters. The Session's reply was that the complainers must produce their documents.

The ringing of a funeral bell may have been a survival from earlier times when bells were rung to keep evil spirits away. In reformed times it was a mark of respect to the dead and a reminder of mortality to the living: "Never send to know for whom the bell tolls. It tolls for thee."

Coffins made by the village joiner were plain boxes, not the highly polished modern type. But the coffin was transformed as it was carried to the grave, solemnly and impressively draped with the church mortcloth. The pall in present day cremation services is a reversion to the mortcloth of times past.

Much thought was given by the Session to providing mortcloths. When the church accounts were balanced in August 1674 it was decided to use the surplus to buy "good velvet as will be a mortcloth". It was decided to charge parishioners using it 30/– Scots. In addition the bellman "for carrying and having a care" of the cloth was to have 4/–. Where a parish had no mortcloth another parish would lend its cloth and so Corstorphine charged outsiders 40/– and the bellman's fee was raised to 6/–.

For the 1674 mortcloth the materials used were velvet, calico, fringes, looping, buttons, and serge for a bag in which to carry the cloth with strings and "knops" (tassels). The cost was £154–4–0 Scots. By 1681 the Session was able to provide a second mortcloth, a "little" one, for the coffins of young people. The velvet cost £56 and the lining £2–8–0. The Gogar burial ground was used by people in the north west part of the parish who around 1700 were borrowing the Cramond mortcloth. The Corstorphine minister reported this to the Laird of Gogar who promised he would "allow no such disorder among his tennents". Augustine Sclate in Gogar was cited to explain to the Session his "breaking the ground and making a grave to Jean Comb who had the Cramond mortcloth contrair to Order". He was warned that any repetition would mean a fine of £6 Scots.

Under the Rev. George Fordyce's control of church affairs a re-appraisal was made in 1712 of the stock of mortcloths. A large cloth was bought from Henry Hathorn, merchant, Edinburgh for £237–14–0 Scots. Hathorn supplied 9 yards super fine black velvet, 9 yards black cloth serge for lining, 100 ounces black silk fringe, tassels and string for the buckram bag to carry the cloth and an ounce of black threads for the tailor sewing the cloth.

This new cloth was hired out at £4 Scots to parishioners and £5 Scots to outsiders. The old large velvet, though "worn", was available at a cheaper price. There was a third large plain cloth. The little velvet cloth cost 2/– sterling and there was a cheaper little cloth one. John Lyon, wright, was instructed to make a chest for holding mortcloths.

Strangers who died in the parish were buried by the church. One such in 1731 was Malcolm Whyte, "a Highland shearer", for whose coffin and grave being dug the Session paid £3–14–0. Again in 1736 the Session gave consideration to mortcloth provision for those they had "were turned old". A large velvet and one for children were bought from Robert Cleland, merchant, Edinburgh, possibly a son of James Cleland who in 1712 bought the property in Corstorphine later known as Dunsmure.

Scotch thrift is evident in the deliberations of the Session in 1754 for by then the second velvet cloth was somewhat worn. The treasurer was to buy a new cloth "either of coarse velvet or of plush". The fringes of the existing best cloth were to be taken off and put on the second cloth to improve it. New fringes were to be got to refurbish the best cloth. These silk fringes bought from Mrs Chalmers cost £58–19–0. This gave the Session three cloths ranging in condition from the new to the "old and bare". In death you got what you paid for.

The same grading of mortcloths appears in funeral charges for 1824: best cloth with hearse £1–1–0; second cloth 8/–; best child's cloth 5/–; second child's cloth 2/6. In 1829 the Edinburgh clothiers, Girdwood and Thomson, supplied a new large and a new small cloth for £27–4–0. When cloth covered coffins were introduced in Victorian times the mortcloth became superfluous and gradually fell into disuse.

In medieval times the gentry enjoyed the right of burial within the church. Though the Reformed Church in 1576 passed an Act prohibiting church burials, a few interments continued for more than two centuries. The last Forrester buried at Corstorphine was the murdered James, 1679, placed beneath the east window. The Watsons of Saughton and Cammo were buried in their vault at the entrance to the south aisle till 1836. Lady Helen, the end of the Watson line, being married to Lord Aberdour, was buried in 1850 on the Morton estate at Dalmahoy.

The most spectacular church burial took place when Harry Aikman in Broomhouse on 9th September 1609 came to the church at midnight to arrange the burial of his wife, Margaret Broun. He was accompanied by James Cleghorn in West Craigs and Andrew Aikman, servant to the Laird of Corstorphine. The church doors were locked so Aikman's party got on the roof with ladders and broke into the building. With spade and picks they dug a grave in the floor.

The next day was the Sabbath. When the last bell for the service had been rung and the congregation awaited the minister, Mr Rutherford, Harry Aikman entered the church with Margaret's corpse. He was accompanied by James Allan in Corstorphine, John Broun in Gogar Mill, James Aikman, Henry Aikman, chirurgeon, and Alexander Liston. When Mr Rutherford went to the pulpit he was "pullit" and Aikman's friends "shote him furth of the dure". Having ejected the minister Harry interred his wife's body. He was reported to the Privy Council who passed him to the Presbytery of Edinburgh to make him give satisfaction for his "insolence".

Registers of death were supposed to be kept by the Session clerk. In 1697 the Corstorphine kirk officer was told to give the name of the deceased to the clerk before the grave was dug and the clerk was then to register it in the deaths register. In practice death registers were neglected: baptisms were given priority and marriages were given some attention. Much depended on the conscientiousness of the clerk. Since the clerk was also the schoolmaster the parish registers should have been kept competently but this is not always so. The interest or lack of interest from the minister was another factor. From the death of Mr Fordyce, 1767, to the coming of David Horne, 1833, there is not the detail of the earlier records. The Registration Act of 1854 made it compulsory for kirk registers to be handed over to the General Registry Office, Edinburgh, where they may be consulted on payment of a statutory fee.

Kirk session records, however, are available for consultation free in the Scottish Record Office, Edinburgh, where most churches have deposited their historical papers. Church account books help to create the social picture. Corstorphine has an account of mortcloths hired 1710–66 with full detail while with less detail there are accounts for 1767–68, 1791–97, 1804–5, 1814–20. The heritors records have brief notes of hired cloths, 1855–60.

Mortcloth accounts are virtually registers of deaths. The old velvet was used in May 1726 for Elizabeth Erskine "a lass belonging to the Trades Maiden Hospital" in Edinburgh. That same year the large velvet cloth and the great bell brought £6 to the funds when Bethia Baird, Lady Cockpen, was buried, presumably in the Watson vault as her first husband was James Watson of Saughton. The large old velvet in 1744 covered Janet Thomson in Carrick Know. In 1749 the large new velvet and the great bell at a cost of £5–10–0 were used for Janet Graham, wife of James Clarkson in Balgreen. Her son, Deacon Clarkson in Edinburgh, gave 12 guineas to the poor of the parish.

Alexander Hardie, farmer, Easter Norton Mains, in 1764 had his large new velvet "in a herse" as he made his last journey to Gogar kirkyard. The hearse must have been got from another parish as there is no mention in the records of a Corstorphine hearse. Christian Ponton in 1764 married Andrew Young of Meadowfield at "Cross Causeys" Edinburgh, the service being performed by the Rev. Walter Ponton, minister of the Tolbooth church. Christian belonged to Dalmeny parish. Ten years later in 1774 Andrew Young, as recorded in the records of Dalmeny church "employed the Herse to carry his wife Christian Ponton her corps to Gogar paid 6/4". She died giving birth to a daughter Susanna.

A chest kept in the church at Corstorphine today may have been the mortcloth chest. The last interment noted in the old parochial register before January 1855 was that of Alexander Elder, railway guard, 26th December 1854.

THE CHURCHYARD

Much of the history of any village lies in its churchyard: "one generation passeth and another generation cometh". In post Reformation Corstorphine the Session and the heritors were concerned to maintain decency in their burial ground. The churchyard in times past was a focal point for the community, the place where people came together before and after sermon time to discuss matters of mutual interest. In some places weekday markets were held in the churchyard. Public notices were affixed to the church door where all would see them.

James, Lord Forrester, 1668 complained that "it was an unhansom thing for any person to pish within the churchyard upon the burral places of Christians". The Session acted at once by placing a notice on the church door to the effect that

An aerial view, pre-1928, showing the crowded housing at the foot of Kirk Loan impinging on what is now the green area to the south of the Old Parish Church. Note also Corstorphine House Terrace (middle top) and Corstorphine Station (top right). *(PB2)*

anyone committing such a nuisance would be fined 6/– Scots. Forrester to prevent any other desecration requested that the churchyard was made secure with gates and door. In 1697 the Session, upset that some notices fixed to the church door were not always "decent", ruled that the minister's approval must be got before a bill was displayed.

Maintenance of the churchyard dykes was essential, not just to mark boundaries but more to ensure order within. Anyone with land adjoining was ordered in 1668 to repair the dyke at their part.

The churchyard in 1673 apparently was used as a short cut because the Session enacted that persons going over the kirkyard dyke would be fined £5 Scots. To enforce this the Session sought the concurrence of the civil magistrate. The same year John Gowans, mason, was employed to repair the easter stile. In addition the easter door of the churchyard was secured, involving the masons in four hours work and the Session in paying for timber, a lock, and "bands" (hinges) as well as drink to the workmen. James Moderall and Andrew Dewar were paid 4/– Scots in 1701 for repairing the path through the churchyard from the south stile towards the north stile. Still today the churchyard path from the High Street to the Glebe is a well trodden road.

Major dyke work went ahead during 1721–22. Sir James Dick, owner of the estate, allowed stones to be removed from the Forrester castle to provide building material. William Henderson in Gogar Mill carted the stones from "the old place". David Mitchell, mason, Gogar demolished the old dyke and built the new. A hundred bags of lime were purchased and bread and ale given to the men who brought the lime. The

Compare this 1980s aerial view with the pre-1928 view. The old houses at the foot of Kirk Loan have been demolished, opening up the churchyard. The circular grassed area and bungalows in Corstorphine House Avenue are also apparent.
(Courtesy RCAHMS, ref. E016506)

beadle, James Hamilton, got sand and was responsible for "souring" (slaking) the lime. By 1820 the dykes again needed attention. Moreover the hedge on the east side was uprooted for it gave shelter for "an abominable nuisance".

Trees were a feature of the churchyard landscape. In 1668 when the ash trees were "failing" Lord Forrester agreed that the old trees should be cut down and sold for their timber value while young trees were planted as replacements. Three ash trees were sold to Leith wrights. In 1679 four trees were sold to Thomas Coe for £23 Scots. Big trees in 1717 were threatening the roof of the church so the Session asked permission from the heritors to sell them and use the money for repairing the church dykes. John Sclate, wright in Gogar, in 1722 bought 40 trees at £4 Scots per tree.

When the church was renovated in 1832 the Session expressed regret at the "want of trees" in the churchyard. They felt that a score planted along the boundary walls would add to the beauty of the setting. At this time the east wall of the churchyard was rebuilt to align it with the wall of the Johnston property. Lime, beech, birch, and sycamore were rejected. Oak, elm and Spanish chestnut were preferred because they could be got from the heritors' plantations. Instructions were also given to clear the burial ground of rubbish. At the end of the 19th century 12 Corstorphine planes were planted.

By the late 17th century the village people were asking for permission to erect memorial stones on family graves. In 1668 Lord Forrester empowered the Session to grant such requests and to fix charges. The maximum fee was 50 merks and the minimum 30 merks. Alexander Clarkson, feuar, in May 1668 paid four rix dollars to put a stone over the grave of his father William. The money on this occasion was given to John Snodgrass for the maintenance of the foundling he had taken into his home.

In 1677 James Allan tailor set up a stone, still standing. Later it was agreed that the bellman would get 6/8 for every tombstone erected. Charges were revised in 1726: permission for a gravestone cost £3 and a headstone 5/– Scots.

Corstorphine in 1820 was uneasy about the activities of grave robbers trading with the School of Anatomy in Edinburgh. The villagers mounted guard over the churchyard. This danger from Resurrectionists may have been the reason for Thomas Mackie choosing to have a small mausoleum in 1821. He was allowed to enclose his tomb with chain or railing and on the north side his enclosure went as far as where the dyke had previously been. Mackie was the husband of Agnes Blaikie, sister of the celebrated Scotch gardener to the French nobility in the decade before the Revolution. To save the village folk watching the churchyard the Session bought from Redpath Brown and Co. 1823–24 safety covers – mort safes – to be put over the graves to hinder removal of corpses. These were hired out, the largest 10/6 and lesser sizes ranging from 8/– to 4/–. The covers were in position for 6 weeks. Any extension of this time was charged at 1/– per week. This arrangement ensured that bodies would be unsuitable for dissection and accordingly would be left undisturbed by the Burke and Hare type of entrepreneur.

Any burial ground long in use inevitably presented in time a problem of space for continuing burials. A lair could be cleared of previous interments and any remaining bones re-interred. The kirk officer at Corstorphine about 1820 in an effort "to secure new graves" removed tombstones. The Session had to threaten loss of pay and dismissal to stop him. No doubt some 17th century stones were destroyed then. George Aitken, mason, who died in 1663, was in a comfortable position. At the time of his death his barnyard was filled with wheat, beir, oats and pease. He had a little old nag and four little kyne. There was his house plenishing and his clothing. His debts were no more than expected – wages to servants, house rent, and rent for land and for his share of the meadow. There were accounts for medicines prescribed for him by Dr Guthrie and David Pringle. In his testament he recommended his soul to his Creator and his final wish was that his body would "be buried in the earth amongst the faithful". The Aitken family were masons and surely brother William and widow Janet would set up a stone.

A large burial area enclosed in 1821 with stonework and an iron rail was erected by John Pettet, tenant of Sir James Baird of Saughton Hall. This annoyed the heritors as he had not asked their permission. About 1890 the Pettet enclosure materials were removed to be used in building the church at Gogar: the inscribed tablet remains on the remnant of the south wall. When Henry Johnston, surgeon, in 1832 wanted the burial space next to his father's family he noted that this ground was covered by two large unclaimed stones and no interment had taken place in the last fifty years. The Johnston ground is opposite the church porch.

James Girdwood's stone beside the window of the south aisle records the family back to 1527 at Langsaughton. The Nimmo family, long farmers at Sighthill, have their genealogy recorded on a tablestone. Set into the exterior south wall is a pedimented memorial erected by William Walker, portioner, who died in 1751. The name William Don also appears on this stone. When Walker and his wife who lived in the Park of Corstorphine had their son, William, baptised one of the witnesses was William Don, servitor to the Laird of Corstorphine, Sir James Dick. Don was Dick's factor.

Other stones recalling village personalities include, near the church porch, the sculptured memorial to Francis Glog who died in 1738. Francis was farmer at Claycott, kirk elder, and kirk treasurer. Two figures depict 18th century farmers sowing and reaping, the reaper sheaf and sickle in hand. Above is a Green Man type of head symbolic in folk lore of fertility and the cycle of life and death in nature and in man. On the reverse side is Father Time. At the side of the path beside the north aisle a stone with the angel and trumpet of resurrection recalls Janet Muirhead, a seventeen year old who died in 1751. Between the porch and the north aisle lies William Hosie, gardener, who for long was in charge of the grounds at Cammo for the Watson family. Still today in the old walled garden at Cammo the 18th century snowdrops which Hosie planted bloom in profusion.

Opposite the great east window rests William H. Marryat 1800–32, minister of Old St. Paul's episcopal church, Edinburgh, and Classics Master at Edinburgh Academy. To the north of the east gable is a boulder of natural rock marking the grave of the shepherd John Foord who was found dead on Corstorphine Hill in February 1795. The rock is reputed to be the stone on which his body was found. The little stone behind Foord's stone is traditionally the grave of his dog.

A victim of early railway history was John Cook, age 23, pointsman with the North British, who was killed by a pilot engine which emerged from a siding while Cook was signalling to an engine proceeding to Haymarket. Cook was standing on the rails at the entrance to the Mound Tunnel on 30th May 1867. The village poet, Robert Cuddie, lies there, too. For the benefit of his widow his verses were published as *Corstorphine Lyrics* in 1878. Though verse, rather than poetry, his works reflect the life of his times. The Hopes of Belmont, distinguished in Edinburgh legal circles, are buried at the east

The 'green-man' fertility symbol with yawning mouth dominates the elaborate decoration on the tombstone of Francis Glog tenant in Corstorphine, d.1738. Francis was an elder and Treasurer of the Parish Church. *(PB2023)*

wall. Under the lamp niche are the Boothbys of Beechwood, parents of Sir Robert Boothby, M.P. Near them is one of Corstorphine's caring physicians, Dr Matthew. The last of the estate owners, the Dicksons, are commemorated near the south aisle.

In the north east corner of the graveyard where he allowed sheep to graze and so incurred the disapproval of the heritors was buried Dr David Scot, minister 1814–34. The original stone enclosure around his grave was later taken down to provide material for building Gogar church. Across from the Mackie mausoleum is the enclosure of the Melville of Hanley

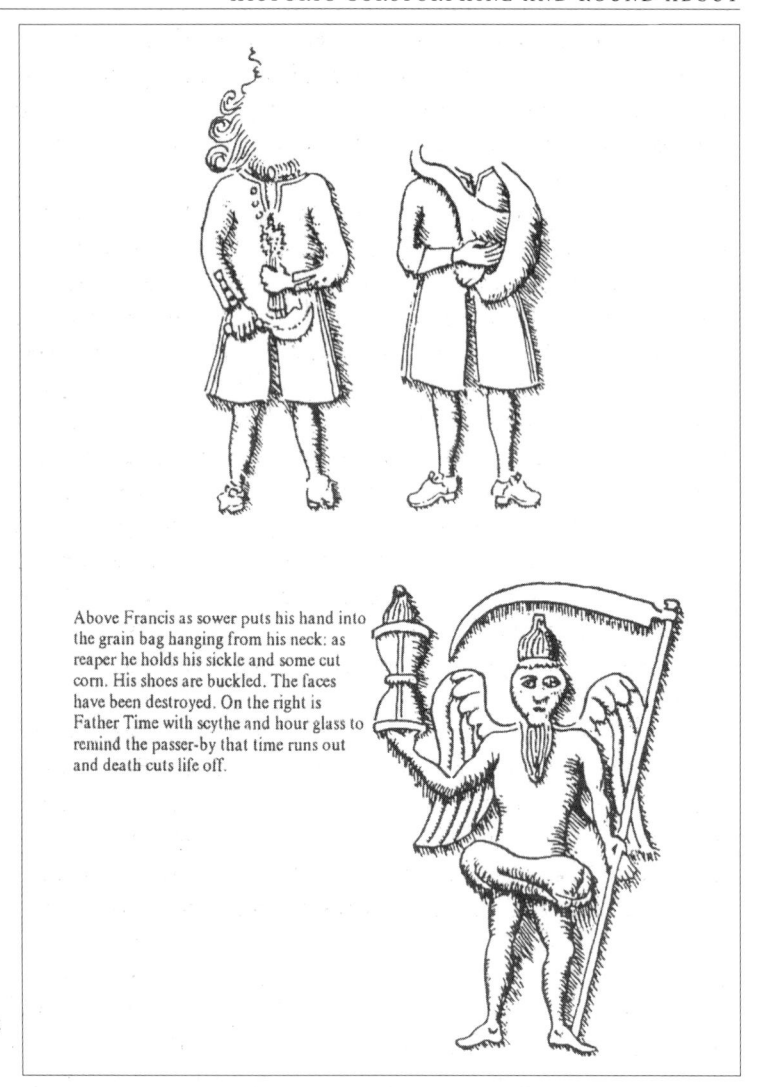

Above Francis as sower puts his hand into the grain bag hanging from his neck: as reaper he holds his sickle and some cut corn. His shoes are buckled. The faces have been destroyed. On the right is Father Time with scythe and hour glass to remind the passer-by that time runs out and death cuts life off.

Details from the tombstone of Francis Glog tenant in Corstorphine, d.1738. *(Courtesy SOAS)*

family. The path which separates these memorials was made by the Rev. David Horne who came to Corstorphine kirk in 1833. He wanted a road from the manse to the church so he was allowed to open a gate in the wall between the Mackie and the Melville enclosures and make a footpath. Today it is a quick cut for less reverend feet travelling between St. John's Road and North Saughton Road.

Beside the south entrance gates to the church and churchyard is a low stone building, which appears to be the survivor of two offering houses, once part of church life in Corstorphine. In 1657 collections were taken at the west door and in 1682 the Session ordered basins to be set at the church doors.

By 1717 the Session were concerned that there were no "sconces" (shelters) for elders standing collecting the offerings. That same year John Lyon, wright was ordered to provide two stools on which the collecting basins could be placed "at the stiles".

There were two stiles, an easter and a wester, and in 1719 John Lyon made a door at the easter stile. By 1721 work started on the offering houses which were sited "at the two entries". Dick of Prestonfield, the owner of the estate, allowed stone to be taken from the old castle. John Sclate in Gogar was responsible for couples and sarking. The doors were made by John Lyon, a local wright. Robert Cumming, slater in the Canongate, used 900 slates and 1,000 slate nails. Bread and ale were provided for the men who brought the slates from Leith. The "cape" (cope) stones came from Queensferry. John Lyon also made seats for the offering houses and put locks on the doors. Chimneys were added in 1723 and two loads of coals for the offering houses appear in the 1725 accounts. John Alexander in 1743 put sarking on the east house and in 1755 slating was done.

The stools and basins which previously had been at the stiles were then moved to the doors of the offering houses. These were usually sturdy stools with stretchers and turned legs. Doubtless some of the existing church pewter plates were used at the offering houses. The offering houses not only provided shelter for the elders on duty but were also convenient places in which to add and to record the Sabbath collections. The Corstorphine offering houses were still in use in 1820 when Archibald Thomson was paid to rebuild them with hammer dressed cope at a cost of £74 sterling. The renovation of 1828 which changed the entrance to the church to the east end and changing fashion in the 19th century led to collections being taken inside the church. The offering houses gradually became disused and in time demolition and alteration of the Kirk Loan side of the church ground left the existing west building as the sole survivor of church architecture long ago.

CRAFT REGULATIONS

In February and March 1673 it was noted in the minute book of the Lodge of Edinburgh (Mary's Chapel No. 1) that "the masons of Corstorphin" who were "at worke of John Gallowayes works" might do the craft in the city harm if not checked. The Lodge feared "great prejudice" as a result of this "incroachment".

The masons concerned were George Aiken, William Aiken, Archibald McAlla, and Edward Cleghorn. They were debarred from operating in Edinburgh for a year and anyone employing them was guilty of "breach of brother love".

Seven years later, 1680, the Masters of Mary's Chapel lifted the ban on the Aikens and McAlla but did not relax the restriction on Cleghorn. Since craft rights were zealously guarded it is interesting that these Corstorphine masons appear to have flouted regulations. They may have been working on a private commission with no intention of setting up in opposition to city masons. This dispute arose a year after David Watson of Saughton was granted permission to use Canongate tradesmen on his mansion at Saughton.

FRIENDLY SOCIETIES: CORSTORPHINE AND SAUGHTON

On 4th August 1789 a group of villagers met "to establish a Fund in order to the relief of ourselves and Brethren in time of necessity". This was the beginning of the Corstorphine Friendly Society. Such societies began in Scotland in the 17th century and were local independent bodies with their own funds. The purpose was to ensure the members against periods of unemployment with consequent loss of earnings when illness struck them, to pay for decent burial for their dead, and to enjoy the fellowship at meetings. The Friendly Society was based on the principle of Self-Help. The motto of the Corstorphine Society was "for ourselves and for all". Contributions varied according to the state of funds. In its early years the enrolment fee was half a crown with quarterly payments of one shilling. Benefits also varied at different times but, on occasions, amounted to three shillings weekly. Members could also claim burial benefit on the death of a wife.

In 1802 a Corstorphine artilleryman stationed at Woolwich wrote home to his mother asking her to keep his name on the register of the Friendly Society. After his discharge he was on his way back to Scotland when he was press ganged by the Navy. In one of the engagements of the Peninsular War he was drowned.

The first banner was bought in 1808 and the second in 1827. Both, though now frail, survive. One may be seen at Ladywell Health Centre. On one side the design shows two members shaking hands across a table on which stands the oak box used to contain the Society's papers: it, too, is still in existence. It had three keys and three keepers. The other side depicts the ancient Cross of Corstorphine in the shape of five trees.

Each year in June the Society met for its annual dinner when the Colours were rouped. The highest bidder then had the honour of heading the procession of members as it went through the parish collecting donations. When the marchers with their band called on Mr Keith at Ravelston in 1816 he gave them "a £1 note". Andrew Erskine, the highest bidder for the Colours in 1821 and a former Preses, fell from grace in 1825 when at the annual general meeting he "was ordered to stand

The banner of Corstorphine Friendly Society, founded in 1789. The centre circle shows the five trees forming the ancient mercat cross of Corstorphine. *(PB1059)*

The oak charter chest, still extant, of Corstorphine Friendly Society, displaying some of the Society's early records, and now in the custody of the Corstorphine Trust. *(s139)*

up". The charge was "that he had been found working dewring the time he was receiving the Societys Sick money". Andrew did not deny the accusation but said "it was not for any interest, but only to trey whither he thought he would be able to work or not". He had to return a week's money to the Treasurer and promise "not to do the like again".

When Cumberland Hill born in Ratho in 1778 decided in 1849 to emigrate to "the Cape of Good Colony" where his son was prepared to keep his parents "for the reminder of their days" he asked for £5 "to provide little comforts for the voyage". The Friendly Society did not deny this request from "Cumby" who had paid his first subscription in 1805.

Families that in later generations left the village remained loyal to the Society. William Keddie, born 1849, whose father joined the Society in 1833, set up in a bakery business at Shandon Place, Edinburgh, and continued to support the Society till his death was noted in the records in 1923–24. The Society came to an end in 1927.

The Friendly Society of the Barony of Saughton started in 1798. It met at Parkhead once in three months on the third Friday of September, December and March at 6.30 in the evening. In 1853 there were 168 members. The Society had income from a flat at 24 Fountainbridge (later premises of St. Cuthbert's Co-operative Society).

Conduct of meetings was strict. All speeches were to be addressed to the Preses, only one member was to speak at one time, and there were to be no interruptions when a member was speaking. Members when speaking were to be "uncovered" and when addressing the Preses speakers were to be "on their feet". For the funeral of a member £4–0–0 was given and for the death of a wife £3–0–0. But a member who made a second marriage (Dr Johnson's "triumph of hope over experience") having had £3 for the first wife had to pay an extra ten shillings on re-marriage.

Members were to be men "of sober habits and sound constitution". The Society was not prepared to be burdened by those whose existing ill health might drain funds or by those whose foolish behaviour might lead to their becoming a burden. No one over 35 years could join. Since life expectancy in the 19th century was 50 for a man and 55 for a woman the age bar is understandable – what insurance companies today term "not a good insurable life". Anyone emigrating could claim benefit when abroad and an emigrant who returned could rejoin as long as his absence did not exceed 15 years. Officials in 1852 came from Corstorphine, Parkhead, Saughton Mains, Slateford, and Hailes Quarry. That year the banner was repaired.

In January 1900 the Liberals under Asquith introduced the old age non-contributory pension of five shillings weekly for those over 70 with an income of less than £26 yearly. Married couples got 7/6. The 1911 National Insurance Act made Friendly Societies the agents for operating the state insurance scheme. The records of the Friendly Societies teach a lesson in humanity and community spirit.

Village End. Looking back into the old village from the west end of the High Street looking east. [GUS]

APPENDIX 1

SERVANTS OF THE KIRK

The line of all who, in any capacity however humble, served the kirk in Corstorphine from Reformation times to 1920 is long. It is deserving of remembrance along with the medieval Provost and his successors for whom a service is held annually.

ELDERS

Dates given are the first, and the last noted in various records. Where the same name appears over a long period it may be father and son. An elder's name with (T) indicates that he also served as Treasurer during part of his eldership.

John Aitken (T) – 1648, 1656
Robert Alexander – (T) 1667
John Allan – 1683, 1698
Thomas Allan (T) – 1705, 1725
Alexander Anderson (T) – 1692, 1722
Rev John Anderson – 1892, 1897
James Asher – 1905, 1908
Alexander Baillie – 1684
Thomas Baillie in Meadowfield (T) – 1652, 1665
Thomas Baillie – 1684, 1709
Thomas Beg – 1677, 1682
James Binny – 1656, 1666
Thomas Binnie – 1825
George Broun in Gogar – 1652, 1666
George Broun in Stennopsmill – 1684
James Broun – 1696, 1705
Mathew Cavenie – 1881, 1909
John Clarkson – 1667
Edward Cleghorn (T) – 1676, 1683: made "ane accompt and reckoning … upon his death bed".
James Cleland (T) – 1741, 1746: Edinburgh baillie: owner of Dunsmuir

George Cochran (T) – 1646, 1656: borrowed from the funds in "tyme of Crumwell" ; kept alehouse ; "not in his power to command Lord Forrester out of his house in time of divine service".
John Comb, farmer Gogar Mains – 1792, 1795
James E. Cowan (T) – 1894
Isaac Cowie – 1909
Sir John Cowper of Gogar – 1646, 1666
John Cunningham, brewer (T) – 1708, 1710
Robert Cunningham (T) – 1701, 1717: deposed drinking
Sir William Cunninghame of Livingston – 1771, 1778
James Davidson – 1898, 1909
John Dickie of Corstorphine Hill – 1741, 1766
Robert Duncan (T) – 1696, 1709
James Dykes – 1681, 1682
Robert Dykes – 1648, 1656
James Eastone – 1692, 1695
Adam Erskine – 1681, 1682
Alexander Ferguson, farmer Larbour (T) – 1747, 1784: tombstone Gogar
John Ferguson, farmer Gogartown (T) – 1727, 1757: tombstone Gogar
Thomas Ferguson, farmer Larbour (T) – 1701, 1741
William Ferguson – 1705, 1709
John Foreman (T) – 1792, 1800
Sir George Forrester – 1648
Sir James Forrester – 1652, 1661
George Foulis of Ravelston – 1652, 1656
Florence Gardner (T) – 1648: titular Provost of Collegiate church
John Gavin – 1898, 1907
George Girdwood – 1667, 1695
James Girdwood – 1677, 1682
Francis Glog, farmer Clayclott (T) – 1705, 1737: tombstone Corstorphine – sculptured sower and reaper
John Gordon, farmer Corstorphine Hill (T) – 1747, 1761
Robert Grahame (T) – 1656, 1678
Sir Francis Grant of Cullen – 1720, 1726
John Grier – 1672, 1676
James Hadden – 1648, 1673
Alexander Hardie, farmer Gogar Mains (T) – 1727, 1745: tombstone Gogar
Henry Hardie – 1682, 1692

James Hardie, farmer West Craigs (T) – 1750, 1778: son merchant Quebec: tombstone Gogar
Thomas Hardie, tenant West Craigs – 1714, 1749: tombstone Gogar
David Heriot, advocate – 1667, 1678: grandson of David Heriot, goldsmith, Edinburgh
William Hill – 1696, 1709
John Hodge – 1656, 1667
John Irving – 1889, 1905
Thomas Jamieson – 1666, 1676
David Johnston, brewer (T) – 1763, 1800: tombstone Corstorphine
James Johnston – 1694
John Johnston – 1701
Dr Thomas Johnston – 1905, 1911
Patrick Johnston – 1684, 1701
William Johnston, brewer (T) – 1727
A. Keith (T) – 1880, 1886
John Kerr – 1889, 1892
Thomas Lauriston – 1656
Dr Henry Leebody – 1905, 1907
Adam Leishman – 1656, 1672
John Leishman – 1684
Florence Liston – 1652, 1666
Thomas Liston – 1646
George McGown, schoolmaster Corstorphine – 1905, 1913
Thomas Mackie – 1826, 1833
Rev. Donald MacLeod – 1909, 1911
Rev. John Mactaggart – 1909
Alexander Maitland – Gibson – 1825
Dr Alexander Matthew – 1898, 1905
John Mitchell, farmer Broomhouse (T) – 1705, 1741
David Morrison – 1684, 1696
William Muir – 1684
James Murray (T) – 1692, 1701
Richard Murray (T) – 1649, 1666: rode to Hamilton to ask Mr Hunter to accept ministry at Corstorphine
Archibald Nimmo – 1705
James Nimmo, farmer Sighthill (T) – 1792, 1800: tombstone Corstorphine
James Nimmo, farmer Gogar Mains – 1825:
son of above James Nimmo
Robert Oliphant, village baker (T) – 1692, 1701

George Paterson – 1677 : Forrester objected to his appointment
Andrew Raburne 1682
William Ramsay of Barnton and Gogar (T) – 1804, 1805
Alexander Reid – 1667, 1676
William Renwick – 1898, 1913
George Robinson of Clermiston, W.S. – 1825
John Shanks – 1607, 1676
Alexander Simpson, schoolmaster Corstorphine – 1814, 1848
Charles Smith – 1898, 1909
James Stevenson – 1648, 1676
John Stewart Crown Chamberlain (T) – 1889, 1893
John Tait – 1676, 1682
Alexander Telfer – 1652, 1654
David Thomson – 1919: author of *The Corstorphine Heirloom* the proceeds of which went to restoring the lamp niche, a project dear to Mr Thomson
Thomas Thomson – 1705
Thomas Tod – 1705, 1712: deposed drinking
John Walker – 1692, 1695
Thomas Walker – 1656, 1678
James Warden (T) – 1705, 1717
James Watson of Saughton – 1646, 1656
Robert Watt – 1792
David Weston – 1881, 1896
James Wightimor – 1684
James Wilkie (T) – 1648, 1684 (possibly a father and son)
James Wilkie – 1725, 1734
James Yorston – 1672, 1682
John Yorston – 1648, 1673
John Yorston, farmer West Craigs – 1696
Alexander Young (T) – 1652, 1653
George Young – 1692, 1701
Thomas Young – 1684

SESSION CLERK: PRECENTOR

The village schoolmaster till the mid 19th century also acted as Session Clerk and Precentor. At Sacrament time a second precentor assisted. The advent of the organ in the late 19th century was the end of the precentor with his tuning fork. Alexander Flemington resigned in 1884 and was the last precentor. He showed the congregation the name of the psalm tune by displaying it on a stand placed at his desk.

The Old Parish Church Choir at the main (east) door c.1880. The Choirmaster, Mr Mollison, is on the left. *(PB625)*

Additional 18th century precentors included: Patrick Petrie 1712; David Lindsay 1720–24; David Watt 1731–32; Francis Mitchell 1738–44; Henry Hews miller Gogar 1745.

The Corstorphine parochial teachers who acted as Session Clerk and precentor were:

Sebastian Parke – 1645
James Chalmers – 1646
William Greg – 1650
Thomas McConchy – 1662
William Wilson – 1689
John Cunningham – 1698
James Coupar – 1699
Laurence Waugh – 1700
William Wood – 1706
Robert Black – 1723
James Mitchell – 1728
Ralph Drummond – 1756
Alexander Bannatyne – 1762
Daniel Ramsay – 1805
Alexander Simpson – 1812
George Manson – 1847
William Duncan – 1863
James Matthew – 1878

In late Victorian times the church choir came into being. The combined position of organist and choirmaster was held by

Joseph Hibbs 1885–92, Daniel McIntyre 1892–94, James Henderson 1895–1903, Charles Hamilton 1904

PIPER TO THE SESSION
Alexander Dobie – 1665

OFFICER, BELLMAN, BEADLE, SEXTON
Walter Landall – 1654–69, 1682
James Simpson – 1669
John Mowat – 1673–76
James Alexander – 1676–82: dismissed insolent to minister
John Knight – 1688–89
William Inglis – 1689
Archibald Inglis – 1692
Andrew Dewar – 1694–1706: "opprobrious speeches against the elders"
William Stevenson – 1706–16: dismissed drinking
James Hamilton – 1716–37
George Sclate – 1737–76
William Blaikie – 1776–1814
John Samuel – 1822
John Smith – 1823
John Smith – 1865: son to above John Smith
Charles Monro – 1866: tombstone with sculptured bell: reputed to have chosen grave near gate to get out first on the great day of Judgement
John Smith – 1882–91
James Orx – 1891–99
James Yule – 1899–1912: emigrated Australia
Walter Clarke – 1911
Andrew Coventry – 1913: enlisted KOSB: duties taken over 1915 by bell ringer Walter Clarke: Thomas Ritchie acted as sexton : Mr Coventry resumed duty on return from war service

CLEANER
Mrs Pratt 1907–12

POST REFORMATION CLERGY
Gogar
Mungo Wood reader – 1561
John Learmonth – 1567
James Hamilton – 1574: minister Kirknewton also acting for Gogar

John Coiss reader – 1574–1576
Andrew Forrester – 1593
William Arthur – 1599

Corstorphine
Mungo Wood reader – 1561: "parson and vicar" Gogar
Walter Lang; said to be reader – 1568–1569
Walter Coupar, reader – 1567–1569
Robert Pont – 1574
John Nimmill, M.A. – 1589–1590
Thomas Marjoribanks, M.A. – 1590
Andrew Forrester – 1590–1598
William Arthur, M.A. – 1599–1607
Robert Rutherford, M.A. – 1607–1616
Robert Lindsay, M.A. – 1612–1626
David Balsillie, M.A. – 1626–1654
Robert Hunter, M.A. – 1655: non-conformist: deprived 1662
William Ogstone, M.D. – 1664–1665
Thomas Mowbray, M.A. – 1665–1666
Archibald Chisholm – 1666–1670
John Pringle – 1670–1672
George Henry – 1672: deprived 1689 for not accepting
    William of Orange
Robert Law, M.A. – 1689–1691
Archibald Hamilton, M.A. – 1692–1709
George Fordyce – 1709–1767
John Chiesly – 1768–1788
Thomas Sharp – 1789–1791
James Oliver – 1792–1814
David Scot, M.D. – 1814–1833
David Horne – 1833 – 1863
Robert Keith Dick Horne – 1863–1881
James Dodds, D.D. – 1881–1895
James Fergusson, T.D. – 1895: full charge 1907–1926
Oswald Bell Milligan – 1927–1940
Foster Franklin, M.A. – 1940–1959
D. Brian Thompson, B.A., Th.M. – 1960–1975
Ian D. Brady, B.Sc., B.D. – 1976–2001
James Bain B.D., Dip.Min. – 2002 –

APPENDIX 2

CURRENCY AND
WEIGHTS AND MEASURES

CURRENCY

In this book, the author uses the abbreviated version of writing amounts of pre-decimal currency.

A sum like Five Pounds Fifteen Shillings and Tenpence is rendered as £5-15-10. A smaller amount such as One Shilling and Sixpence appears as 1/6. Ten shillings appears as 10/-

The three values were familiarly spoken of as "L.S.D". (Latin: *Libra* = Pound, *Solidus* = Shilling, *Denarius* = Penny). The sign we still use for Pounds (£) is simply an L with a stroke through it to show that it is a short form of *Libra*. When decimal currency was introduced in 1971, only Pounds and Pence were retained, and Shillings were dropped. The method of indicating "pence" was changed from "d" to "p".

Scots currency existed until 1707 when it was abolished following the Union between England and Scotland. Scots currency had been roughly the equivalent of the English currency until the latter part of the 14th century. It then began to depreciate over a long period. By 1707, Scots currency was reckoned to be approximately worth One-Twelfth the value of Sterling. Thus **£1 Scots** was worth only One Shilling and Eightpence Sterling at the time of the Union with England. To put it another way, £12 Scots were needed to match the value of £1 Sterling.

The amount most frequently occurring in accounts other than the Pound Scots was the **Merk Scots**. A Merk was worth two-thirds of the Pound Scots, i.e. Thirteen Shillings and Fourpence Scots, or One Shilling and a Penny-Halfpenny Sterling.

It is normal, when dealing with pre-1707 amounts in Scotland, to add "Scots" after the sum, to show that it is the Scots currency being referred to, not Sterling; for example, "£5-15-10 Scots", although this is often implied rather than stated.

A **rex dollar** was a silver coin of European origin which, because of our close trading links with Europe, circulated in Scotland from around 1600 onwards, rather as the Euro does today. In the period 1650-1700 a **rex dollar** was worth roughly £3 Scots, or Five Shillings Sterling.

WEIGHTS AND MEASURES

In this book, the main old measure of weight appearing in the text is "boll", usually by reference to a quantity of grain or meal. **1 boll of bear** [barley] weighed 140lbs (63.5kg) approximately, but as usual in Scotland, the amount could vary from locality to locality.

In 1661 a commission was set up to regulate weights and measures in Scotland, resulting in a set of national standards controlled by certain burghs. In 1824 weights and measures were standardised by Act of Parliament at Westminster, and the whole of the UK followed the Imperial System from then onwards.

INDEX

Note: Index entries in italics are chapter headings/sub-headings.

Aberdeen Militia (Napoleonic War) – 158, 234
Adam Forrester's Chapel – 5
Adamson, James, joiner – 90
Adamson, Robert, joiner – 90
Adamson, Robert, wright – 241
Aikman, Harry, in Broomhouse – 62, 243-4, 185
Aisle, Niddrie's – 43
Aitken, John, mason – 106, 141
Aitken, Mr, ironmonger, Hanover St (Edinburgh) – 95
Ale, Selling – 208
Alexander, John, wright (Corstorphine) – 112
Allan, Alexander, wright – 108
Alms House, The – 36
Amulree House (Mansion House) – 118, 170, 202
Anderson, Alexander, baxter, Hermiston – 109
Arabic Numerals – 48
Army – 68, 120-30, 208
    Men and Supplies – 137-139
Apprenticeships – 48, 216
Archaeology – 1
Armour – 7-8, 13-15, 125
Arthur, Wil, prebendary – 31
Arthur, William, reader at Gogar – 264
    Minister, Corstorphine – 52-53, 264
Artillery – 124, 138, 254
Aubigny, Sieur de – 7-9
Ayres, Justice – 181

Baillie/Forrester (landowner):
    Corstorphine – 5-35, 41, 54, 59, 63, 83, 85, 88, 99, 105, 112, 117, 125, 140-141, 144, 168, 189, 225, 243, 245
Bain, James, Minister – 264
Baird (landowner): Saughton – 26, 88, 94
Balgonie – 24
Ballantine, James and Gardiner, stained glass artists (Edinburgh) – 103
Ballantine, James and Sons, stained glass artists (Edinburgh) – 101
Balsillie, Mr David MA (Minister):
    The First Reconstruction – 54-5; also 264

Bannachtyne, Nicholas, Provost – 12, 18, 20, 22, 96, 99
Bannatyne, Alexander (schoolmaster) – 156-157
Baptisms – 231-236 See also 46, 93, 104, 130, 226, 228
Barclay, Andrew, wright, Abbeyhill (Edinburgh) – 108, 109
Barn, The Teind Yard and – 116
Barnton – 23, 71, 75, 164
Baron Courts: Saughton and Corstorphine – 181-185
Baron Courts see also Law and Order
    Baillies – 182
    Corstorphine – 52, 145, 181-185
    Saughton – 181-185
Beggars & vagrants – 65, 218
Beginnings – 1
Bell Tower, The – 40-43
Belmont – 239
Benefactors – 20
Black Market Poultry – 189
Black, Robert (schoolmaster) – 154
Blackhall – 82, 217
Blakie, Charles – 165
Bleachfield – 132
Board, The School – 162
Bonfires – 39, 55, 154
Bonner, Mrs (Schoolteacher) – 173, 177
Books, bookselling and libraries – 24, 173
Boothby, Sir Robert – 251
Borthwick, Niniane, prebendary – 31
Bothwell, Richard, prebendary – 30
Brady, Ian, Minister – 264
Brewing & distilling:
    Corstorphine – 208-211
    Drunkenness – 147-150, 209
    Excise – 208-211
    Gaugers – 210-211
    Process – 209
    Selling ale – 208-211
Bridges see Roads and Bridges
Broom see Farms
Broun: Gorgie – 156
Building, The Church – 85
Brown, Christopher D – 38
Brown, Thomas, architect (Edinburgh) – 94

Bruce, Charles, glazier (Edinburgh/Corstorphine) – 88
Brucehill – 239
Bryson, Nathaniel, stained glass artist, 8, Leith Street Terrace (Edinburgh) – 96, 102
Building, The – 85-99
Building materials: – 85, 91, 96, 106, 110
    Nails & slates – 85, 92, 106, 110
    Thatch – 106-7
    Timber – 85, 106
Burial grounds – 221, 243, 245
    Body snatchers – 78, 248
    Corstorphine – 3, 76, 85, 89, 91, 221, 230, 240-5
    Early sites – 1-3, 26
    Edinburgh – 69, 191
    Gogar – 46, 241, 244
Burlaw Courts – 185
Burn, William, architect (Edinburgh) – 13, 45, 78, 86, 94-5, 101
Bursaries – 143, 169
Burton, Alexander, glazier – 100

Cairncross, Robert, Provost – 23
Candlemas gift to schoolteacher – 153
Candlemas "bleeze" – 154
Cammo (New Saughton), Watsons, Saughton – 33, 47, 75, 88, 90, 117, 124, 130, 135, 156, 186, 208, 219, 222, 233, 243, 250
Canals – 74
Caring for the Poor – 217-222
Carrick, Alexander, carver (Edinburgh) – 84
Catechism – 43, 144, 163
Catstane – 1
Celandine flower – 8
Chalmers, James, schoolmaster – 141, 143, 223, 262
Chalmers, Dr. Thomas – 79, 159
Chalmers, P. MacGregor – 83
Chamberlain, Neville – 126-7
Chapel, Adam Forrester's – 5
Chapter House: The Sacristy: The Seal – 35
Charles I – 55, 123
Charles II – 55, 125
Chaucer – 24

267

Chepman, Malcolm, prebendary – 30
Chiesly, John (Minister) – 70-73, 264
Child labour – 74-75
Children's names – 234
Chisholm, Archibald, Episcopal
  Minister – 59, 64, 145, 264
CHURCH IN CORSTORPHINE, THE:
  BEGINNINGS – 1
Church Building, The – 85
Church, The Collegiate – 9
Church of Scotland see Churches
Churches: Aberdeen – 19
Churches: Corstorphine: Chapels – 1-9
Churches: Corstorphine: Collegiate &
  Parish – 1
  Adam Forrester's Chapel – 5-9
  Airman burial – 243
  Altar slab – 34
  Altars – 4, 6, 8, 12-14, 35, 96
  Alterations: 1646 – 56, 85-88
  Alterations: 1828 – 13, 46, 78, 86,
    94, 100, 151, 161
  Alterations: 1905 see Restoration
    1905
  Arabic numerals – 48
  Baird loft – 88, 91/2
  Baptisms see main entry
  Bannachtyne stone – 112, 18, 20, 96
  Baptismal laver – 231-232
  Beginnings – 1
  Bell   40-43, 91, 99, 207, 241, 244
  Bell tower see Tower
  Benefactors – 4-11, 16-22, 219
  Bruce seat – 88
  Chaplains' houses – 4, 10-11, 19-20,
    32
  Chapter House – 35-36
  Choir boys – 9, 11, 140
  Choir stalls – 16
  Church hall – 25, 28, 82
  Churchyard see Burial grounds
    main entry
  Collections – 69, 76, 82, 112, 116,
    153, 215, 236, 252/3
  Collegiate Church, The – 9-14
  Communion – 36, 46, 83, 90, 93,
    101, 111-16, 204, 227
  Congregational examination –
    50-53, 60
  Conventicles – 60
  Cromwell – 57, 90, 111, 120-26
  Cross of gold – 19, 73
  Cross slabs – 46/7
  Cups, Communion – 113-114
  Darge chair – 29
  Deacons – 202
  Disruption – 77-81
  Dissolution – 26
  Dower House, The – 32-35
  Dunsmuir seat – 92
  Elders – 51-2, 56, 65, 73, 89, 111, 115,
    201-4, 213, 258

Eleis seat – 90
Evangelist stone – 45
Excommunication – 24-25
Fast day – 112
Finance – 9, 11, 18-19, 53, 55-56, 88
Font & laver – 46, 231-232
Forrester loft: – 89-90
  monuments – 7-9, 13-18
  stone – 47
Glebe – 26, 53, 63, 110, 225
Greenlaw breviary – 30-31
Heating – 94
Henderson, George, architect –
  13, 95-96
Heraldry see main entry
Heriot seat – 92-93
Heriot stone – 11, 46
Heritors – 68, 94
Hospital (Alms House) – 36-38
Hour glass – 81
Kennedy, Bishop – 19
Kirk Loan gate – 83
Lamp Acre – 38-40, 143, 152
Lamp Niche – 38-40
Laver – 231-232
Libel (accusation) – 222
Manse – 25-29, 53, 54, 64, 78,
  104-111
Marriages see main entry
Masons' Marks – 99
Ministers: – 50-85, 116-119, 264-265
  "Election" (1709) – 68
Myrton Seat – 91
Myrton laver – 231-232
Niddrie's Aisle – 43-44
Offering Houses – 252-253
Organ – 97
Our Lady Kirk – 3-4, 52
Papal Recognition – 18-20
Paraphrases – 72
Parish:
  Medieval – 3-13
  Post-Reformation – 48-116
Patronage – 11, 22, 32-33, 49, 59, 70,
  72, 77-81
Place of Repentance – 56, 63,
  89-90, 92, 125, 203, 207
Poor see Poor Relief
Poor's Box money, theft of – 52
Porch – 87, 89
Prebendaries – 10-11, 19, 29-32
Precentors – 78, 82, 116
Priests' Door – 45-46, 48
Provosts – 4, 11-12, 18-19, 21-25,
  104-105
Psalm Tunes – 149
Pulpit – 61, 91, 93, 96-97
  the "Tent"-116
Ratho – 3, 19-20, 48-50
Ravelston – 55, 90-91
Restoration
  1905 – 84-85, 95-97

Roull – 22-23
Sacristy (later, vestry) – 12, 35, 96
St. Conan's Church, Loch Awe,
  seat at – 87
St. John the Baptist – 6, 38-39
St. Mary – 3-4
Saughton – 51, 55
Seal (of Collegiate Church) – 35-36
Seating – 62, 86-95, 237
Secession – 72, 233-234
Services:
  Medieval – 13, 19, 21
  Reformed – 43, 61, 65,
    111-114, 144
Session: –
  Discipline – 201-204
    see also Fornication
  Records – 52, 56, 58-59, 63,
    66-67, 73, 83, 148-149,
    157, 205-253
Skene drawings – 86-87
South Aisle – 6-7, 12-13, 43-45, 47
Spur Silver – 9
Stewart, Bernard, Lord of
  Aubigny – 7-9
Stipend – 53, 54 55-56, 59, 60, 64,
  69, 72-73, 116, 120
Sundials – 45
Teinds see main entry
"Tent" Preaching – 116
Testimonials (certificates of good
  character) – 65, 126, 148-149, 150,
  217-218
Tod Stone – 46
Tombs – 13-18
Tower – 40-43, 53, 225
Unions (ecclesiastical) – 51-52,
  54-55, 117
Visitations – 25, 51-52, 81-82, 149
Walker & Don Monument – 250
Watson (of Saughton) stone – 47
vault & seat – 90
Weather, seasons & services –
  57-58, 69, 112, 203
Windows – 6-7, 13, 52, 85-86,
  99-104
Churches: Corstorphine: Episcopal –
  53-54, 172, 239
Churches: Corstorphine: Free Church
  (St. Ninian's) – 80
Churches: Corstorphine: Roman
  Catholic – 168
Churches: Edinburgh: –
  Fortrose Cathedral – 23
  Gogar – 3, 11, 46, 50-54,
    69, 249
  Greyfriars – 65
  Hamilton – 22
  Holyrood – 2, 3, 18, 21, 49, 50, 51,
    52, 53, 54, 116, 117
  Lothian – 1
  Queensferry, South – 45

INDEX

St. Cuthbert's (West Kirk) – 2, 39, 53, 55, 65, 103, 117, 142, 238
St. Giles' – 4, 7, 55, 99
West Kirk (St. Cuthbert's) – see above, St Cuthbert's (West Kirk)
Churchyard, The – 245-253
    grave robbers, safeguards against – 248-249
Claycott (Clayclote) – 250
Cleghorn, Edward, mason – 254
Cleland (Clelland), James, baillie and merchant in Edinburgh – 92
Clerkington – 19, 24, 49, 51, 117 (Rosebery)
Clermiston, Robinson family of – 234-235
Clothes & Clothing
    Medieval – 13-16
    Mourning – 240-245
Cock fighting – 76, 154
Coinage (at the Union of 1707) – 67
Coiss, John, reader at Gogar – 264
Cok, George, prebendary – 30
Cole, Alexander, prebendary – 30
Colinton School Board, fees – 143
Collections, National – 215-216
Collegiate Church, The – 9-14
Coltbridge – 122, 148, 195, 196, 197
Commissioners of Supply – 131, 138-139
Commissions for the Surrenders of Superiorities and Teinds – 55, 117
Commonties see Pasturage
Communion, Sacrament of – 111
Concealed Pregnancy – 191
Corstorphine Bequest (fund for the poor) – 219
Corstorphine Castle – 74, 122
Corstorphine Friendly Society – 76, 254-257
Corstorphine Hill House – 46-47
Corstorphine House – 209
Corstorphine, Marion (abandoned child) – 230
Corstorphine Mineral Well – 74
Corstorphine Muir see Cramond Muir
Corstorphine Old Parish Church –
    Heraldry – 7, 8, 13, 16-18, 41, 44, 47, 94
Corstorphine Rotary Club,
    gift of lamp to Church (1958) – 40
Coupar Angus, effigy at – 7
Coupar (Cowper) of Gogar – 57, 62, 121, 123
Coupar, James (schoolmaster) – 150
Coupar, Walter, reader – 264
Courts, Baron – 181
Courts, Burlaw – 185
Cowper, Walter, reader – *50*, *117*
Craft Regulations – 253-254
Crag, Alexander, Provost – 22

Craigs:
    East – 182, 188, 215, 229
    West – 181, 182, 187, 230
Cramond Muir – 228
Cramond
    Collection at Kirk (1690) – 216
    Comb's mill at – 211
    Inglis of – 60
    Kirk Cramond – 12, 24
    Men pressed for military service from (1756) – 138
    Minister at
        John Hamilton – 65
        Robert Walker – 118
    Mortcloth borrowed from – 242
    Southfield farm in – 205
    Witnesses from, at witchcraft trial – 226
Cranshaws, Berwickshire, teinds of – 118
Creich, Patrick, prebendary – 31
Criminal Matters – 188-189
Cripple John's Acre – 142-143
Crocket, Mr (Alexander), slate merchant, Leith – 110
Cromwellian campaigns – 90, 111, 120-127
Cromwellian Times – 120-127
Cross of Corstorphine – 160
Cross of gold ("croix d'or fin") – 19, 73, 170
Cruickshank, Helen B (poet, Corstorphine) – 23
Cuddie, John, gardener, Corstorphine – 98
Cullen, Sir Francis Grant, Lord, Senator of the College of Justice – 69
"Cunning" (rabbit) – 227
Cunningham, Laurence, mason – 106
Cunningham, John (schoolmaster) – 146-150. See also 66
CURRENCY AND WEIGHTS AND MEASURES, – App 2
Currie
    Military recruitment in – 138
    Minister at – 65
    School board of, fees – 143
    Teinds of – 117
Curror, sir John, prebendary – 30

Dalmahoy
    Alexander – 49
    Half – 49
    sir John – 31, 49
De Halis, Jac de, prebendary – 30
Defence of the Realm, 1660-1787:
    Quartering – 127-132
Denny, Patrick, prebendary – 31
Dick family, of Corstorphine and Prestonfield – 93, 114-115, 247
Dickson family, of Corstorphine – 97, 101, 114-115
DISRUPTION, TO THE – 77-85

Dixon, Mrs Elizabeth Thomson or – 28
Doctors see Medicine
Dodds, Dr James (Minister) – 82-83; also 28, 264
Douglas, George, prebendary – 31
Douglas, James, Provost – 22
Douglas, John, prebendary – 31
Douglas, Robert, prebendary – 31
Douglas, Robert, Provost – 24
"Dower House, The" – 32-35
Downie, John, in Corstorphine – 115
Drainage and Sewerage – 95, 109, 163, 164, 165
Drummond, Ralph (schoolmaster) – 156
Drunkenness see *under* Brewing and distilling
Duff, John, Minister – 60, 264
Dunbar, William (poet), "Lament" – 22
Duncan, William (schoolmaster) – 162
Dunfermline, Andrew Forrester, Minister in (1598) – 52
Dunsmuir (Orchardhead) – 92

Early Seventeenth Century, The – 53
Edinburgh
    Airport – 1
    Bedlam – 217
    Blind Asylum – 159, 217
    Castlehill
        Bell founders' workshop in – 41
        Execution at – 188
    Churches see Churches: Edinburgh
    City guard house – 197
    Correction house – 207
    Gillespie's Hospital – 159
    "Happy Land", Leith Wynd – 200
    Heriot's Hospital clock *(ref)* – 196
    Incorporation of Calton, meeting *(ref)* – 196
    Mercat Cross, execution at (1664) – 190
    Monteith's Close – 23
    Morningside Lunatic Asylum – 222
    National Monument (Napoleonic wars), contribution to – 216
    Orchardfield (Bread St area) – 24
    Parliament Square *(poetic ref)* – 180
    Public Dispensary, contribution to – 217
    Quarrell Holes, encounter with the Devil at (witchcraft case) – 226
    Royal Infirmary, payment to – 230
    Tanfield, Free Church Assembly at (1843) – 79
    Tolbooth
        imprisonment in (1711) – 137
        (1813) – 198
        instructions to Keeper of (1771) – 193

Tollcross *(ref 1553)* – 24
Trades Maiden Hospital, burial of "lass belonging to" (1726) – 244-245
EDUCATION – 140-181
Education – Corstorphine:
  Bursaries – 143, 169
  Candlemas Gift to schoolmaster – 153
  Catechism – 144, 163
  Certificates of merit awarded to pupils – 167
  Cleaner – 164
  Collegiate Church – 140
  Drill (for boys) – 165, 169
  Examination Day, Corstorphine
  Female School – 175-176
  Fees – 140, 153, 154, 156
  Female Industrial Home – 200
  Female schools – 145, 172-177,
    Sewing teacher – 193
  Free Church School – 177
  Glebe – 26, 53, 63, 109, 110, 225
  Grants *see main entry*
  Hours and holidays – 150-157
  Infant mistress – 169
  Lamp Acre – 38-40, 142, 152
  Management – 140-153
  Mars Training Ship – 165
  Meals – 170
  Non-Parochial – 143, 145, 156, 177-179
  Oath of Allegiance – 145
  Parish School: – 140-171
  Playground Games – 179-180
  Poor scholars – 140, 144, 153, 154, 156
  Presbytery, powers of, in educational matters -159
  Privies *see* Toilets
  Punishment
    of pupil, for stealing – 169
    of schoolmaster for "immoral conduct" – 158-160
  Qualifying Examination – 169
  Ramsay, Daniel, schoolmaster – 157-160
  Reports, Scotch Education Department – 164, 166-167
  School and schoolhouse – 140-145, 152-158, 160-163
  School board – 162-171
  School song – 170
  Schoolmaster's land – 141-142
  Scotch Education Department *see* Reports
  Simpson, Alexander, schoolmaster – 160-162
  Staffing conditions – 14-146
  Toilets – 163, 164, 165
Education, school at Gogar – 152
  Midlothian, petition by schoolmasters in – 157

Tutors – 74-75, 77, 78
EIGHTEENTH CENTURY, THE – 68
Eighteenth Century [School]
  Masters – 150
Eleis
  of Stenhouse – 54, 88 91, 117, 186
  of Stenhopmiln – 90
Emigration, support for – 176
Engagement, The – 120-121, 123
Erskine, Adam, mealmaker – 182
Examination Day – 175-176

Fairgrieve, James, builder – 95
Fair at Innerleithen – 186
Falconer, P A (Headmaster) – 170
Farms and Farming:
  Broom (flower) *see* Whins
  Claysair, lease of ground at – 118
  Cocks Croft – 5
  Crops – 74, 249
  Feast and term days
    St. John the Baptist – 6, 38
  Gardener's croft – 4
  Horses *see main entry*
  Infield *see* Pasturage *(main entry)*
  Lerbour/ Larbour – 72
  Meadowfield – 11
  Oxen – 225
  Outfield *see* Pasturage *(main entry)*
  Paddockholm ("Paddowholme") – 118
  Pasturage *see main entry*
  Potatoes – 74
  Poultry and eggs – 189
  Redheughs ("Reidhews") – 26, 117
  Rent (land at Cramond) – 205
  Roum (fodder) – 186
  Sacristans/ secretaris lands – 117
  Shearers – 211, 214, 221
  Soumes (units of pasture) – 185
  Stock – 204-205, 249
  Teinds *see main entry*
  Threshing mills – 74
  Wages (of ploughmen) – 74
  Weather –
    Adverse weather (1798) – 220
    Excessive rain (1655) – 57
    Excessive rain (1658) – 58
    Severely cold Spring (1740) – 220
    Severe Winter (1795) – 220
    Severe Winter (1881) – 165
  Whins – 154
Female Education – 172-177
Female Industrial Home – 199
Female Schools – 145, 172-177
Fergusson, James (Minister) – 83-85; *see also* 169, 264
Ferries, Andrew, builder – 95
Ferrybank House, feu duty of – 37
Fetternear Banner – 30

'Field of Flashes' – 124
Finance, national – 130
  Hearth Tax – 133-135
  Poll Tax – 135
Firearms and swords – 188, 194-195
Fire, two houses destroyed by, – 219
Fixby (house), baptism at – 99
'Flashes', Field of – 124
Flooding – 110, 152
Font – 46
Food and Drink:
  Dinner – 68
  Fruit and vegetables – 68
  Meat: – 68
  Pies – 68
  Poultry – 68, 189
Foord, John, shepherd – 250
Forbes, Duncan, prebendary – 30
Fordyce, George (Minister) – 68-69.
  See also 106, 113, 152-153, 230, 234, 236, 242, 264
Fornication – 205-208.
  See also 66, 89, 232-233
Forrest, Thomas, glazier (Edinburgh) – 92,106
Forrester/Baillie (landowner):
  Corstorphine – 5-35, 41, 54, 59, 63, 83, 85, 88, 99, 105, 112, 117, 125, 140/1, 144, 168, 189, 225, 243, 245
Forrester, Andrew, Minister – 50-52, 264
Forrester – Heraldry – 7, 11, 13-18, 44, 94
Forrester, Robert, Provost – 23
Forrester's Chapel, Adam – 5
Forstur, Will, prebendary – 30
Foulis (landowner): Ravelston – 129
Foundlings – 227-231
Foundlings and fostering – 74-75, 227-231, 234-235
France and Corstorphine – 8
Franklin, Foster, Minister – 264
Frazer, George, architect (Edinburgh), Auditor of Excise – 110
Freemasonry – 84-85, 253-254
Friendly Societies:
  Corstorphine and Saughton – 254-257
Friendly Societies – 157
  Corstorphine – 157, 254-256
  Saughton – 256-257
From the Outside: Sundials – 45
"Fugies" (runaway cocks) – 154
Funerals – 240-245
  coffins – 241-243
  meals – 241
  mortcloths and bells – 242-245
Furniture and furnishings
  Beds and bedding – 173
  Cabinets and chests – 173
  Carpeting – 173
  Chairs – 173
  Grates and chimneys – 145-146
Galloway, Alexander, prebendary – 30

INDEX

Gardens and Gardening
    Abbeyhill, Thomas Allan,
        gardener there – 233
    Corstorphine, John Cuddie,
        gardener there – 98
    Manse garden – 109
    William Lithgow,
        gardener there – 213
    Gogar's fruit garden, theft from – 214
    Ravelston garden, break-in – 78
Gardner, Florence, Provost – 25
Gawinok, Andrew, prebendary – 30
Gib, Adam, Secession Minister at Edinburgh – 72, 77, 233-234
Gibsone of Pentland, Sir John – 33
    Lady Gibson, his widow – 33
Gibson Lodge ("Dower House") – 32-35
Gill, Alexander, prebendary – 31
Girdwood Family of Saughton and Corstorphine – 103
Glasse, Patrick, Covenanter – 60-61
Glebe, Corstorphine – 26, 53, 63, 109, 110, 225
Glenorchy, Lady – 71-72
Glo(a)g, Francis, farmer at Claycott – 250
Gogar: –
    Cromwell's presence at – 122-124
    Gogar Burn – 124
    John Sclate, wright in – 248
    Lamp Acre – 38
Gorgie Mill, John Brown in – 44
    John Weir, labourer at – 138
Grange see Kirkcaldy of Grange
Grants –
    Use of schoolroom – 163, 164, 166
    State grant to school staff salary – 163
    State grant to school (Payment by Results) – 164
Grave Slabs – 46-48
Grave robbers, safeguards against – 248-249
Gray, Ironmonger, George Street (Edinburgh), *ref* – 164
Gray, James, advocate and prebendary – 31
Greenlaw Breviary – 30-31
Greenlaw, sir John, prebendary – 30-31
Grieve, Denholm, Forrester and Mackenzie, builders – 95

Hairdressing (periwig maker) – 228
Haldan(e) of Saughton, James – 90
Halis, Jac de, prebendary – 30
Hamilton, Anne, Duchess of – 58, 189
Hamilton, James, acting Minister for Gogar – 264
Hamilton, organ builders (Edinburgh) – 97
Hamilton, Archibald, (Minister) – 64-67; also 132, 146, 263
Haw, Patrick, prebendary – 30

Hay, Henderson, Tarbolton, Architects – 95
Hearth Tax, The – 133-135
Helping Others – 216-217
Henderson, Dr – 221
Henderson, George, Architect of the 1905 Church restoration – 95-96
Henderson and Wilson, church furnishings (Edinburgh) – 96
Henry, George, Episcopal Minister – 60-64, 151, 233, 264
Heraldry
    Canting – 23
    Corstorphine Old Parish Church – 12, 13-18, 23, 41, 44, 47, 94
    Forrester – 7, 11, 13-18, 44, 94
    Scott – 25
    Watson – 47
    Wigmar – 44
Herdman, Mrs John, Hazelbank – 102
Hermiston Myre – 186
Hermiston House – 94
Heron, peutherer – 115
Hope of Belmont, James – 95
Horne, David (Minister) – 78-80; see also 110, 240, 244, 252, 264
Horne, Robert Keith Dick (Minister) – 81-82, 264
Horses, saddlery, stabling
    see also Smiths
    Coaches – 68
    Horse from Flanders – 23
Hosie, William, gardener at Cammo – 250
Hospital, The: The Alms House – 36-38
Howisone, John, prebendary – 30
Housebreaking, Theft and – 214
Household Economy:
    Cook, Hugh Smelie, professional cook – 234
    Cutlery – 173
    Food and Drink
        Dinner (1709) – 68
        Meat and poultry – 68
        Pies – 68
        Wine – 68
    Kitchen Equipment
        Tableware, glass – 173
        Wines, ales, sprits – 68
Hunter, Bernard, prebendary – 31
Hunter, Mr Robert, MA (Minister) – 57-59; also 264
Hunting – Linlithgow and Stirlingshire Hunt *(ref)* – 240
Huntingtoun of Corstorphine (place name) – 185
Hutton, General (re Corstorphine Church, 1818) – 20
Imrie, William, wright (Corstorphine) – 93
Industrial Home, The Female – 199
Infanticide case – 191-194

Infield see Pasturage
Inglis, James, prebendary – 31
Innerleithen Fair – 186
Inns, Taverns, Hotels:
    Coltbridge – 195
    Corstorphine (Provost's House) – 27
Irish families (Irish Corner) – 38
Ireland's Block – see Mansion House

James IV – 8, auditor to 23, 39
James V, chaplain to – 23
James (VI) – 54
James VII – 64
Jameson and Ramsay, masons, Edinburgh – 110
Jewellery (watch) – 195, 197
Johnston family, Corstorphine
    David, brewer, 73
    Dr Thomas of Corstorphine House, 105
    Jean (daughter of William, brewer, 193
Juniper Green – 94
Justice Ayres – 181
Justices of the Peace – 186-188

Kain see Rents
Keith family, Ravelston – 234
King, Clement, prebendary – 31
Kirk Session, The – 201-245
Kirkcaldy of Grange, (Sir William) – 181
Kirkland, Mr, surgeon – 220
Kirkliston – 207
Knights Hospitallers (St John of Jerusalem) – 104
Knights Templar ("Templars") – 6
Knox, James, slater – 95

Lamp Niche, The: The Lamp Acre – 38-40
    Corstorphine – 38-40
    Gogar – 38
Landowners:
    Baird: Saughton – 26, 27, 88, 91, 94
    Coupar (Cowper): Gogar – 57, 62, 91, 121, 123
    Dick: Corstorphine: Prestonfield – 70, 93, 114, 247
    Dickson: Corstorphine – 91, 97
    Forrester/Baillie: Corstorphine – 3-38, 44, 49, 50, 54, 55, 63, 64, 70, 83, 86-90, 94, 112, 117-118, 121, 123, 125, 126, 140, 141, 145, 168, 185, 189-190, 245, 248
    Foulis: Ravelston – 129, 145
    Keith: Ravelston – 234
    Myrton: Gogar – 231
    Watson: Saughton: New Saughton (Cammo) – 70, 88, 90, 91, 121, 124, 184, 233
Lang, Walter, 'said to be reader' – 264
Langside, Battle of *(ref)* – 181

Lauder, George, prebendary – 31
Law, Robert, Minister – 64, 264
LAW AND ORDER – 181-257
Law and Order: see also Witchcraft
   Assaults, brawls, civil disturbance
      – 4, 139, 185, 188-189, 199-201,
      210, 214-215, 230
   Baron Courts: Saughton and
      Corstorphine-181-185
   Baron Courts, Baillies – 184-185
   Burlaw Courts – 185-186
   Concealed pregnancies – 191,
      193-194
   Execution – 182, 188, 190, 191, 199
   Female Industrial Home – 199-201
   Heritable jurisdictions, abolition
      of – 183-184
   Illegal trading – 181
   Justice Ayres – 181
   Justices of the Peace – 138-139,
      186-189
   Justiciary, High Court of – (ref)
      159, 188-189
   Marital ill treatment – 180, 206,
      214-215, 218
   Murder and manslaughter –
      182, 188-199
   Prison, use of Corstorphine
      Church as – 53, 183, 225
   Prostitution – 215
   Theft – 125, 182-183, 186-187,
      199-200, 214
   Transportation – 193-194, 200, 207
Laver, the Myrton – 231-232
Learmonth, John, Minister at Gogar –
   263
"Leather ordnance" – 124
Leith Wynd (ref) – 196
Leith,
   "Granoreum" in – 24
   Garrison at (1661) – 128, 129
   Press gangs in – 139
Leslie, David (Lord Newark) – 120-124
Liberton, teacher at – 154
Libraries, books
   New kirk session minute book
      (1646) – 56
   New pulpit Bible – 78
   Parish library – 78
   Reference to Chaucer ("Chaser") –
      24
   School text books – 173
   School library – 174
   Scottish Prayer Book – 55
Lindsay, Robert, Minister – 54, 264
Linen bleaching – 132
Linlithgow and Stirlingshire Hunt (ref)
   – 240
Lister, plumber (Corstorphine) – 96
Lithgow, William, gardener – 213
Lizars, David, tenant in Damhead near
   Gorgie – 138

Lodge of Edinburgh (Mary's Chapel
   No 1) – 253-254
Lodge of St John, Corstorphine – 84-85
Lowis, sir Adam, prebendary – 31
Lunn, John, builder (Edinburgh) –
   95, 110
Lyon, John, wright (Corstorphine) –
   106

Makgill, Alexander, advocate and
   provost – 24-25
McAlla, Archibald, mason – 254
McGibbon, Charles, builder – 95
McGill see also Makgill
   Hew, prebendary – 31
McGown, George W T (schoolmaster)
   – 168-169
McRabbie, Reuben, periwig maker
   (Edinburgh) – 228
Mackie, Thomas (Pinkhill) – 248
Maitland, Jane H., school in
   Corstorphine run by – 177-179
Maitland of Haltoun (Hatton), Charles,
   Lord Treasurer Deputy – 31-32
Major, John (Historian) – 40
Manse, The – 104-116
Mansion House – 118, 170, 202
Manson, George (Schoolmaster) – 162
Maps and Plans, references to:
   Corstorphine village, 1777 – 141
   Marches between Damhead and
      Balgreen, 1797 – 141-142
Marjoribanks, Robert, prebendary – 30
Marjoribanks, Thomas, prebendary –
   (1548) 30, (1562-67) 31
Marjoribanks, Thomas, Minister (1590)
   – 264
Marriages – 236-240
Marriages:
   Corstorphine marriages at Ratho –
      50
   Money collected at marriage – 62
   Promise of marriage – 56
   Tocher (dowry) – 59
Marryat, William, minister and
   teacher – 250
Mars Training Ship – 165
Mary Queen of Scots (ref) – 181
Masons see Lodge of Edinburgh
   Lodge of St John, Corstorphine
Matthew, James (schoolmaster) – 163,
   167-168
Meadowfield see Farms
Medicine:
   Abortion (plea to induce) – 206
   Anatomy (dissection) – 199
   Cholera (1832-33) – 78, 161, 221
   Druggist (apothecary) – 59
   Herbal (to induce abortion) – 206
   Illness – 50, 226
   Mental health – 213 (alleged
      idiocy), 217

Midwives – 206
Plague – 21, 56, 206, (cholera) 221,
   226
Practitioners – 57, 103,199, 221, 251
Treatment – 217, 221
Melville of Hanley family, tomb – 251
Men and Supplies – 137-139
Merchamston, James, Provost – 23
Merschel, John, prebendary – 30
Midsummer rituals – 38
Militia – 127-133
Millar, J and Sons, masons – 96
Milliagan, Oswald Bell, Minister – 264
Mills and Milling:
   Brown, John, in Gorgie Mill – 44
   Cramond parish (Mauslie) – 205
   Erskine, Adam, mealmaker – 182
   Gogar, Harry Hews, miller of – 116
   Gorgie – 44, 138, 156
   Millers, prejudice against – 214
Mineral Well, Corstorphine – 74
Mitchell, David, mason – 108
Mitchel, Francis, mason
   (Corstorphine) – 93, 110
Mitchell, James (schoolmaster) –
   154, 156
Mitchelson, Samuel, lawyer (1765) –
   32-33
Monro, Dr Alexander (Senior and
   Junior) – 199
Monro of Culcraggie, William – 57
Montrose, (James Graham, 1st
   Marquis of) – 120
Moodie (Mudy) of Dalry and
   Saughtonhall, Thomas – 40
More, William, Lord of Abercorn – 4
Morehead, Dr Robert, Episcopal
   Clergyman – 77, 172-177
   Mrs, (Founder of female school) –
      172-177
Mortcloth chest – 245
Mortuary – 38
Mossman, William, mason –
Moubray, Martin, clerk in GPO
   Edinburgh – 193
Mowbray, Thomas, Episcopal Minister
   – 59-60, 264
Mudy see Moodie
Murrayfield – 195, 199
Murrayfield Murder, The – 194-199
Music (at school) – 162
Musselburgh – 128, 217
Myrton (landowner): Gogar – 43
Myrton laver – 231-232

Napoleonic Wars, baptisms during – 234
National Collections (of money in
   church for worthy causes) –
   215-216
National Covenant – 55
National Napoleonic War Memorial,
   contribution to – 216

INDEX

Neilson, Hew, apothecary – 59
Nether Cramond – 56
New Lanark – 75
New Saughton (Cammo), Watsons, Saughton – 33, 47, 75, 88, 90, 117, 124, 130, 135, 156, 186, 208, 219, 222, 233, 243, 250
Niddrie's Aisle – 43-44
Niddry – 43-44
Nimmill, John, MA – 264
Nimmo family, farmers in Sighthill – 250
Nisbet, Dean – 151
Numerals – 48
Nurseries *see* Gardens

Oakland – 105
Ogstone, William, Episcopal Minister – 59, 264
Oliver, James (Minister) – 73-77; *see also* 40, 264
Orchardhead (Dunsmuir) – 92
Orkney, St. Clair of – 14
Other Schools – 177-179
Over Bow, Edinburgh – 36-37
Outfield *see* Pasturage
Oxen (in witchcraft case) – 225

Papal Recognition – 18-20
Parish Church, The – 3
PARISH LIFE – 120-140
Pasturage
    Common (outfield) – 185
    Infield – 186
Peace, Justices of the – 186
Peacock, Alexander, mason – 93, 110
"Penicuik Ploughman" (nom de plume) – 77
Penny, John, prebendary – 30
Pilgrimages – 24, 39
Plans and Maps – 141-142
Playground and Street Names – 179-180
Police – 197
Poll Tax, The – 135. *See also* 182
Pont, Robert, Minister – 264
Poor, Caring for the – 217
Poor Relief
    Alms House – 36-38
    Finance – 62, 64, 67, 70, 73, 88, 116, 222, 229, 233, 245
    Poor's box – 43
        theft from – 52
    Relief – 20, 65, 204, 217-222, 245
Population, Corstorphine (1793) – 74
Post Office, Edinburgh, clerk in – 193
Poultry, Black Market – 189
Prebendaries, The – 29-32
Pregnancy, Concealed – 191
Pressed military service – 137-139
Primrose, John, mason (Edinburgh) – 99
Pringle, John, Episcopal Minister – 60, 264

Privies at school – 163-165
    Conversion to water closets – 165
Profaning the Sabbath – 211-214
Provost's House, The – 25-29
Provosts, The – 21-25
Punishment
    At school, for stealing – 169
    Of schoolmaster, for "immoral conduct" – 158-160
Punton, (Deacon) Alexander, wright – 93, 110

Qualifying Examination (introduced 1903) – 169
Quarry, Ravelston – 197
Quartering – 123, 126, 127-132

Railways – 250
Ramsay, Beatrix (1646) – 32
Ramsay, Daniel (schoolmaster) – 157-160
Ramsay, sir James, prebendary – 30
Rannie, Mungo, brewer and baillie in Portsburgh, Edinburgh – 27
Ratho – 3, 18, 19-20, 32, 49
    Mr Robertson of – 71
Ravelston – 195
    Quarry – 197
Reconstruction, The First – 54-58
Recreation and Sports
    Quoits (1708) – 213
    Children's games – 179-180
Redheughs *see* Farms
Reformation Settlement, The – 48
REFORMED PARISH CHURCH, THE – 50
Regulations, Craft – 253-254
Reid, John, wright, Belmont Foot – 95, 110
Rents:
    Farm *see* Farms
    Kain (1696) – 182
Restoration to Revolution, 1662-89 – 59-64
Rewll, Andrew, weaver in Corstorphine – 188
Rhind, Birnie, church furnishings – 96
Richardson, Dr (James), Inspector of Ancient Monuments – 14
Rinde, Margaret, shearer – 214
Roads and bridges
    Accidents – 111, 216
    Corstorphine churchyard – 245-253
    Flooding –
        Manse and glebe (1777) – 110
Robinson of Clermiston, George – 141, 221 235
Robinson, Elizabeth – 235
Roseburn: – 142
    see also Coltbridge; Mills and Milling House – 122
Roseleaf Cottage – 127

Roull (Rowll) of Corstorphine, Provost – 22-23
Roups
    Provost's House (1767) – 27
    Alms House (1810) – 37
Royal Midlothian Yeomanry Cavalry – 199
Rutherford, Robert, Minister – 54, 264

St. Cuthbert – 1
St. John The Baptist *see* Churches, Corstorphine Collegiate & Parish Church *see* Churches, Corstorphine
St. Ninian's Church (Free Church) *see* Churches, Corstorphine
Sabbath Profaning the – 211-214. *See also* 66
Sacrament of Communion – 111
Sacristy, The – 35
Saddlery *see* Horses
Samuel, John, wright – 93
Samuel, Thomas, wright (Corstorphine) – 93(twice)
Samuel, William, mason (Corstorphine) – 97
Saughton: New Saughton (Cammo), Watsons – 33, 47, 75, 88, 90, 117, 124, 130, 135, 156, 186, 208, 219, 222, 233, 243, 250
Saughtonhall, Baird of – 26, 91-92
School and Schoolhouse – 140-179
School Board, The – 162-170
Schoolmaster's Land – 141, 160
Schools, Other – 177
Sclate, Augustine, weaver, West Craigs – 234
Sclate, John, wright in Gogar – 248
Scone, John of, mason – 99
Scot, Dr David (Minister) – 77-78; *see also* 230, 251, 264
Scott of Buccleuch, Sir David – 24
Scott, Alexander, Provost (1529-44) – 23-24
Scott – heraldry – 25
Scott, ironmonger, Grassmarket (Edinburgh) – 164
Scott, J. and T., church furniture (Edinburgh) – 96
Scott, James, Provost (1532-64) – 24
Scott, Robert, prebendary – 31
Scott, Sir Walter – 175, 176, 211
Scott, Thomas, prebendary – 30
Scott, William, Provost (1564-68) – 24
Seal, The – 35
Seatoune, John, goldsmith (Edinburgh) – 114
Selling Ale – 208-211
Selway, (George Upton) – 25, 34
SERVANTS OF THE KIRK – App 1
Session, The Kirk – 201
Seton: Niddry – 43-44

Settlement, The Reformation – 48
Sharp, Thomas (Minister) – 73
Ship, the *Crawford*, bound for America – 193
Simpson, Alexander, schoolmaster – 160-162
Simsone, William, prebendary – 30
Skene of Rubislaw, James, drawings by – 86
Slabs, Grave – 46
Slander and Strife – 214-215
Slateford, dissenters' church at – 72
Smelie, Hugh, professional cook – 234
Smith, John, mason – 110
Smiths, smiddy,
    At Loanhead of Corstorphine – 189
    Profaning the Sabbath by horse-shoeing – 213
Snuff – 222
Societies, Friendly: Corstorphine and Saughton – 254
Society in Scotland for Propagating Christian Knowledge – 216
Somers and Douglas, glaziers (Edinburgh) – 110
Soumes (units of pasture) – 185
Soup kitchen – 221
Spinning – 174
Squire, John, mason – 99
Stained and painted glass – 99-101
Statistical Accounts of Scotland – 20, 34, 46, 73-74, 124
Steeple *see* Tower
Stewart, Janet, sewing teacher (infanticide case) – 191-194
Story, Alex, prebendary – 30
Story, Hector, prebendary – 30
Street Names, Playground and – 179-180
Stuart Granolithic Stone Co. Ltd. – 96
Sundials – 45
Swinton, David, prebendary
Swinton, Captain John – 189-191
Sycamore, Corstorphine – 63, 74, 112, 168

Tait, Mr, Architect – 94
Taxation –
    Hearth Tax – 133-135
    Poll Tax – 135
    Window Tax – 33
Teind Yard and Barn, The: Stipends – 116
Teinds, Teind Sheaves, Yard and Barn – 10, 24-25, 29, 35-36, 48-49, 55, 88, 116-119
"Templars" – 6

Templelands – 11, 37
Thatchers' wages – 109
Theft and Housebreaking – 214
Thompson, D Brian, Minister – 264
Thomson, Archibald, wright – 97
Thomson, Elizabeth, school assistant – 165
Thomson, R C, market gardener – 168
Thomson, Robert, market gardener – 162
Thomson, Thomas, prebendary – 30
Thomson family, Gibson Lodge – 34
To 1698: Schoolmaster's Land; The Lamp Acre – 140-146
To the 1872 [Education, Scotland] Act – 160
To the Disruption – 77-85
Tobacco and pipes – 68
Tombs, Forrester *see* Church, Corstorphine, Collegiate and Parish, Forrester Monuments
Tombs, The – 13
TOWARDS RESTORATION – 81
Tower, The Bell – 40
Tranent – 4
Transport: *see also* Railways *and* Roads and bridges
    Carriages, coaches and carts –
    Coach hire – 68
    Glasgow mail coach – 195
    Telegraph coach – 197
    Horses – 23, 68
    Railways – 250
    School transport from Gogar – 169
Transportation: The Female Industrial Home – 199-201
Treasures Within: The Font: Grave Slabs: Numerals – 46-48
Trees –
    Destruction of – 221
    Planting – 248
    see also Sycamore, Corstorphine
Trotter: Mortonhall – 69, 230
Turnhouse Aerodrome, Chaplain to Royal Flying Corps – 83

Vagrants & beggars – 65, 218
Vance, Patrick, prebendary – 31
Verulam, Earl of – 86

Wages:
    Agricultural – 74
    Thatchers' – 109
Wallace, John, tailor (Corstorphine) – 97
Warden, James (Church Treasurer) – 204-205

Wardlaw of Riccarton, James – 44
Water of Leith – 122, 142, 148, 152,
Watson (landowner): Saughton: New Saughton (Cammo) – 33, 47, 75, 88, 90, 117, 124, 130, 135, 156, 186, 208, 219, 222, 233, 243, 250
Watson – Heraldry – 47
Waugh, Laurence, Schoolmaster – 150
Weather
    Adverse weather (1798) – 220
    Drought (1652) – 57
    Excessive rain (1655) – 57; (1658) – 58
    Severe Spring (1740) – 220
    Severe winter (1795) – 220; (1881) – 165
    see also Churches: Corstorphine: Weather
Webster, Gordon, stained glass artist (Edinburgh) – 104
WEIGHT AND MEASURES, CURRENCY AND – App 2
Weir, John, labourer at Gorgie Mill – 138
Wells – 47, 161
Wemyss, Colonel, General of Artillery – 124
Wemyss's "leather ordnance" – 124
West Church (St. Cuthbert's)
    see Churches
West Craigs, Augustine Sclate, weaver in – 234
Whins – 154
White, David, thatcher – 108
Wigmar, heraldry of – 16, 41, 44
Wilkie, James, prebendary – 31
Wilkieson, John, prebendary – 30
Wilkieson, sir Thomas, prebendary – 30
Wilson, Daniel, mason – 108
Windows, The [Church] – 99-104
Witchcraft – 222-227
Women workers – 208
Wood, John Philp, local historian – 20, 28, 33, 73
Wood, Mungo,
    'parson and vicar' at Gogar – 50, 263
    reader, Corstorphine – 264
Wood, William, schoolmaster – 66, 151-154

Yorston: Corstorphine – 137, 188, 239
Young, John, prebendary – 31
Young: Meadowfield and Redheughs – 245